Ancient History from Coins

Coins are a rich source of information for the ancient historian; yet too often historians are uneasy about using them as evidence because of the special problems attached to their interpretation. *Ancient History from Coins* demystifies this specialized subject and introduces students to the techniques, methods, problems and advantages of using coins in the study of ancient history.

Christopher Howgego shows through numerous examples how the character, patterns and behaviour of coinage bear on major historical themes. Covering the period from the invention of coinage (*c.* 600 BC) until the reign of Diocletian, this study examines topics ranging from state finance and economic history to imperial domination and political propaganda.

Students and teachers of ancient history will find *Ancient History from Coins* an indispensable guide to using the evidence provided by coins in their studies.

Christopher Howgego is the curator responsible for Roman coins at the Ashmolean Museum in Oxford, and a lecturer in Roman numismatics at the University of Oxford. He has taught and written extensively on ancient coinage.

Approaching the Ancient World
Series editor: Richard Stoneman

The sources for the study of the Greek and Roman world are diffuse, diverse, and often complex, and special training is needed in order to use them to the best advantage in constructing a historical picture.

The books in this series provide an introduction to the problems and methods involved in the study of ancient history. The topics covered will range from the use of literary sources for Greek history and for Roman history, through numismatics, epigraphy, and dirt archaeology, to the use of legal evidence and of art and artefacts in chronology. There will also be books on statistical and comparative method, and on feminist approaches.

The Uses of Greek Mythology
Ken Dowden

Art, Artefacts, and Chronology in Classical Archaeology
William R. Biers

Reading Papyri, Writing Ancient History
Roger S. Bagnall

Ancient History from Coins

Christopher Howgego

London and New York

First published 1995
by Routledge
11 New Fetter Lane, London EC4P 4EE

Simultaneously published in the USA and Canada
by Routledge
29 West 35th Street, New York, NY 10001

© 1995 Christopher Howgego

Typeset in Baskerville by Florencetype Ltd, Stoodleigh, Devon

Printed and bound in Great Britain by
Biddles Ltd, Guildford and King's Lynn

British Library Cataloguing in Publication Data
A catalogue record for this book is available from the British Library

Library of Congress Cataloguing in Publication Data
A catalogue record for this book has been requested

ISBN 0–415–08992–1
 0–415–08993–X (pbk)

For Anthony

Contents

Plates

Plates appear between pages 170 and 171. A detailed key may be found on pp. 162–70. Numbers in square brackets in the text refer to the coins in the plates.

Figures

Preface

This book is intended for students and teachers of ancient history who want to know how the study of coinage can be of interest to them. Its aim is to show how the character, patterns, and behaviour of coinage bear on major historical themes, and to introduce the principal numismatic approaches by reference to some of the more cogent examples. In addition, it is hoped that individual chapters will be of some use as essays in interpretation for those who already have a knowledge of numismatics. The book covers the period from the beginning of coinage, one side or other of 600 BC, until the reign of Diocletian. Where appropriate it ranges backwards to look at the history of money before coinage, and onwards into the fourth century AD to bring out contrasts with what happened earlier.

The first chapter is concerned with money, an important branch of history for which coinage is naturally a major source (although documentary evidence is important where it exists, particularly for describing money-use). The second discusses some of the aspects of the production of coinage which are fundamental to an appreciation of how to use coins as an historical source. The central chapters explore the relationship between empires and local coinages as an aspect of imperialism, and the implications of political iconography for state ideology. The final two chapters are broadly economic. I had intended to write on trade rather than circulation, but it became increasingly clear that to do so was to prejudge important questions, and to circumscribe radically the range of issues which may be illuminated by the movement of coin. The final chapter looks at what may be learned from coinages under pressure, about the nature of financial and economic crises.

The treatment is thematic, therefore, and the focus is on historical topics. A sketch of the history of coinage is given in chapter 1, and numismatic methodology emerges as the book progresses, but neither is the main object of the exercise. Good introductions to both are available already (history: Carradice and Price 1988; Kraay 1976; Mørkholm 1991; Crawford 1985; Burnett 1987; methodology: Crawford 1983a; Burnett 1991).

No attempt is made to catalogue the historical events or other phenomena recorded on coins (and sometimes only on coins). The use of coins in a purely documentary fashion may be important, but it is too obvious to require a book to describe it.

I opted for the title *Ancient History from Coins* because the book deals with historical questions which arise out of the existence and nature of coinage, rather than to demonstrate what coins can tell us that other sources cannot. Coins are one source among many which contribute to our knowledge of the past, and no source can (or, at any rate, should) be viewed in isolation. If any reader feels that the title is inadequate because the book concerns the relationship between coinage and history, rather than a one-way flow from coins to history, I should be delighted by the criticism. I should also like to apologize to anyone who regards my use of the word 'ancient' as unwarranted. Much of the ancient world is not treated here, but the coverage does extend beyond Graeco-Roman civilization and beyond the Mediterranean, and I could not think of a better word.

There is a natural tendency for numismatics to become a specialist discipline, because it has its own substantial body of material and methodology, and because its practitioners tend to be employed in museums rather than in universities. If this book goes any way towards preventing such an unwelcome academic division it will have been well worth the writing.

Acknowledgements

I am very grateful to Robin Osborne, François de Callataÿ, Greg Woolf, Hans-Markus von Kaenel, John Lloyd, and Alan Bowman for the time and care they took to comment on earlier drafts of chapters 1 to 6 respectively. Part of chapter 1 was read to the International Conference on Economic Thought and Economic Reality in Ancient Greece, held at Delphi in September 1994. Suggestions by participants, and particularly by Sitta von Reden, have given greater depth to the discussion of the development of money in the Greek world. Roger Bland kindly gave permission for the reproduction of the graph on p. 117, and helped me to obtain illustrations of coins from the British Museum to supplement those from the Ashmolean. Henry Kim and his computer ingeniously provided the map for p. 5. Natalie Frio-Hamel coped patiently and efficiently with several drafts of untidy and minuscule manuscript. The photographs taken in the Ashmolean are the expert work of Anne Holly.

This book has been written in the ever congenial surroundings of the Heberden Coin Room, with constant support and stimulation from colleagues who are also friends. It was finished during a period of sabbatical, generously granted by the Visitors of the Ashmolean Museum. The whole process has been made very much more enjoyable by the award of a Research Fellowship at Wolfson College, Oxford.

Helen has lived with the work from its conception, and been a constant support, but I am sure she will not mind if this book is for Anthony, who was born the day after the text was completed. I wonder what he will make of it.

Abbreviations

AIIN	*Annali: Istituto Italiano di Numismatica*
AJN	*American Journal of Numismatics*
Annales ESC	*Annales: Économies, sociétés, civilisations*
ANRW	*Aufstieg und Niedergang der römischen Welt*
AS	*Anatolian Studies*
BCH	*Bulletin de correspondance hellénique*
BICS	*Bulletin of the Institute of Classical Studies of the University of London*
CH	*Coin Hoards* vols 1–8, London: Royal Numismatic Society, 1975–94
CIG	*Corpus Inscriptionum Graecarum*
CIL	*Corpus Inscriptionum Latinarum*
C.J.	*Codex Iustinianus*
CR	*Classical Review*
CRAI	*Comptes rendus de l'Académie des Inscriptions et Belles-lettres*
C. Th.	*Codex Theodosianus*
Dévaluations I	*Les "dévaluations" à Rome: Époque républicaine et impériale (Rome, 13–15 novembre 1975)*, Rome: École française de Rome, 1978
Dévaluations II	*Les "dévaluations" à Rome: Époque républicaine et impériale 2 (Gdansk, 19–21 octobre 1978)*, Rome: École française de Rome, 1980
Dig.	*Iustiniani Digesta*
Econ. Hist. Rev.	*Economic History Review*

HSCP	*Harvard Studies in Classical Philology*
INJ	*Israel Numismatic Journal*
JdAI	*Jahrbuch des Deutschen Archäologischen Instituts*
JHS	*Journal of Hellenic Studies*
JNES	*Journal of Near Eastern Studies*
JNG	*Jahrbuch für Numismatik und Geldgeschichte*
JNSI	*The Journal of the Numismatic Society of India*
JRA	*Journal of Roman Archaeology*
JRS	*Journal of Roman Studies*
JS	*Journal des Savants*
MN	*Museum Notes*, American Numismatic Society
NC	*Numismatic Chronicle*
N. Circ.	*Numismatic Circular*, London: Spink and Son
NNM	*Numismatic Notes and Monographs*, American Numismatic Society
OGIS	Dittenberger, W. (1903–5), *Orientis Graeci Inscriptiones Selectae*, Leipzig: Hirzel
OJA	*Oxford Journal of Archaeology*
P. Bad.	Bilabel, F. (1923) *Griechische Papyri: Veröffentlichungen aus den badischen Papyrus-Sammlungen* 2, Heidelberg
PBSR	*Papers of the British School at Rome*
P. Panop. Beatty	Skeat, T.C. (1964) *Papyri from Panoplis in the Chester Beatty Library Dublin*, Dublin: Hodges Figgis and Co
P. Ryl.	Hunt, A.S. *et al.* (eds) (1911–52) *Catalogue of the Greek and Latin Papyri in the John Rylands Library, Manchester*
P. Sarap.	Schwartz, J. (1961) *Les archives de Sarapion et de ses fils*, Cairo: Institut français d'archéologie orientale
QT	*Quaderni Ticinesi: Numismatica e antichità classiche*
RA	*Revue archéologique*
RBN	*Revue belge de numismatique*
REA	*Revue des études anciennes*
REG	*Revue des études grecques*

RIC	*The Roman Imperial Coinage* vols 1–10, London: Spink, 1923–94
RIN	*Rivista italiana di numismatica e scienze affini*
RN	*Revue numismatique*
RPC I	Burnett, A., Amandry, M., and Ripollès, P.P. (1992) *Roman Provincial Coinage I: From the Death of Caesar to the Death of Vitellius (44 BC – AD 69)*, London: British Museum Press and Paris: Bibliothèque Nationale
RRC	Crawford, M.H. (1974) *Roman Republican Coinage*, Cambridge: Cambridge University Press
SAN	*SAN: Journal of the Society for Ancient Numismatics*, Santa Monica, California
SM	*Schweizer Münzblatter*
SNR	*Schweizerische numismatische Rundschau*
Syll.[3]	Dittenberger, W. (1915–24), *Sylloge Inscriptionum Graecarum*, 3rd edn, Leipzig: Hirzel
WA	*World Archaeology*
ZNUJ	*Zeszyty Naukowe Uniwersytetu Jagiellonskiego*
ZPE	*Zeitschrift für Papyrologie und Epigraphik*

Chapter 1

Money

THE HISTORY OF COINAGE

A coin is a piece of money made of metal which conforms to a standard and bears a design. This book is concerned with the Greek tradition of coinage, which spread as far as India and Britain in antiquity. The earliest Indian coinage of the mid-fourth century BC may, or may not, have owed something to Greek inspiration through Persia, but in any case Indian coinage was certainly influenced by the Greek tradition from the third century BC (Cribb 1983). Chinese coinage, introduced a mere century or so after the Greek, was an entirely separate development, and thus is not considered here.

How can one justify calling the tradition Greek, when a reasonable case can be made that coins were first struck in the kingdom of Lydia? The primacy of Lydia should not be taken for granted. No great weight can be put on the fact that the earliest written source, a sixth-century writer (Xenophanes) quoted in a thesaurus of the second century AD, claimed that coinage was a Lydian invention (Pollux IX, 83). Even if the quotation is genuine, the claim need not be true (cf. Kraay 1976: 313). The case rests on the preponderance of Lydian coins in the earliest datable archaeological context for coinage, and the consideration that Lydia possessed the natural sources of electrum, the alloy of gold and silver from which the earliest coinage was made (Hdt. I, 93; V, 101). Against this it is perhaps worth emphasizing that the earliest archaeological context is in the Greek city of Ephesos.

Wherever the earliest coins were actually struck, it is valid to interpret coinage as a Greek phenomenon. The most important reason is that coinage spread rapidly throughout the Greek world, but was slow to take root elsewhere. Within the Persian empire coinage was produced in the sixth century BC only in hellenized areas (western Asia Minor, Cyprus, Cyrene). The Phoenicians struck no coins until the middle of the fifth century. The Carthaginians produced their first coinage in Sicily in the second half of the fifth century. Etruscan coinage was plentiful only in the third century, although there were a few issues in the fifth and fourth.

The other reason is that Lydia, for all its political power, was itself under marked Greek influence (Boardman 1980: 97). Lydian art was thoroughly permeated by East Greek styles, and the Lydian capital at Sardis even had an *agora* (Hdt. V, 101; elusive to the archaeologist: Hanfmann 1983: 34, 69, 72–3). It would be dangerous to go too far in this direction. After all, the transformation of Sardis into a Greek *polis*, both physically and in terms of political institutions, did not take place until the third century BC (Sherwin-White and Kuhrt 1993: 181; Hanfmann 1983: 109–38). To claim coinage as a purely 'Greek invention' would be to miss the possibly important point that coinage developed where Lydian and Greek cultures interacted. Nevertheless, coinage soon became a Greek phenomenon. The Greek, or at any rate hellenized, context of the earliest coinages is important for understanding the historical significance of the introduction and spread of coinage (see pp. 14–18).

Renewed excavations of the Temple of Artemis at Ephesos have undermined older conclusions about the chronology of the earliest coins based upon the sequence of structures on the site (Bammer 1990; 1991). Now we can say only that the earliest context for electrum coinage is underneath the temple of *c.* 560 BC to which the Lydian king Croesus contributed. Arguments from art history and the date of the pot in which some of the coins were found (*c.* 650–625 BC) have been used to push the date of the beginning of coinage back well into the seventh century, but they cannot be conclusive (Weidauer 1975; Williams 1991–3). The style of coins may be conservative, comparison between large pots and tiny coins is problematic, and poor workmanship is easily mistaken for archaism. An old pot may contain more recent coins. In default of convincing new evidence it is better to emphasize the secure *terminus ante quem* of *c.* 560 BC, and to admit that we are not sure how much earlier coinage began.

The coins from underneath the Artemision of 560 BC were in the form of lumps of electrum made to a weight standard, some unmarked, some with just punch marks, some with striations on one side and punches on the other [3], and others with true designs and punches. The temptation to divine an evolutionary sequence is to be avoided (Price 1983). All are in the same archaeological context, and one typeless nugget was stamped with the same punch as a coin which has the design of a lion's head on the other side (Karwiese 1991: 10).

We know nothing about the function of the earliest coinage. Theories that coins were first used to pay mercenaries, or for a wider range of standardized payments by and to the state, are consistent with the character and behaviour of the coinage (Cook 1958; Kraay 1976: 317–28). Literary and documentary evidence is, however, quite inadequate to allow us to decide between competing hypotheses.

We know remarkably little even about the authorities behind the issue of the earliest electrum coinages. The most common type of coin at the Artemision depicts a lion's head (the smallest fractions have a lion's paw) and sometimes bears an inscription [4–5]. A second inscription is known from a related issue not found at the Artemision [6]. All these coins are assumed to be Lydian because of their commonness and wide distribution (forty-five were found at the Phrygian capital of Gordion), and because the inscriptions are not in Greek. It has been generally accepted that the inscriptions, which may be transliterated as VALVEL and RKALIL, represent the names of individuals, but they may also be taken to refer to the mint (Carruba 1991). A related issue has confronted boars' heads and an inscription (Bammer 1991: 67). Some other types have been associated with Greek cities; the most convincing example is the attribution of coins with a seal to Phocaea, where the seal (*phōkē* in Greek) became a standard part of the type [2].

Some scholars have been convinced that the earliest coins were produced by individuals rather than states (whether kingdoms or cities), partly because of the great variety of types (e.g. Furtwängler 1986; Price 1983). The same conclusion was once drawn for the same reason about the earliest (silver) coinage of Athens [e.g. 19]. This view cannot be disproved, but there is no certain case in the whole of antiquity of coins being produced by individuals. At some periods states produced coinages *for* individuals (see pp. 33–4), but that is an entirely different matter. Furthermore, it is easy to find examples of later state coinages with a multiplicity of types (Furtwängler 1982). Among the early electrum the large number of types gives a mistaken impression that there was also a large number of mints. In a number of cases different types share the same reverse punches, showing that they are likely to have been produced at the same place (Weidauer 1975).

The famous type which appears to have the inscription 'I am the badge of Phanes' adds some plausibility to the case that some coinages were personal [1]. However, the interpretation of the inscription has been challenged (Kastner 1986), and, even if Phanes is a personal name, we do not know who this Phanes was (might he have been a tyrant, or other kind of ruler, or a person responsible for a state coinage?; Furtwängler 1982: 23–4). One might argue that it is invalid to infer from the absence of later examples of personal coinages that the earliest coinages were not personal. The earliest coinages might in principle have been different. However, the spread of coinage does seem to make sense in the context of the development of the *polis* as state (see pp. 14–18), and the onus of proof is upon those who wish to argue that the earliest coinages were personal.

Electrum coinage was replaced in Lydia by a coinage in gold and silver, probably under Croesus (*c.* 561–547 BC), but possibly only under the Persians (547 BC onwards) (Carradice 1987a) [27–8]. The Persians continued to produce gold and silver coinage until the time of Alexander [29–30], but most Greek cities turned exclusively to silver. It is sometimes said that electrum was abandoned because the natural alloy contained varying amounts of gold and silver, and hence the value of any given coin was uncertain. This explanation may not be valid, because analyses have now shown that the alloy of some of the Lydian electrum coins was controlled (Cowell *et al.* forthcoming). Thus it may be significant that there is archaeological evidence for the separation of gold and silver at Sardis *c.* 620–550 BC (Hanfmann 1983: 34–41; Waldbaum 1983: 6–7). Major electrum coinages of controlled composition were produced at Cyzicus [32], Mytilene, and Phocaea until the fourth century BC.

Outside western Asia Minor the chronology of the spread of coinage is highly uncertain. For the sixth century there is only one datable archaeological context, namely the foundation deposits under the Apadana at Persepolis.[1] To this evidence may be added the reasonable suppositions that the greater part of the substantial coinage of Sybaris in south Italy was produced before the city was destroyed in 510 BC [12], and that the coinages of some of the later colonies were not struck until after the cities were founded (for example Abdera in *c.* 544 BC, and Velia in *c.* 535 BC) [25; 11]. There are perhaps no other secure chronological pegs for dating coinage in the sixth century. Archaeological fixed-points, or more usually *termini ante quos*, multiply from the early fifth century. Careful analyses of hoards which contain coins from different mints allow chronological conclusions about the

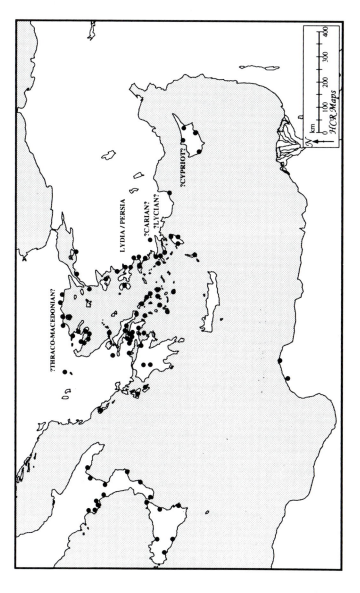

Figure 1 Approximate spread of minting up to 500 BC; some attributions are uncertain, and chronologies are often doubtful (Map courtesy of Henry Kim)

coinage of one city to be extended to coins struck elsewhere. Thus we can be reasonably confident of the stage reached by many coinages by the early fifth century. Estimates of how long it took to produce the coins struck before that stage are used to establish the date of the start of the various coinages. This is really guesswork, and unwarranted precision is a great danger to the subject.

Such agnosticism should not be allowed to detract from an important perspective. Arguments from silence are always dangerous, but the paucity of early archaeological contexts for coinage is striking. New evidence may bring surprises, but at the moment there is little reason (apart from later literary references) to push the start of silver coinages back much before the middle of the sixth century. This means that the spread of coinage throughout the Greek world was rapid. By 500 BC there were established coinages in mainland Greece, Italy, Sicily, and the hellenized areas of the Persian empire (including Cyrenaica) (Fig. 1).

In a few cases the diaspora of East Greeks in the face of Persian pressure allows the process of the spread of coinage to be traced. Abdera, founded *c.* 544 BC from Teos, adopted the same coin type as its mother city, but differentiated its coinage by showing the griffin facing in the opposite direction [25 cf. 9]. Velia was founded by Phocaean refugees *c.* 535 BC; it adopted a style of coinage familiar from the homeland and quite unlike the incuse coinage of the other Greek cities in south Italy [11]. Samians who fled to Zancle in Sicily after the Ionian Revolt struck coins showing the lion scalp from the statue of Hera on Samos and, on the other side, a Samian galley [13]. The East Greek diaspora, ties between mother-city and colony, and trade all provided mechanisms for the spread of coinage, but the rapidity of the spread is better explained by the economic, political, and social transformation of the Greek *polis* which made the Greek world ripe for coinage (see pp. 14–18).

Considerations of the function of early Greek coinage must take into account the range of denominations available. It has been argued that the minimal supply of low denominations in all but a few states means that coinage was of little use in a retail context (Kraay 1964). This observation does not take into account the fact that market exchange was itself undergoing a process of development at the time of the introduction of coinage (see pp. 16–17), and the factual base of the claim has also shifted. Metal detectors and greater scholarly awareness have increased our estimate of the incidence of fractional coinage.

Kraay properly observed that the high value of electrum means that even the smallest electrum coin was still worth something like a day's wage (he did not mean to imply anything about the existence of wage labour in sixth-century western Asia Minor). There is another perspective. The smallest electrum denomination, one ninety-sixth of a stater, weighs *c.* 0.15g [7]. The smallest Athenian silver fraction so far discovered is one sixteenth of an obol, and weighs a staggering 0.044g (Pászthory 1979). Thus in some contexts coins were made just as small as possible (it is very hard to imagine how coins as small as this were actually handled).

That issues of fractional coinage in the archaic period might be substantial may be illustrated by one example. A sixth-century hoard from western Asia Minor contains 906 silver coins of the same type, in three denominations (*CH* I, 3; Kim 1994) [8]. The two smallest denominations average *c.* 0.43g and *c.* 0.21g, and were struck using nearly four hundred known obverse dies. This suggests an original production of at least several million coins, and much higher figures are possible (cf. pp. 30–3). By any standards that is a large issue. Ionia was a region which enjoyed a relatively good supply of fractional silver, and in this respect continued the traditions of the electrum coinage. A single instance is no substitute for a much-needed survey of the incidence of fractional coinage throughout the Greek world (cf. Kim 1994). Even so, this one example is sufficient to show that a significant supply of fractions need not be predicated upon the kind of widespread state pay seen in democratic Athens (cf. pp. 18–19).

Thus it now appears that the quantity of fractional coinage in the late sixth and fifth centuries was greater than was thought a few decades ago, but it would be quite wrong to give the impression that a good supply of fractional coinage was ubiquitous in the Greek world. The development of a token base metal coinage for small denominations remains an important watershed. The low value of base metal (usually bronze) meant that even small denominations were large enough to handle without undue difficulty. There was a north Etruscan tradition of using base metal by weight as a form of money, which on archaeological evidence went back at least to the sixth century BC. This tradition was continued by the Romans in a modified form until the Second Punic War (see p. 112). Elsewhere bronze was a token coinage from the first (Price 1968; Picard 1989). This may help to account for the opposition to its introduction, which is recorded at Athens in the fifth century BC (Athenaeus XV, 669 D), and may be inferred from penalties in a law about the introduction of bronze coinage from Gortyn in the middle or second half of the third century BC (*Syll.*[3] 525; Austin 1981: 185–6, no. 105).

Athens adopted a regular bronze coinage only in the third quarter of the fourth century BC (Kroll 1979) [24]. Elsewhere in mainland Greece the coinage of Archelaus I of Macedon shows that a bronze coinage had been introduced by the end of the fifth century, and excavations at Olynthos (destroyed in 348 BC) demonstrate that it was a widespread phenomenon by the middle of the fourth century. The bronze coinages of some cities in south Italy and Sicily began earlier. Those of Thurium and Acragas, at least, started before 425 BC (Price 1968; 1979b). A separate development from base metal money in the form of arrowheads, through wheel money and dolphins, to round coins took place in the region to the north and west of the Black Sea between the mid-sixth and mid-fourth centuries BC (Stancomb 1993).

At the other end of the denominational scale Persian gold darics [30], Lampsacene gold, and Cyzicene electrum [32] were used as 'international' currencies until the time of Alexander. Indeed, electrum seems to have become a standard coinage for the Black Sea region. An international role was taken on by the gold coinage produced in the name of Philip II of Macedon [43]. The role of 'Macedonian' gold was greatly extended under Alexander, who struck gold throughout his empire as far east as Susa [44]. Gold coinages continued to be produced extensively in his name until *c.* 280 BC, but later became confined to the Black Sea area and western Asia Minor, and ended by *c.* 200 BC (Price 1991a). Some of the successor kings produced gold coinages in their own names, but one gets the impression that the Ptolemaic series was the only really substantial regal gold coinage (even that was on a small scale after *c.* 180 BC) [78–9]. To the west Carthage struck a gold coinage from early in the fourth century down to the destruction of the city in 146 BC [81]. Over the years this coinage became significantly debased with silver (see pp. 113–14).

The nature of the roles of the major gold and electrum coinages is unclear. They circulated widely and some were used for payments between states. It would be interesting to know to what extent such coinages were also used for internal payments in cities which had no (or very little) gold or electrum coinage of their own.

It is also worth asking why civic gold and electrum coinage is so rare. There were some sizeable issues which extended over a reasonable period. The electrum of Cyzicus, Mytilene, and Phocaea has already been mentioned, and one might add the gold of Lampsacus and Syracuse in the fourth century, and of Ephesos and Rhodes in the late hellenistic period. Most other issues were exceptional, and may often be associated with emergencies (see pp. 111–13). We know that both Athens and Rome stored gold against dire necessity, on the Acropolis and in the *aerarium sanctius* respectively. It remains unclear why there were not more regular gold coinages. Prudence (i.e. saving for emergencies), alternative uses (cult objects etc.), and the high value of gold (making inconveniently high-value coins) may have played a part. Access to mines clearly lay behind most of the major series, but gold was surely available more widely than is implied by the production of coinage. Was there some taboo that gold should not be generally used for coinage unless absolutely necessary?

The conquests of Alexander were important in spreading the use of other types of coinage as well as gold. Before Alexander, the western part of the Persian empire had seen an inflow of Greek silver (see pp. 95–8). Coins were struck in the hellenized areas from the sixth century, and in the fourth century BC imitations of Athenian owls were produced from Egypt to Babylonia (Nicolet-Pierre 1986; Price 1993) [38–9]. There was even a minor bronze coinage minted in Egypt before Alexander (Price 1981). Imported silver may have been treated as bullion, but local production, particularly of bronze, is an indication of some type of coin-use. The use of weighed silver as a medium of exchange was probably widespread, and can be seen, for example, in the Treasury Tablets of *c.* 467/6 BC from Persepolis (Hallock 1960). The use of coin before Alexander in areas away from the Mediterranean may well have been minimal. The important and complex Babylonian business documents of the descendants of Egibi in Babylonia (690–480 BC), and of Murashu in the fifth century BC, indicate silver as the principal means of exchange, but reveal no trace of coinage (Bogaert 1966: 125). On the other hand the aramaic documents from Elephantine in the south of Egypt begin to mention Greek coins, as opposed to silver by weight, in the last decade of the fifth century BC (Naster 1970).

Under Alexander gold and silver down to one obol was struck at Babylon and Susa [44]. Although the precise context is unclear, one cannot help noting in this regard that a Babylonian astronomical diary recorded under the year 274/3 BC that purchases in Babylon and the (other) cities were made with copper coins of Ionia (Sachs and Hunger 1988: 345, no. -273, 33′). Bronze coinage was minted at Susa and Ecbatana before the end of the third century BC, and the Seleucids were producing coins at Bactra by *c.* 285 BC. As Seleucid control was gradually withdrawn an independent regal coinage began in Bactria soon after the middle of the third century BC [75]. Around 200 BC a Bactrian Greek king initiated a Greek coinage in western India which continued until the early first century AD. The Greek tradition of coinage was taken up by the Kushans in northern central India and Afghanistan, and further west by the Parthians and then the Sassanians.

To the north of the Greek world the influx of Greek coinage through mercenary pay and other means gave rise to imitative coinage from the beginning of the third century BC. These so-called Celtic coinages spread from the Danube to Britain (Nash 1987). Macedonian coinage provided much the most influential prototypes, with the silver of Philip II and Alexander being copied in the Danubian region [49], and the gold being the most prolific model in central and western Europe. Gallo-Belgic coins reached Britain perhaps as early as the third century BC, but in quantity not before *c.* 150–100 BC. Potin (cast bronze) coinages began to be produced in Britain *c.* 120–80 BC, and a gold coinage at least by the 60s BC. From the last third of the century until the Roman invasion in AD 43 Britain had increasingly Romanized coinages in debased gold, silver, and bronze (Haselgrove 1993) [150–2].

Rome itself had adopted coinage under Greek influence at the end of the fourth century BC. Initially Rome drew on the Etruscan custom of using cast bronze by weight, as well as on the Greek tradition of silver and token bronze coinage. Briefly the two traditions were fused, but cast bronze (by then in the form of round coins) was abandoned in the course of the Second Punic War [84].

The same war saw the silver and bronze coinages supplemented by some issues of gold [88–9], but afterwards there was no gold coinage until the time of Sulla, and no substantial issues until 46 BC [104]. Why this was so remains a mystery, as we know that gold in the form of booty poured into Rome. A similar question hangs over much of Greek numismatics (see pp. 8–9).

The creation of something like a regular gold coinage from 46 BC was a development of major importance (Howgego 1992: 10–12). The coining of gold greatly increased the total value of the coinage in circulation. Gold coinage may even have become the most valuable component of the coin supply by the Flavian period, to judge from the finds at Pompeii (Duncan-Jones 1994: 70–2). The predominance of gold in the later Roman Empire may have been more marked as issues of silver declined, but the contrast with the principate should not be drawn too dramatically.

Roman silver coinage had displaced the silver of the Greek cities in Italy in the course of the third century BC. The story of how a standardized Roman coinage came to be used to the exclusion of other types of coinage in the whole of what was to become the Roman Empire is a complex one. The telling of that story has been one of the major achievements of Roman numismatics in recent decades. Some strands will be sketched in chapter 3. Local coinages some-times ended after annexation, but others were taken over by the Romans. Local systems of denominations became assimilated to, or were replaced by, the Roman. Local coinages lasted longer in the east than in the west, and local bronze usually persisted longer than silver. By the time of Diocletian the whole of the Empire shared a stan-dardized coinage produced at a network of regional mints, the distribution of which reflected quite closely the financial organization of the Empire.

The final imposition of a standardized coinage was not uncon-nected with the decentralization of minting for the imperial coinage. Decisive steps in this direction were taken from the 250s AD. Before that Rome (and Lugdunum for part of the first century AD) had provided a gold coinage for the whole of the Empire, a silver coinage which came to dominate in the west, and to be used increasingly in the east, and a bronze coinage for the west. That this had been possible is a tribute to the extent to which the Roman economy was integrated for certain purposes (see pp. 100–1). It is notable that, before the 250s, decentralized production of imperial coinages tended to be associated with disunity caused by warfare (whether against external enemies, as in the Second Punic War, or the civil wars of the late Republic and Empire).

The system of denominations based on the denarius, introduced in the Second Punic War, lasted remarkably well [90]. Some im-portant changes took place over the centuries, most notably the retarrifing of the denarius from ten to sixteen asses *c.* 146 BC, the creation of a regular gold coinage from *c.* 46 BC, the reorganiz-ation of the base metal denominations *c.* 23 BC, and the introduction in AD 215 of the so-called 'antoninianus' [140], which progressively replaced the denarius in circulation between the 240s and the early 270s. The system, nevertheless, remained in essence the same, until it was changed out of recognition in the second half of the third century.

Developments in the third century were complex, and are not well understood (see chapter 6). What is clear is that financial crises caused the dramatic debasement of the silver coinage, down to 2 per cent silver in the 260s, and an increasing paucity of gold coinage. The gold coinage was also debased, although to a much smaller extent than the silver, and its weight became very erratic. Lower denominations in base metal temporarily came to an end. Reforms under Aurelian and Diocletian failed to restore stability for long. The base silver and bronze continued to be subject to repeated reforms in the fourth century. Silver remained less important than it had been under the Republic and Principate, although issues in the second half of the fourth century were not small. The gold coinage was restored to full purity under Aurelian, and under Diocletian it was again struck to a standard weight. The gold 'solidus' was minted at 72 to the pound from the time of Constantine, and in notably large quantities from the 320s to the 360s [176]. The use of gold became dominant in important sectors of the Roman economy, most notably in the extraction of revenues in money by the state. The gold 'solidus' was to outlast the Roman Empire in the west, and was continued under the Byzantine empire in the east.

WHAT DIFFERENCE DID HAVING A COINAGE MAKE?

For the historian there is little point in tracing the outlines of the history of coinage without asking how having a coinage mattered. Coinage is a particularly useful form of money, but in assessing its historical impact it is important to remember that it is not the only form. Money may be defined with reference to its various functions as a store of wealth, a measure of value, and as a means of payment and exchange (Polanyi 1968). Certain commodities, particularly metals and grain, performed some or all of these roles long before the introduction of coinage.

The use of commodities and property as a store of wealth is so banal that it cannot be taken to indicate money-use, but one cannot fail to be impressed by the widespread adoption of measures of value in early literate societies. A mere five hundred years or so after the introduction of writing at the end of the fourth millennium BC we find such measures recorded in Babylonia and Egypt (Foster 1977; Powell 1990; Chassinat 1921). Measures of value may not have been absolutely ubiquitous in literate societies; no trace of any has been found in the Mycenaean Linear B texts (Finley 1981: 206). It is possible, however, to be misled by the very particular nature of the archives which we possess (the Linear B tablets also lack almost any reference to trade, but one would not wish to argue for the absence of trade) (Uchitel 1988).

Measures of value might remain just that. From one relatively well-documented Egyptian context of the mid-second millennium BC there is no evidence that commodities used to measure value (copper, silver, and grain) were also employed as a means of exchange (Janssen 1975). They were used to arrive at notional equivalences in barter, but took no physical part in the transactions (unless, of course, they were the object of one side of the exchange). Mesopotamian civilization represents a marked contrast. Already from *c.* 2,300 BC we find silver and grain being used not only as a measure of value, but also as a means of exchange. In the best-documented 'commercial' contexts considerable sophistication is apparent. For example, a detailed study of Ur in the period 2,000–1,700 BC reveals the use of silver for sales, wages/rations, rents, taxes, loans (with interest also in silver), and for gifts. Silver was the main means of financing trading expeditions, and merchants were used by both temples and the palace to convert revenues in kind into silver to be stored in the treasury (van der Mieroop 1992).

The form in which silver was used as money in some contexts comes close to falling within the definition of a coinage. The silver was sometimes cut up according to an identifiable standard. It might be in scrap, coils, rings, irregular ingots and the like, but not always (Powell 1978; Bivar 1971). In south-east Anatolia *c.* 730 BC large cast ingots were inscribed in Aramaic with the name of a local ruler (Barrekub) (Balmuth 1971; Furtwängler 1986: 157), and an Assyrian document of 694 BC which describes the building programme of Sennacherib at Nineveh refers in a simile to the casting of half shekel pieces (Luckenbill 1924: 109, col. VII, 18).

Our picture of money before coinage in the Greek world is much less clear. Money is absent from Mycenaean documents, as already noted. Homeric evidence is problematic as it relates to various periods of active composition (from Pre-Palatial Mycenae to the later eighth century BC) in an oral tradition, and arguably reflects more the heroic self-definition of an elite rather than all-pervasive modes of behaviour (Sherratt 1990). At any rate Homer reveals a world which seems to make sense when viewed as a society in which reciprocity (gift exchange) and hierarchical redistribution were dominant. Certain types of goods circulated in closely defined contexts. Gifts circulating among those of top rank included finished objects of metal, cattle, and women (Morris 1986: 9). Meat and related products (hides and textiles) seem to have been controlled from above and redistributed down the social structure (Redfield 1986: 35). There is no trace of money as a means of exchange in this world, and not much room for it, although cattle were used in some contexts as a measure of value (Finley 1981: 236; Macrakis 1984).

We cannot trace the process of the emergence of money in the Greek world. Ethnographical evidence favours the emergence of money from regimes of value used, for example, to mediate prestige or social patterns. Apparently no case has been recorded of money developing out of barter (Crump 1981: 54, 88–90, 114–15; Humphrey 1985). It is possible, however, that anthropology is misleading in this respect, as it has been able to witness the emergence of money only in relatively 'backward' societies which exist in the context of a wider world in which money is already the dominant means of exchange. Anthropology is useful in revealing our own cultural assumptions, and in suggesting alternative models. It raises possibilities, but it cannot determine the answer to the question of how money actually developed in Greece. Economic theory is able to demonstrate how money might in principle have evolved out of barter, and it would be unwise to discard the possibility, especially given the ubiquity of barter (Anderlini and Sabourian 1992; Humphrey and Hugh-Jones 1992).

Anthropological models have been used to suggest that money in the Greek world may have been developed in the spheres of marriage (dowries), vengeance (fines), and gift exchange (from which, it is argued, state pay, liturgy, and social lending are derived) (von Reden forthcoming b; cf. Seaford 1994: 191–234). This approach is clearly helpful in suggesting origins other than barter for money within a purely Greek context, although it is also possible that money-use in the Near East provided a stimulus. By the time of the introduction of coinage, dowries, fines, and gift exchange seem inadequate to account for why coined money was normally, and perhaps always, struck by the state (see pp. 3–4), and why coins circulated between states right from the start (see pp. 95–8).

A differentiated analysis of spheres of money-use may tend to obscure the salient feature that the same class of physical object (coinage) came to be used to mediate in a wide range of spheres. The use of coinage presumably led to the transfer of values (and ideas) between such spheres as dowry, fine, gift, payments by and to the state, and commercial exchange. Indeed, it is important to ask why a single means of exchange came to be used in all these spheres. The use of coin by the state to make payments is presumably part of the answer, but to be effective payments must be useful to the recipient. Some recipients will have been able to return the coins to the state to settle obligations such as enforced contributions, taxes, or fines, but it is tempting to see the usefulness of coin for market exchange as underpinning the whole system.

Whatever the processes involved, it does seem that the Greek world had taken significant steps towards the use of money before the introduction of coinage. Etymology, later literary stories (of dubious value), and some archaeological finds suggest, but do not prove, that iron spits were used as a form of currency before coinage. Other utensils, such as tripods and bowls, may have served a similar purpose in some areas (Kraay 1976: 213–15). Finds of gold, silver, and electrum bars adjusted to weight standards in Greek contexts of *c.* 700 BC or earlier may possibly be an indication of the use of precious metals as money in some form (Furtwängler 1986: 156). Solon's laws reveal that before coinage the administrative subdivisions of Athenian tribes (*naucraries*) already dealt in silver for some purposes (Arist., *Ath. Pol.* 8, 3). The introduction of coinage is itself an indication that the economy and society were not of the Homeric type. But, as we have seen, coinage had very nearly been 'invented' in earlier Middle-Eastern contexts (see p. 13). It is not so much the 'invention' of coinage as its rapid spread which is a persuasive indicator of the transformation of the Greek world, and which demands explanation.

Similarities in the character and behaviour of coinage throughout the Greek world strongly imply that it is right to try to interpret coinage as a single phenomenon. The immediate context in which coinage was adopted, and the ways in which coins were used, will have varied somewhat from place to place. Thus the incidence of fractional coinage was not uniform from region to region (see pp. 6–7), and south Italy adopted a distinct method of manufacture for its 'incuse' coinage [12]. The predominant impression, however, is one of similarity. With few exceptions, pure silver was the preferred metal, standard large coins fell in a narrow range between 12g and 17.2g, coins were issued by states, and the issuing authorities were identified by types which tended to remain unchanged (Kraay 1976: 317). A broadly uniformitarian explanation thus seems appropriate.

At one level the rapidity of the spread of coinage was allowed by the diaspora of East Greeks in the face of Persian expansion, the maintenance of links between mother-city and colony, and by patterns of interchange in the Mediterranean, which went back to the eighth century BC and beyond (Purcell 1991; Sherratt and Sherratt 1993). Such links may have been a precondition for the rapid spread of coinage, but they do not explain it. Interchange of goods (including trade) does not require a coinage (see chapter 5).

The cultural background to the spread of coinage was a Greek world in which peer polity interaction[2] operated both unconsciously and through deliberate competition to ensure the widespread adoption of a whole range of phenomena, from military techniques and political structures to particular crafts and tastes (Snodgrass 1986). The *polis* was a key institution in this process. Although it was never dominant in all areas, its influence as a cultural construct established certain norms. One can readily imagine a degree of competitiveness in the decision to assert civic identity by producing a coinage. It is true that a significant number of polities struck coins rarely or not at all, and presumably depended on coins minted elsewhere. For example, only 60 out of the 205 states which paid tribute to Athens struck their own coins between 480 and 400 BC (Nixon and Price 1990: 156). Nevertheless, there was a significant tendency for richer states to mint for themselves, and the 'political' aspect of coinage is one to be reckoned with (see chapter 3). If peer polity interaction is a persuasive background for the rapid spread of coinage, again it seems insufficient to answer the question of why coinage in particular became one of the phenomena characteristic of the Greek world.

The explanation is rather to be found in the receptive ground provided by the radical transformation of the *polis* in the sixth century BC. The interaction of economic, social, and political changes was complex. The spread of coinage may itself be seen both as caused by such changes, and also as an agent in the process.

At the economic level the most significant aspect of the transformation of the *polis* was the growth in the extent of market exchange ('commoditization') (cf. Appadurai 1986). The key period is variously located from before 700 to after 500 BC by historians, according to whether they place emphasis on the archaeological evidence for inter-regional trade, or on the persistence of literary expressions of distaste for trade and the market (Morris 1986; Redfield 1986). To accept that there was a real change is not to deny the existence of elements of market exchange earlier. Such elements were demonstrably present in the classic 'redistributive economies' of the ancient Near East (Yoffe 1981). Reciprocity, redistribution, and market exchange are most profitably viewed as 'ideal types' used to characterize predominant economic activity. The different categories could, and did, co-exist. By the same token, significant elements of reciprocity/gift exchange can be found in Athenian society of the fifth and fourth centuries BC. The interest-free *eranos* loans are a persuasive example (Millett 1991: 109–59). The market, however, gained a new centrality, arguably symbolized by the development of the *agora* in the period 700–600 BC (Morris 1991: 40; Snodgrass 1991: 10–11). The force of that symbolism depends on our judgement as to whether the *agora* had a commercial role from the start, and to whether the commercial aspect of the *agora*, whenever it developed, represented a real increase in market exchange, or simply a relocation of trade from elsewhere (von Reden forthcoming a: 105–6). That the developed *agora* had political, judicial, social, and religious roles in addition to being a market place is no argument against the symbolism, but does serve to remind us of the inextricable ties between all these aspects.

The encroachment of market exchange freed wealth from the closed aristocratic spheres of gift exchange. This had a social impact, especially as wealth became the defining characteristic of social hierarchy (from the time of Solon at Athens). Wealth might now pose a threat to the traditional family/cultic power-bases (cf. Redfield 1986; Davies 1984: 105–14).

The blow to local aristocratic patronage was compounded at a political level by the strengthening of the centralized power of the *polis* as state. The citizen body was radically reorganized under the umbrella of the *polis* (one thinks of the reforms of Cleisthenes at Athens) (Murray 1990). The relationships of power became defined in a constitutional form, and a way was paved to democracy (which some cities took and others did not). The growth of state authority may itself have been favourable to coinage, which was issued by the state, and to a degree regulated and guaranteed by it (von Reden forthcoming a). The development of a coinage was one aspect of a more fundamental tendency in the archaic period to define values and to codify, and thus to establish norms which could be enforced (Austin and Vidal-Naquet 1977: 56–8). It is in this connection that one can appreciate the semantic connection between *nomisma* (coin) and *nomos* (law) (Will 1955: 9–10).

One might be tempted to answer the question 'What difference did having a coinage make?' with reference to increased economic sophistication. One might point to deposit-banking (in which the banker works with the money deposited by a client) as a concrete example of a financial form which developed as a result of the introduction of coinage (especially if it is accepted that it grew out of moneychanging) (Bogaert 1966: 135–44; 1968: 305). However, this may be to overstate the importance of the development (Millett 1991: 203–6), and in any case this type of answer surely misses the main point. Considerable sophistication in the use of money was achieved in the great redistributive economies of the Near East long before the introduction of coinage (see p. 13). It is perhaps also flat-footed to ask whether the limited denominational structure of early coinage implies that it was not intended to facilitate retail trade (see pp. 6–7). Rather the spread of coinage had a complex relationship with the increasing importance of market exchange. Retail trade was itself evolving. The spread of coinage arguably furthered the processes of commoditization and social and political change which gave rise to it. To see the causes and significance of the spread of coinage in the radical transformation of the Greek *polis* satisfactorily explains why coinage long remained an essentially Greek phenomenon (see pp. 1–2). This broad perspective invites large questions. Does the development of coinage help to explain why Greek society was less 'feudal' than, say, Persian? And to what extent did the working of Athenian democracy depend upon coinage?

USE OF COINAGE: ATHENS

In order to see how coinage came to be used we rely heavily upon the survival of written sources. The lack of documentary evidence explains why it is possible to hold widely differing views about such topics as the function of the early electrum coinage, or coin-use in 'Celtic' societies. Detailed pictures are possible at the moment only for Athens in the fifth and fourth centuries BC, and for the Roman Empire. Work still to be done on the papyrological evidence may well add Ptolemaic Egypt to the list.

Whatever the situation earlier, it is likely that the advent of state pay at Athens significantly extended the use of coinage within the economy (Rutter 1981). Naval and military pay was essentially a development of the long campaigns under the Delian League. General military pay had arisen from earlier subsistence payments before the Peloponnesian War. Enormous sums might be spent on campaign: 1,200 talents on the suppression of the Samian revolt in 440/39 BC;

over 2,000 talents on the siege of Potidaea in 432–430/29 BC. From
the 450s there was pay for jurors (theoretically 6,000 of them) and
for attendance at the Council; from 404/3 BC also for the Assembly.
In the 330s the total cost of such political pay would have been rather
under 100 talents each year (Hansen 1991: 315–16). In addition
Pericles introduced a 2 obol payment to allow every citizen to attend
the theatre, and there was also the mysterious *diobelia* (if it was not
identical with one of the other payments already mentioned). Aristotle
(*Ath. Pol.* 24) claims that more than 20,000 persons were maintained
out of the proceeds of the tributes and the taxes and the contributions
of the allies. To this may be added those engaged in the periodic
building programmes. Some global sums are known from the
Parthenon building records of 447/6– 433/2 BC (e.g. 16,392 drachmas
for sculptors working on the pediment in one year), and individual
pay rates are recorded for the Erechtheion in 409/8–407/6 BC (e.g.
a drachma per day for sawyers) (Fornara 1983: xxiv, 137).

There is an obvious connection between state pay and the production of denominations small enough to allow a daily wage to be
paid and used (see pp. 6–7). Pay both presupposed and encouraged
a cash-based market. The connections, and assumptions about the
market, are well brought out in a vignette from Aristophanes, *Wasps*
785–93 (422 BC). The state treasurer had run out of small change,
so he gave two jurors one drachma, which they changed in the fish
market. One might compare the assumptions implicit in Thucydides'
statement that when the fleet left for the expedition to Sicily everyone
took money for private expenses over and above their pay, and soldiers
and merchants also took money for the purpose of trade (Th. VI,
31; see p. 91).

The regulation of the markets in Athens and the Peiraeus required
a total of ten *agoranomoi*, ten *metronomoi*, and ten (later thirty-five) *sito-
phylakes*, to supervise the market in general, weights and measures,
and the sale of corn, flour, and bread respectively (Salmon forthcoming). Some indication of the scale of the retail trade at Athens
may be gleaned from the occupation of slaves recorded when they
gained their freedom (Davies 1984: 48). Not surprisingly domestic
slaves held first place, but the second largest group was in retail.
(There is a bias here. The large numbers of slaves engaged in heavy
manual work, in the mines for example, were unlikely to be manumitted.) There is a reasonable amount of evidence for prices,
particularly in Aristophanes and in the inscriptions recording the sale
of the property confiscated from those who profaned the mysteries

and mutilated the herms in 415/14 BC (Ehrenberg 1951: 219–52; Pritchett 1956; 1961; Amyx 1958). The daily wage typically varied from half to one and a half drachmas [cf. 22].

Credit was important in enabling the coinage in circulation to work harder. Lending might be impersonal or embedded in social relationships (the absence of an interest charge, or a low interest rate, is characteristic of the latter). Sources for impersonal loans included usurers (*obolostatai*), pawnbrokers, shopkeepers (for purchases on credit), corporate bodies (demes, temples at a deme level, cult organizations), banks (typically for non-citizens, especially those engaged in trade, and for citizens with no other recourse), and professional moneylenders (especially for the finance of overseas trade through maritime loans) (Millett 1991).

The scale of credit is difficult to assess. Socially-embedded lending (including *eranos* loans) seems to have been pervasive. On the impersonal side, banks were important enough for part of the *agora* to be reserved for them before 411 BC (Bogaert 1968: 61). The largest banks lent on a substantial scale: when Pasion leased his bank to Phormion it had 50 talents out on loan. Bank credit is likely to have been much less important than maritime loans, which were taken out by merchants or shipowners and secured on the cargo or the ship (Millett 1983). The familiarity with which such loans are treated in law-court speeches leaves the impression that a significant proportion of Athens' overseas trade was financed by that means (Millett 1991: 188). On the negative side, Athens never evolved any systematic means for transferring money from one place to another without the physical movement of coinage, and indeed there are only three known cases of arrangements to circumvent such movement, none of them directly involving banking institutions (Millett 1991: 8). In so far as trade relied on the movement of coin (see pp. 92–5) it remained hampered by the cost, inconvenience, and insecurity of moving coin about.

The evidence for credit in money is, nevertheless, an impressive testimony to the extent of money-use. The financial importance of leasing tells the same story (Osborne 1988). Rents were normally reckoned and paid in coin (Davies 1984: 55; Osborne 1988: 323). The leasing of the mines and of sacred land by the city and of land by other corporate bodies (tribes, demes, phratries, religious organizations) was on a considerable scale. Evidence for leasing by individuals goes back to the end of the sixth century BC, and rents from houses and farmland were a common constituent of income for a man of substance from as early as our evidence goes (Davies 1984: 49). Rented private buildings were mostly confined to Athens itself, the Peiraeus, and Eleusis, and they were largely taken up by visitors, resident aliens, and freed slaves (none of whom could own landed property). Thus the Old Oligarch included among the advantages of the holding of law cases at Athens the opportunities it provided for renting out lodgings, carriages, and slaves (Ps. Xenophon, *Ath. Pol.* I, 17). The leasing of farmland was partly a result of the scattered pattern of landholding, but the rich also needed cash from their estates.

The cash demands on the rich for private expenditure, liturgies, the *eisphora*, and philanthropy had important consequences. It meant that country estates had to bring in cash, whether through rents or the sale of produce. This implies a substantial cash market for agricultural goods (Osborne 1991). The countryside was thus not free from the cash economy, although market exchange for cash may not have been prevalent in rural areas. Neither literary evidence nor archaeology reveals any markets in Athenian territory outside Athens itself, the Peiraeus, and Sounion. Up to five different *agoras* may be attested for the deme of Sounion, but it was an exceptional area. The silver mines radically altered normal village life (Osborne 1987: 78, 108). Elsewhere the countryman, like Theophrastos' Rustic (12–14), might go to the town to make purchases. Loans by demes and temples at a deme level should imply some need for coin in rural areas. This type of credit might be substantial: at one point *c.* 450–440 BC the Temple of Nemesis at Rhamnous had 51,400 drachmas out on loan in fixed sums of either 200 or 300 drachmas (Fornara 1983: 90–1). Nevertheless, it is unlikely that the countryside was heavily monetized. Presumably barter and socially embedded exchange played a greater role there. It remains hard not to be impressed by the high level of monetization in the town. For Aristotle barter was characteristic of the past and of uncivilized tribes, but not (by implication) of his own society (Arist., *Pol.* 1257a).

Documentary evidence does not permit an account of the spread of money-use throughout the Greek world and beyond. We cannot assume that there was a continuous development towards greater monetization in any one area, and certainly cannot argue from one area to another. The spread of the circulation and production of coinage is suggestive in general terms, but neither the presence nor even the production of coinage in a given area is a sure indication of the extent and nature of the use of money. There can, however, be little doubt that the conquests by Alexander and by Rome marked important stages in the spread of coin-use and the development of monetization in east and west.

USE OF COINAGE: ROME

Under the Roman Empire it is again possible to examine such topics in some detail, and across a much greater geographical area. The papyrological evidence from Egypt is far superior to evidence from any other region, with the consequent dangers of extrapolation. It is obvious that levels of monetization will have varied throughout the Empire, and over time. However, where evidence exists, contrasts are not as great as they might have been, and something of a general picture does emerge. As at Athens (see p. 21), the absence of coinage was seen as an attribute of an ideal primitive community, or as a noteworthy feature of remote and backward areas. The extensive documentary evidence has been reviewed elsewhere, and space dictates that only the conclusions may be given here:

> the normal use of coin as a means of exchange was ubiquitous in the Roman world. That is to say that coin was used both in towns and in areas of settled agriculture, and in the 'less developed' as well as the 'more sophisticated' provinces. . . . The overall picture . . . is that money was the dominant means of exchange for goods, at least in the cities, but that agricultural produce, particularly corn, played a substantial role alongside money in taxation, rents, wages, and credit. The use of money in all these areas shows how money use was embedded in the structure of the economy, and the use of kind does not need to be explained by a shortage of coin. Nevertheless, the use of kind within important areas of the economy restrained the level of monetization, and money use remained relatively unsophisticated.
>
> (Howgego 1992: 30)

In other words Rome, like Athens, never developed any systematic means for transferring money other than by the movement of coin. The only apparent exceptions were the transfers of tax revenues by the state (in some cases) and the use of private connections by the elite (see p. 90). There was no negotiable paper, bill of exchange, or the like.

The use of money was integral to the Roman Empire when viewed (as all empires can be) as a system for extracting surplus production (see p. 39). So again, when asking what difference did having a coinage make, we may adopt a provocatively broad perspective. How would the Roman Empire, any more than Athenian democracy, have worked without coinage?

Chapter 2

Minting

WHERE DID THE METALS COME FROM?

Patterns of coinage were constrained by, and cannot be understood without reference to, the availability of bullion. Here we touch the very springs of history. The connections between metals, coinage, and power are sometimes obvious. The splendour and empire of Athens were built upon the mines of Laurion and tribute in silver from the allies. Gold mining in the territory of Krenides fuelled Macedonian ambitions under Philip. Alexander's capture and coining of Persian treasures from 333 BC is on any reckoning to be counted as one of the great turning points of history, monetary and otherwise. Rome fed upon the stored-up wealth of the hellenistic world, and the systematic extraction of mineral resources within the Empire. The dwindling supply of precious metals in the Roman world was one of the aspects of the crisis of the third century AD (see p. 137).

Literary evidence for the sources of metal for coinage refers not only to mines and booty, but also to indemnities, gifts, purchase, and the melting of wealth stored up in various forms (cult statues, offerings, crowns, vessels, furniture, building ornamentation, and bullion) (Howgego 1990: 4–7). Old or foreign coins might also be restruck. How cities with no access to mines obtained the metal for coinage – by what mix of warfare, trade, and taxation, or whatever – is a major historical problem.

Scientific analysis goes some way to providing clues. Considerable caution is required in drawing conclusions from trace elements in coinage because even within a single mine such elements may vary greatly. Trace elements may be used effectively to discriminate between coins of different mints, but they are much less useful as a way of identifying the original source of the metal. Lead isotope analysis has proved more promising. The principal source for Greek silver in the archaic period was silver-bearing lead ore. The isotopic composition of the ore was 'frozen' at the time of mineralization, and is not altered by refining or re-melting. The lead isotope reading is thus like a fingerprint which may be used to compare coins with samples of ore from a suspected source. Unfortunately, for the technique to be valid one has to make the rigid assumption that metal from different sources has not been mixed. Many coinages are likely to have been produced from re-used and mixed metal, but the technique has been applied with some success to silver coinage of the archaic period (the assumption being that early coinages are less likely to have been produced from re-used metal) (Gale, Gentner, and Wagner 1980; Price 1980).

Among the interesting results is the observation that the Aeginetans coined silver from the mines on Siphnos. The precise nature of the connection between Aegina and Siphnos is unknown, but the Aeginetans were famous as traders. The upshot is clearer. Aegina produced what was probably the most substantial (some judge the only substantial) silver coinage of the sixth century BC [16]. The wealth of both islands is well known (one thinks of the Temple of Aphaia on Aegina, and of the Siphnian treasury at Delphi) (cf. Hdt. III, 57–9).

At Athens it appears that the use of Laurion silver for coinage was only occasional before 500 BC. It is surely no coincidence that the coinage of Athens, unlike its pottery, came to dominate foreign markets only from the fifth century BC (see p. 97). The bonanza of the 480s has left its trace in coin issued at the time 'probably representing one of the most intensive periods of minting in the history of Greek coinage' (Price and Waggoner 1975: 63) [20].

Corinth is a good example of a city with no mines in its territory [17–18]. It may have had access to silver through its colonies in northwest Greece, but, interestingly, lead isotope analysis shows that Corinth was using Laurion silver as early as Athens itself. Now we are at least in a position to ask whether some degree of dependence on Attic silver explains why Corinth (surprisingly) produced little coinage at least during the earlier part of the Peloponnesian War (Mattingly 1989).

Lead isotope analyses are not available for later periods, but it is tempting to single out one unsuspected development which has been identified by trace element analysis. The dramatic rise in the platinum content of the Roman gold coinage during and after c. AD 346–88 indicates that a major new source of gold was being exploited (Morrisson *et al.* 1985: 92–5). This may well have been more important in establishing the dominance of gold in the late Roman economy than Constantine's coining of the treasures of pagan temples. The location of the new source of gold remains unknown.

WHAT IS A MINT?

Metals were converted into coinage at a mint, but what is a mint? As with many simple questions the answer turns out to be a little complicated.

Representations of minting scenes, surviving dies, and scientific examinations of the coins themselves give some idea of the technology involved in the manufacture of coins (Vermeule 1954; Malkmus 1989–93). Coins were cast only when they were too large to be struck [e.g. 84] (some forgers also used casting as the easiest way to copy official coins). The vast majority of ancient coins were manufactured by striking a blank between two engraved dies, the upper (reverse) set in a punch, and the lower (obverse) set in an anvil. Striking is much more efficient than casting for mass production.

The titles of various mint-workers and functionaries are known from Trajanic inscriptions found in the vicinity of the Roman mint. Their posts and occupations hint at much: the contracting of operations, the preparation of metals, the engraving of dies, the striking of coins in workshops, the presence of quality controllers (*aequatores*), a cashier? (*dispensator rationis*), and bankers? (*nummularii*) (Alföldi 1958–9). The organization of coin production into a number of workshops (*officinae*) is recorded on coins from the reign of Philip (AD 244–9), and certainly goes back earlier (Carson 1956) [142]. It is important not to be seduced by such information into making the assumption that all mints were substantial and permanent enterprises.

Certainly, at major mints with a regular output of coinage we may envisage a building complex dedicated to the purpose. Such establishments might stand idle when no minting was taking place. A papyrus of 258 BC reveals just such a situation: work at the Ptolemaic mint at Alexandria had been halted through a bureaucratic muddle (Austin 1981: 410–11).

Archaeology helps to fill in the picture. The Athenian mint from the end of the fifth century to the late first century BC has been identified at the east end of the south side of the *agora* (Camp 1979). The building contained bronze bars with discs cut from similar bars, together with evidence of metal refining. Inscriptions relating to the mint were found near by. The mint was a large establishment, 27 m by 38 m, on strong foundations 1 m thick, and consisted of a number of rooms of various sizes around an open courtyard. We happen to know that the workers in the mint were public slaves (Lewis 1990: 257).

At Rome the mint was on the Capitoline during the Republic. The mint was moved, probably after the fire in AD 80, to part of the site of Nero's *Domus Aurea*, which was returned to public ownership under the Flavians. A fragment of the *Forma Urbis*, a map of Rome on marble, gives some idea of the ground plan (Rodriguez-Almeida 1980: 63–5, Figs 16, 17). Remains of the building itself have been plausibly located under the church of S. Clemente, *c.* 400 m east of the Colosseum (Coarelli 1985: 192–5). It was a long rectangular building with a width of *c.* 30 m, and of unknown length. It had two main storeys, the lower of which was divided into two floors in the earliest phase of the building. The exterior of the building was formed by a substantial wall, probably with only one entrance and no other openings. The lower floor was composed of a large number of rooms arranged around a courtyard with a peristyle. The complex may have continued to function as a mint until the late fourth century AD.

Few other official mints of the Graeco-Roman world have been located. This is surprising given the large numbers of cities which produced coins, and the apparent implication of the evidence from Athens and Rome that mints could be found in the centre of cities (where excavation has been most intense). A number of explanations are to hand.

Most civic coinages were highly sporadic, often with decades between issues. In these circumstances, it may well be that there was no mint building as such. The technology of coinage was not that complicated, and premises may have been used only as required (especially if they already had metal-working facilities). The buildings of smaller mints, in so far as they were permanent, may have had no distinct typology, and thus remain unrecognized.

When mints were closed in an orderly fashion there would be few diagnostic traces for the archaeologist to find, apart from evidence for some type of metal working. Precious metals would have been removed, and dies destroyed, or perhaps dedicated in temples (as we know happened in 406 BC at Athens and in 166 BC at Delos; Robert 1962: 18–24). Hasty abandonment may account for our greater ability to locate forgers' workshops (King forthcoming). Finds of coin blanks have been the principal category of evidence used to suggest the location of official mints. Silver blanks survive from Eretria and Chalcis on Euboea, but their archaeological contexts are not known (Consolaki and Hackens 1980: 286–9). Finds of bronze blanks are more numerous. They date from the late fifth to the second century BC, and range from Italy to Aï Khanoum in Bactria (Cantilena 1989 with references; Oeconomides 1993; Bernard 1985). Often it is not clear whether the findspot is to be identified as the mint or not. Blanks from a temple at Argos are more plausibly taken to have been deposited after the mint was closed, rather than as evidence for minting in the temple itself (Consolaki and Hackens 1980). The identification of the workshop which produced blanks for Ptolemaic bronzes at Paphos on Cyprus does seem secure (both moulds and blanks were found, together with evidence for metal working; Nicolaou 1990). The mint at Halieis in the Peloponnese has also been located with some plausibility. Bronze blanks were found in a building 10 m by 11 m, the back wall of which was formed by the city wall. It stood on strong foundations, and had a central column. It has been suggested that the building served other purposes, as well as being the mint (Boyd and Rudolf 1978: 339).

It is possible that in some contexts official coins were produced in multiple small establishments, rather than in central mints. This seems to run counter to the dictates of security (one thinks in this context of the massive wall around the mint of Rome, and of the cohort attached to the Roman imperial mint at Lugdunum). Nevertheless, some scholars have interpreted the widely dispersed finds of dies of the early principate in Gaul as evidence of decentralized minting (Amandry 1991), and a passage of the fifth-century ecclesiastical historian Sozomen relating to late antique Antioch has been taken in the same way (Liebeschuetz 1972: 57–8).

The word 'mint' is normally used by numismatists to mean the establishment which produced the coins of a given city, on the assumption that it was located in the city named or alluded to on the coins. In the vast majority of cases that assumption is likely to be correct, but it cannot be (or, at any rate, has not been) proved. The use of the same die to produce coins for two or more different cities raises the possibility that one mint might strike for cities elsewhere. On the one hand, such die-sharing occurs in certain well-defined contexts, which implies that the phenomenon was not a general one. On the other hand, it may be noted that die-sharing between cities could occur only when the same type was used on one side of the coin at both cities. Obviously, if coins of two cities do not share a type there is no possibility of die-sharing between them, even if the coins were produced at the same establishment. In the latter case the identity of the mint might be recognizable in principle through similarities in the engraving of the dies, in techniques of manufacture, and in metallurgy. Such similarities might well pass unnoticed, and in any case are difficult to interpret. Thus 'centralized' minting probably remains undetected in certain contexts.

A further complication is that even the sharing of dies between cities does not necessarily mean that their coins were produced in the same mint. Die-sharing between mints may arise also from the transfer of dies from one mint to another, most obviously when a new mint is being set up. Thus as the minting of regal coinage spread in the wake of Alexander's conquests a die was transferred from the established mint at Sidon to a new mint at Ake (Price 1991a: 37). Dies might be transferred in other contexts, which are reasonably easy to envisage in the case of the decentralized minting of regal and federal coinages (examples are known from the Seleucid, Ptolemaic, and Attalid kingdoms, and from the Achaean League) (Thompson 1968: 100–2 for the last). Die-sharing between mints is so uncommon in hellenistic contexts that it is more plausible to interpret the practice by the transfer of dies, rather than as evidence for the striking at one establishment of coins in the name of different cities (Mørkholm 1982b).

The systematic, as opposed to occasional, sharing of dies between cities is more likely to arise from centralized minting. It is clear that in the late fifth and early fourth century BC Neapolis struck silver coins for other cities and peoples in Campania (Rutter 1979: 75, 82–3, 102). In the late fourth century BC the mint of Neapolis was responsible for the earliest token bronze coinage in the name of the Romans, which has a tell-tale inscription in Greek. The phenomenon of die-sharing between cities was at its most extensive in the late second and third centuries AD, when it has been detected in the Danubian provinces, the Peloponnese, Asia Minor, and Syria (Grunauer-von Hoerschelmann 1982–3; Kraft 1972; Johnston 1982–3; Butcher 1986–7; 1988b). It is not surprising that there was some degree of collaboration in the production of civic bronzes for hundreds of cities, many of which were relatively insignificant, and struck coins only occasionally. For the most part we cannot tell whether that collaboration was a matter of central minting, or merely of the transfer of dies (perhaps by itinerant die-cutters or mints). In some cases, however, the combination of die-sharing and distinctive techniques of manufacture or metallurgy allows us to be certain that one civic mint actually produced coins for other cities (e.g. Syrian Antioch for a number of cities in northern Syria and for Philippopolis in Arabia within the period *c.* AD 218–54; Butcher 1986–7; 1988b) [168].

The pattern of production at the major precious metal mints might also be complex. At certain periods Rome produced regional-style silver coinages (as well as base metal) to be put into circulation in Cappadocia, Syria, Egypt, and elsewhere in the east. The clearest example is an issue of Syrian-style tetradrachms under Philip I in AD 244, which has Greek inscriptions, but carries the Latin mintmark MON. VRB. [169]. The phenomenon is perhaps not so surprising when one reflects that the Rome mint produced coinage for all the provinces in the west. The only difference is that coinage in the west was standardized, but coinages for the east were produced to conform to regional styles and weight standards. In addition to Rome, the mints of Alexandria and Antioch also struck silver coinages for other provinces in the east (Burnett 1987: 31; Butcher 1988a: 36–7).

Thus mints might be permanent or temporary establishments, or indeed itinerant, in some cases moving with a campaign (cf. Mørkholm 1982b: 211), or with the emperor (in the case of the late Roman 'comitatensian' mint) (Hendy 1985: 386–94) [182]. Dies might be moved from one mint to another, and a mint in one city might produce coins for another city or region. Some understanding of such complexity has been gained by numismatic scholarship in recent decades, but it is important not to over-react to such revelations. In the vast majority of cases there is no reason to doubt that coins were struck where they appear to have been. Complex collaboration took place in certain well-defined contexts (although some, no doubt, still escape us).

HOW LARGE WERE ISSUES?

The study of the dies used to mass-produce coinages sheds light not only on the organization of minting, but also on the duration and scale of production. Just as coins from the same dies were normally produced at the same place (with some exceptions, just discussed), so coins from the same dies are also likely to be contemporary with each other. How 'contemporary' depends upon the intensity of production (dies wore out or broke through use). In the hellenistic period some silver coinages were dated by month, and thus allow an investigation of the duration in use of individual dies (Mørkholm 1983b; de Callataÿ forthcoming a) [53]. At mints with a substantial and regular coinage dies lasted on average three to five months, and sometimes rather less (the dies of Mithridates did not normally last longer than a month). In mints with a smaller output dies might continue in use for up to five years. The Roman world reveals extremes. Some scholars have estimated that the intensity of production of denarii in the mint of Rome in the late Republic meant that dies might need to be discarded after less than a day (Carter and Nord 1992). By contrast, in the discontinuous civic mints of the east there is a case of a single die being used for two issues eighty years apart (the die was presumably in storage for the intervening period) (Mørkholm 1983b: 16). Such an exceptional instance should not be allowed to distract from normal patterns, but it does warn us not to accept without consideration the assumption that coins from the same dies were closely contemporary (a danger in Greek numismatics, where our understanding of chronology often depends heavily on die-studies to supplement hoard evidence).

For the historian far and away the most important consequence of the study of dies is that it allows an estimate to be made of the size of issues of coinage. No mint records survive from the ancient world, and thus all attempts at quantification must start from the surviving coins. The original number of dies used for an issue must be calculated, and multiplied by the average number of coins produced by each die.

The original number of dies is calculated by statistical extrapolation from the number of dies observed in modern study, on the basis of the amount of duplication in the existing sample of coins. It is good practice to express the result not as a single estimate, but as a range between which one can be confident that the correct number lay. Where the existing sample of coinage is poor relative to original production, margins for error may be very wide (Esty 1986).

Some degree of comfort may be obtained by comparing estimated totals for dies with the relative frequency of issues in hoards. Under ideal circumstances a large hoard will reflect coinage output reasonably well, provided that allowance is made for the progressive loss of earlier coins from circulation (Volk 1987). Indeed, following Crawford's pioneering work on Roman Republican coinage, it has become quite normal to use hoard evidence to extrapolate from the evidence of die-studies of particular issues to estimate the size of issues for which die-studies have not been performed (*RRC* pp.

640–94; Duncan-Jones 1994: 113–15; de Callataÿ forthcoming b). This method is both fruitful and theoretically sound, although it must be remembered that it carries its own margins for error. For example, the pattern of frequency of issues may vary, sometimes markedly, between hoards from different regions (e.g. Duncan-Jones 1994: 120–2). So one has to find a way to combine evidence from different regions in order to obtain a balanced view of original production. However sensibly done, any such procedure involves an element of guesswork.

More problematic is to move from a relative estimate of coinage output (expressed in terms of dies) to an absolute one (expressed as a number of coins). Some assumption about the average productivity of dies is required. The only firm evidence from antiquity comes from the epigraphic record of the bullion used for a silver coinage of the Amphictions at Delphi *c.* 338–333 BC, which may be compared with the number of dies used to produce that coinage (Kinns 1983). Uncertainties in the reading of the inscription and some unknown factors leave some room for doubt, but the average production from each stater obverse die probably fell between 23,000 and 47,000 coins, and between 11,000 and 28,000 for each reverse die. This evidence gives some feel for possible orders of magnitude, but we have no reason to regard the figures as typical.[1]

Clearly the actual output of individual dies may vary enormously, but there may also be significant variation in average output between issues, and within single issues over time. Most obviously output per die will have varied according to the metals involved, the size and type of the coins, the quality of the die, the skill of the mint workers, and whether or not the dies were used until they broke. We cannot estimate the variability of output with any accuracy for the ancient world, but the records of dies used and bullion coined in England between 1281 and 1327 provide a suggestive analogy from a pre-industrial context. The average production from dies at different stages within this period varied from 5,000 to 74,000 (Mate 1969; Howgego 1992: 3).

With such considerations in mind it can be seen that there is danger of over-optimism about what may be achieved. Calculations are likely to mislead unless margins for error are stated, and then multiplied through every stage of complex calculations. Studies of output are of fundamental importance when properly and cautiously applied. For example, they suffice to demonstrate the small scale of Roman coinage relative to that of Carthage and even of some Italian cities prior to the Second Punic War (Burnett 1987: 12–14; 1989, 41–8), or to emphasize the low total value of the Roman provincial bronze coinage produced at the relatively important mint of Corinth from 44 BC to AD 69 (Howgego 1989). In both cases the calculations allow us to exclude certain explanations of the function of the coinages concerned. Die-studies are often sufficient to distinguish periods of high and low production, and are useful as long as the evidence is not pushed too far. Thus we may see how the output of certain coinages increased dramatically at times of war or of monetary reform, but the idea that calculations may be accurate enough to allow detailed year-by-year comparisons with estimates of state expenditure is a fantasy.

Some of the excesses of quantitative numismatics have been subjected to more detailed criticisms elsewhere (Howgego 1992; Buttrey 1993; 1994), and indeed notes of caution were sounded long ago (Grierson 1968). A much more balanced approach is now emerging (de Callataÿ forthcoming b). The present author's cautious view about the spurious accuracy with which many quantitative studies have been presented explains why the present book does not give the approach as much space as might seem warranted by the optimism of some recent work.

WHY WERE COINS STRUCK?

That attempts have been made to compare the output of coinage with state expenditure is natural enough. Until recently it has been orthodox to argue that coins were struck for no other purpose than to allow states to make payments, with little or no regard to how they would be used subsequently. This view gained strength from the perception that state payments were the only way in which coinage might enter circulation.

In certain contexts, at least, there were other ways. Individuals might bring their own bullion to a mint to have it coined. An inscription of the third century BC records that a certain foreigner, Polycharmos by name, lent a hundred gold staters to the city of Olbia on the security of some sacred vessels. When the city could not repay the loan Polycharmos took the vessels to the mint to have them coined. In the event the vessels were saved by a benefactor (*Syll.*[3] 495). In a similar vein the pseudo-Aristotelian *Oeconomica* (1350 b) mentions that the Persian Didales took silver to Amisos to get it minted for his troops. Our evidence is so haphazard that we have little idea how widespread such practices were. In Athens the mint was in principle accessible in the *agora*. By contrast, the degree of centralization of minting in the Roman world means that it would have been difficult for the vast majority of the population to get gold or silver to a mint. It is thus somewhat surprising that there is some evidence that the state minted coins for individuals in the Roman Empire of the fourth century AD, and perhaps also under the late Republic (Howgego 1990: 19–20).

In areas which operated closed monetary systems (see pp. 52–6) there had to be some way in which those coming from outside could exchange foreign coin. A Ptolemaic papyrus of 258 BC records that the mint (for a fee) restruck foreign coin for 'the foreigners who came here by sea, the merchants, the forwarding agents and others' (Austin 1981: 410–11).

In addition to state payments and minting for individuals, coins might have been put into circulation by 'selling' them to the public, or to moneychangers who would then 'sell' them to the public. There is no direct evidence before the time of Anastasius, but a report of Symmachus (*Rel.* 29) in AD 384–5 shows that moneychangers were forced to sell gold solidi to a state treasury for a fixed quantity of base metal coin. Some such practice may have been used to inject new base metal coin into circulation and (presumably the point of the exercise) to extract gold for the state. In this context we should like to know what the bankers (*nummularii*) attached to the mint at Rome actually did (Andreau 1987: 202).

Thus other possibilities exist, but the weight of evidence suggests that state expenditure was far and away the most important means by which coinage was put into circulation in most ancient contexts. The medieval situation was different. Individuals and institutions other than the state minted as well, and coinage was struck primarily for individuals. The contrast between antiquity and the Middle Ages (in the west) may have been overdrawn, but the shift to minting predominantly for individuals is one aspect of the transformation from the late antique to the medieval world (Hendy 1988; 1991; 1993).

Even if one accepts that in antiquity the majority of coins were put into circulation by means of state payments, it does not mean that expenditure was the only consideration in striking a coinage. Other elements might enter into decisions about whether to re-mint old coins before putting them back into circulation, and about which denominations to strike (it is difficult to imagine how the requirements of state expenditure led to the production of so much small change). There is a considerable amount of ancient evidence for alternative motives to coin, which has been gathered elsewhere, and so may be summarized here. These motives:

> included not only technical monetary factors, such as re-coinages connected with monetary reforms or closed currency systems, the need to renew worn coin or to standardize a disparate accumulation, and, perhaps, the terms of monetary alliances, but also the substantial concerns of profit, pride, and politics. . . . Furthermore, the denial . . . that coined money had in the ancient world an economic reason for existence seems to run counter to the evidence for measures taken in reaction to popular pressure to ensure the smooth functioning of the currency as a means of exchange, and fails to explain adequately steps taken to improve the supply of coinage at times of shortage. It is the clear testimony of ancient authors that coins could be struck to facilitate exchange between individuals, the payment of taxes and external trade.
>
> (Howgego 1990: 24–5)

It follows that, although patterns of coinage may reflect patterns of state expenditure, they need not.

COINAGE AND STATE EXPENDITURE

Some doubt has been cast upon assumptions about an automatic connection between coining and state expenditure, and on the degree of accuracy attainable in estimating the size of coinages. A further basic problem is that states might make payments not only in new coin, but also in the old coin which flowed back into their treasuries through a mixture of tribute, taxes, rents, confiscations, booty, bequests, and the like. Foreign coin, bullion [cf. 183–4], and even credit might also play a part in certain contexts. The unknown mixture of such elements in state payments renders even more uncertain the relationship between patterns of production of new coin and patterns of expenditure (Howgego 1990: 11–15). By way of example a detailed study of Roman coinage in the reign of Domitian has shown that new coinage is unlikely to have accounted for much more than a tenth of state expenditure in any given year (Burnett 1987: 95; based on Carradice 1983). Other tentative estimates of coin production from Nero to Marcus Aurelius suggest that new coinage was normally (but perhaps not always) well below the level of state expenditure (Duncan-Jones 1994: 45–6, 111–12, 167).

Despite the problems involved, it remains true that the interpretation of coin production in the light of state finances has been one of the most productive approaches of recent decades, and that it is folly to attempt to interpret the purpose of a coinage without trying to gain some idea of its scale (hence the great importance of Crawford's work on the Roman Republic, *RRC* pp. 633–707). The related topic of what happened to coinages at times of crisis in state finances has also been a fruitful field of research and debate (see chapter 6).

Even where numismatic approaches do not greatly supplement what we know already, they may be of use in rooting general perceptions in the material evidence. Thus it may be helpful to be told that the building of the Athenian fleet in the 480s BC to fight the Persians coincided with 'probably . . . one of the most intensive periods of minting in the history of Greek coinage' (see p. 25) [20], or that there was a significant increase in coinage in many regions of Alexander's empire when a substantial part of his army was paid off and sent home from *c.* 324 BC (see p. 50), or that Rome's massive coinage in 90 BC during the Social War was larger than that in any other year of the Republic (*RRC* 340; Burnett 1987: 92) [95].

We would have expected a substantial production of coins in all these contexts. It may also be instructive to consider unexpectedly large coinages, as it forces us to ask what lay behind them. Thus a variety of apparently civic or local coinages struck within, or adjacent to, the empires of Persia, the Attalids, and Rome may plausibly be interpreted as vehicles for the financial concerns of the imperial power (see chapter 3). That is an advance in our knowledge: not all Roman coins (for example) looked like Roman coins.

Military expenditure looms large in numismatic studies. To a degree that is no more than a reflection of the preponderance of the military in the budget of most substantial ancient states, but it is perhaps worth reflecting that not all expenditures were military. We may think among other things of food for free or subsidized distribution, games, cash handouts to the populace and the military, public works, public servants, settlements (of colonies or individuals), and external payments (bribes, ransoms, subsidies, and indemnities). Specific coinages may be associated with at least some of these categories (Howgego 1990: 9–11). For example, food may be illustrated nicely by the denarii of *c.* 100 BC which are inscribed to show that they were struck to purchase corn (*ad fru(mentum) emu(ndum)*) (*RRC* 330; Garnsey 1988: 198–9) [94].

External payments are a particularly tricky category: why was there any need to coin payments destined to go abroad, rather than just sending the bullion, old coin, or whatever was to hand? That is a difficult question to answer, but there are coinages which seem to have been struck for export in one form or another: for example the tribal coinages of north Greece in the late archaic and early classical period (see p. 96), or the Attic weight coinages struck in and around the Attalid kingdom (see pp. 54–6). Perhaps some recipients simply preferred coin in a recognizable and standard form. Not all external payments provoked coinages, however. It has been aptly pointed out that the largest indemnity ever imposed by the Romans – on Antiochus III – failed to affect the scale of production of Seleucid coinage (Le Rider 1993b; Sherwin-White and Kuhrt 1993: 215 for problems caused by the indemnity).

Given that coinage might be connected with non-military expenditure, and that it need not be connected with expenditure at all, we need some methodology for recognizing military coinages. Five possible indicators have been identified elsewhere, and examples given of each (Howgego 1990: 8–9). They are: military inscriptions on the coins, highly specific military typology, an unambiguously military context, a monetary phenomenon apparently explicable in no other way, and clear literary evidence that a particular coinage was struck for military purposes. None of these indicators is compelling in all cases, but at least they provide a basis for plausible argument. It is obvious that many military coinages will have displayed none of these indicators, but it is unclear how we are to recognize them.

Where the chronologies of coinages are imprecise and warfare frequent there may sometimes be a temptation for scholars to associate one with the other. The danger of circularity of argument is obvious. Where chronologies are known precisely much may be achieved. The coinages of Mithridates VI of Pontus were dated by the year and the month (de Callataÿ 1987) [57]. Years of intense production, and arguably all years of coining, reflected periods of warfare. The one apparent exception – the intensive output for two years prior to Mithridates' invasion of Bithynia in 73 BC – may be explained plausibly as reflecting a period of preparation for warfare. In the same vein, within each year of coining, production was most intense between April and June, the time of preparations for, and the start of, campaigns.

The annual dating of some Roman coinages also allows precise interpretation. Walker conclusively demonstrated how coinage in the east under Nero followed Corbulo's campaigns from Asia Minor to Syria [155], and how coinage in Syria reflected the period of the First Jewish Revolt (Walker 1976–8, III: 112–17). As with the Mithridatic coinages it is not only the intensity of such coining which is interesting; one may in principle see the preparations before the outbreak of actual warfare reflected in the patterns of coinage.

Thus both the quantitative approach and the interpretation of coinages in the context of state finance have much to offer the historian, provided that they are applied with an understanding of the methodological problems involved, and of the limits of the techniques available.

Chapter 3

Empires

COINAGE AND IMPERIALISM

Empires are political systems based on the actual or threatened use of force to extract surpluses from their subjects. . . . Pre-industrial empires could not support large governmental institutions and so secured their power by promoting a community of interest among élites within the empire, and a sense of imperial membership based on participation in ruler worship and adherence to imperial cultural and symbolic systems. Economically, however, empires were first and foremost tributary structures, and much of the limited energy at their disposal was devoted to ensuring adequate supplies of cash, labour and agricultural produce from the areas under their control.

(Woolf 1992: 283)

The topic of imperialism embraces both territorial expansion and the exercise of power. The spread of use of an imperial coinage, or of symbols relating to imperial control (for example, ruler portraits) on local coinages, may mirror the expansion of an empire. The types of some imperial coinages reveal martial ideologies and claims to rule, and thus have a part to play in debates about the causes of imperial expansion. Was expansion merely accidental, or reluctant but inevitable, the normal result of relationships between states, or a quite deliberate objective (Garnsey and Whittaker 1978: 1–6)? The imperial coinage of Rome parades an imperial ideology in by far the most blatant and systematic way, although aspects of the theme go back to Alexander (see p. 64) [45].

Numismatics also illuminates the exercise of power. This is not surprising since the extraction of tribute in cash (but not always in cash) is central to the definition of an empire with which we began. The ruling power might impose its own coinage, or its own weight standards and systems of denominations, or remain laissez-faire about existing coinages. Dominance by imperial coinages or imperial models of coinage need not have been brought about by political or administrative acts. Other possible causes include acculturation and some forms of economic subordination (for example, the inability to coin owing to the draining of supplies of precious metals by imperial authorities, or the lack of any fiscal or other need for subject polities to produce their own coinages).

It is wrong, however, to exclude imposition from consideration, and to deny that there is a connection between coinage and autonomy. In an important treatment of the subject Martin showed that Philip II of Macedon did not suppress coinage in Thessaly (Martin 1985). He went on to broaden his thesis by denying that there were any cases of suppression of local coinages by imperial powers for political reasons, and that there was any connection between coinage and sovereignty. He was correct to point out that the ancient world lacked a theoretical definition of sovereignty which embraced the right to coin. However, the degree of autonomy enjoyed by subject cities (or peoples) within empires was the result of a series of negotiations and accommodations. Coinage may be seen as one of the media through which this negotiation might take place. As regards suppression Martin dismissed too readily the most convincing cases with which he dealt (fifth-century BC Athens and Ptolemaic Egypt), and did not deal at all with another compelling example (Rome).

Two considerations may help to restore some plausibility to the subject. First, in some contexts permission to coin might be granted by imperial powers. For example, the Seleucid Antiochus VII is said to have conceded the right to coin to the Jews under Simon (142–134 BC)(I Maccabees 15, 6–7). Such a concession is possible, as Judaea remained a Seleucid dependency until 129 BC (cf. Sherwin-White and Kuhrt 1993: 228). The case is problematic in that no coinage can be assigned to Simon. Either the right was revoked or it was never granted, but even if the story is unhistorical it still reveals the plausibility of the concept. Not so ambiguous are the many cases of the granting of permission to coin under the Roman Empire (*RPC* I: 1–3). Patrae, for example, owed its right to coin to the indulgence of Domitian (*Indulgentiae Aug. Moneta Inpetrata*), probably after the right had been withdrawn under Vespasian (Levy 1987).

The second consideration is that the removal of the yoke of empire might result in a burst of coinage. Under Ptolemaic dominion, with its tightly controlled monetary system (see pp. 52–4), the cities of southern Asia Minor had not minted. When Seleucid control was reasserted in the area from *c.* 221 BC a degree of autonomy seems to have been allowed. A number of cities instituted new dating eras in recognition of their new status, and began to strike silver coins (Price 1991a: 346–68). Posthumous 'Alexanders' were struck in the very first year of the new eras at Phaselis, Perge, and Aspendos [67], and in year 3 at Sillyum. Side began to strike silver with civic types (Athena and Nike) at about the same time [68]. The connection between the new political situation and the outburst of coinage is clear.

Likewise, as Seleucid control was gradually withdrawn from eastern Cilicia, Syria, Phoenicia, and Palestine from the 130s to the 80s BC a number of cities began to strike silver coinage, often dated according to the new eras which again marked the new status of the cities (Mørkholm 1983a; 1984; Spaer 1984). Aegae, Seleucia Pieria, Laodicea, Tripolis [74], Sidon, Tyre, and Ascalon all struck within the first six years of their new eras. The coins of Elaeusa, Seleucia, Laodicea, Tripolis, and Ascalon all blazoned their new autonomy. Again it is hard to deny a connection between coinage and autonomy. In a similar vein both Jewish revolts under the Roman empire evoked nationalistic coinages with new eras celebrating freedom (Millar 1993: 366–74 for context) [158–9].

Given that (in some cases) imperial powers could grant permission to coin, and that some cities or peoples reacted to restored freedom by producing their own coinages, it seems reasonable to conclude that some connection was felt to exist between coinage and political autonomy. Pride in the assertion of civic identity is not to be underestimated (Howgego 1990: 20–1). It may have played a role in spreading the practice of coining throughout the Greek world (see p. 16). There is some clear evidence for later periods, most notably in an honorific inscription from Sestos which belongs after the end of the Attalid kingdom (*OGIS* 339; Austin 1981: 348–52). The inscription is explicit about why the people decided to strike its own bronze coinage: the first reason given was that the city's coin type should be current. It is tempting to single out also an inscription from Perge which records a series of acclamations in honour of the city in AD 275–6 (Weiss 1991). Although it is not clear to which type of coinage reference is being made, the acclamation 'Hail Perge, honoured with silver coinage' neatly encapsulates the link between coining and civic pride.

From one perspective the continuation into the third century AD of local coinages in the eastern half of the Roman Empire may be seen as a cultural phenomenon (see pp. 58–9). The production of coinage by a community in its own name implied that it was independent (in the narrow sense that it was not part of the territory of another community; it did not need to be either free or autonomous in the technical sense used by the Romans of a relatively small number of privileged cities). The vast majority of coinages were produced in the name of *poleis*, although some issues were minted by independent tribal groupings usually in the process of coalescing around a centre which would become a *polis* (Mitchell 1993 I: 87, 95, 113, 176). Coinages might also be produced in the name of the provincial *koina*, which comprised groups of *poleis*, or by client kingdoms. The salient point is that coins were never struck by villages, which by definition were communities subordinate to *poleis*, despite the fact that in physical terms larger villages might be virtually indistinguishable from *poleis* (Mitchell 1993 I: 177–87).

Not all *poleis* struck coins, but it is apparent that the production of coinage could be intended precisely as a demonstration of *polis* status, and of the hellenization implied by that. Under the Roman Empire the *polis* came to be regarded as the administrative and cultural norm, and *poleis* were established in areas where they had not existed before (although the *polis* never became dominant everywhere). Many of these new cities issued coins, and in some cases the intention to demonstrate status is apparent. For example, Pompey organized Pontus into the territories of eleven *poleis*, some of which were new or recent foundations. Under the Roman governors between 61 BC and 46 BC seven cities in the joint province of Bithynia and Pontus had coins issued in their name. The degree of similarity between the coinages suggests either initiative from a central authority or at least collaboration between the *poleis* (Mitchell 1993 I: 32; *RPC* I: 336) [63]. The coinages may be seen as part of the deliberate creation of a structure of *poleis*. Three centuries later the emperor Philip (AD 244–9) founded a city, with the status of a *colonia*, at his presumed birthplace 80 km south-east of Damascus. Coins were produced in the name of the new city of Philippopolis, but they were actually minted at Antioch [168]. The coins may be seen as one aspect of the creation of the elaborate new Graeco-Roman city (see p. 30; Millar 1993: 156, 531).

Under the Roman Empire the issuing of a civic coinage no longer represented a claim to political autonomy as it had been understood earlier, but a coinage still implied that the issuing authority was an independent community on the Graeco-Roman model. That strengthens rather than weakens the case for some connection between coinage and autonomy in earlier periods. It was precisely the phenomenon of the Roman Empire which altered the definition of a *polis* away from political autonomy, and towards an administrative and cultural construct. In the eastern half of the Roman Empire the capacity to issue coinage became a recognizable part of that construct, in much the same way as public buildings (cf. Mitchell 1993 I: 80–1, 198; Millar 1993: 256–7). The point may be underlined by the observation that the transformation of the *polis* into the city of late antiquity, which entailed a diminution in the role of cities, brought civic coinages to an end (see pp. 138–40).

One should not consider just the right to coin. Coinage may be seen as symbolic at two levels. The use of a single coinage throughout an empire (whether exclusively or not) is a symbol of cohesion and belonging, affirmed by constant use. It is part of the active definition of what it means to be a subject/citizen of the empire. At the second level, the typology of the coins may itself be symbolic. This is most obvious in the case of portraiture, which implies that the individual represented is in some way symbolic of the state. The affirmation of worldly power through coin portraiture is nicely encapsulated in Christ's words 'of whom is this image and the inscription?', 'give to Caesar the things which are Caesar's' (Matt. 22:17–22; Mark 12:13–17; Luke 20:21–6).

Millar has remarked of the burst of portraiture after Octavian secured sole rule:

> we should not minimize the colossal change which had come over the symbolic character of the coinage, both Roman and non-Roman. . . . What we have is . . . a set of visible and uncontrovertible examples of how people construed the world in which they lived; or, to put it another way, of the symbols which they thought it appropriate to display publicly.
>
> (Millar 1984: 45)

The typology of coinage, alongside other articulations of power like the imperial cult, imperial statues in public places, and imperial inscriptions on buildings, brought the reality of empire into the lives of all its subjects.

The reactions of the ruled are seldom apparent. However, the local elites of the Roman Empire cooperated with, and ultimately identified themselves with, the ruling power. Thus it came about that Roman provincial coinage illustrates the beneficial ideology of rule which was the natural outcome of their position (see pp. 84–7).

Coinage thus reflects in complex ways the relationship between ruler and subject. Its representational art is both a means of active self-definition, and a way to maintain dominance. At a more general level our emphasis on the political/military and economic forces which held empires together is in danger of diverting attention away from the importance of symbolic power (cf. Woolf 1990: 54–5).

The object of this chapter is to review the impact on monetary systems of the 'empires' of Athens, Persia, Philip II, Alexander, the Seleucids, Ptolemies, Attalids, and Rome. These examples have been chosen to illustrate a range of possibilities, and because adequate evidence and good modern treatments are available. There would be value in undertaking a similar type of analysis for other kingdoms and empires, say the Antigonids, or Carthage, or Parthia, or Sassanian Persia. The use of coin images and inscriptions to represent power and policy will be discussed more fully in chapter 4, although some aspects of the typology of imperial coinages are mentioned here.

ATHENS

The date of the Athenian decree enforcing the use of Athenian coins, weights, and measures is notoriously problematic, although on any account it belonged in the period *c.* 450–414 BC. The balance of probabilities now favours the 420s or later. What is clear is that copies had to be set up in the market places of cities throughout the Athenian 'empire' (a number of fragmentary copies survive), and that the decree is uncompromisingly imperialistic in tone (Meiggs 1972: 405). As regards coinage the decree enacts that the secretary of the Athenian Council is to add the following to the bouleutic oath: 'If anyone mints silver coins in the cities and does not use Athenian coins or weights or measures but [foreign coins], weights and measures, [I shall punish him and fine him according to the previous] decree which Klearchos [proposed].' The mention of the previous decree presumably implies that some such enactment goes back earlier than the decree we have (Lewis 1987; Mattingly 1987).

The decree appears to mean what it says about the exclusive use of Athenian coin [21]. Attempts to interpret it as meaning that Attic weight (not necessarily Athenian) coins should be used, or that Athenian coinage is to be used for the purposes of calculation only, seem precluded by arrangements mentioned in the decree for individuals to convert foreign coin into Athenian. Quite how this worked is another matter: it is hard to envisage individuals from throughout the empire bringing coin to the mint at Athens, as the decree seems to specify.

One might also question whether it ever proved possible to enforce the intentions of the decree. Hoard evidence for the chronology of a number of important mints in north Greece (including Abdera, Aenus, Acanthus, Mende, and Maroneia) makes it difficult to postulate significant gaps in the output of civic coinage in the north Aegean between 450 and 425 BC (Price 1987b). The type of evidence we have for the chronology of such coinages (hoards and die-studies) means that short gaps in production (say up to ten years) might be impossible for us to detect. The decree might be after *c.* 425 BC – making continuity between 450 and 425 irrelevant – but even here there is a problem. There is practically no hoard evidence to show that Athenian coin played an important role in the north Aegean at any period in the second half of the fifth century BC. One would have expected the contrary, if Athenian coin had been the only currency for a significant period. This absence of evidence may not, with total confidence, be taken as evidence of absence, but it is worrying.

Another concern is that we have no trustworthy evidence of resentment of the measure. There is a joke in Aristophanes (*Birds* 1040–1) which may be relevant, but there is no actual mention of coinage in the text, and it is a brave editor who amends the text of a joke (cf. Meiggs 1972: 168, 587). Furthermore, the foundation charter of the Second Athenian Confederacy of 378/7 BC, which forbade certain aggressive measures which Athens had adopted in the fifth century, does not mention coinage (Martin 1985: 206–7).

So there are problems not only about the date of the decree, but also about the manner and extent of its implementation. On the other hand, it does seem clear that the Athenians thought that they could legislate for their Aegean empire in this way. It has been argued that the intention of the measure was purely to facilitate military and administrative payments, and the receipt of tribute and dues, through universal use of a standard coinage. It is hard to believe that that is the whole truth. The Athenians might have specified that the coinage of the allies all had to be on the same weight standard and of the same fineness, but they did not (Will 1988). They imposed, or tried to impose, the coinage of Athens itself. Finley rightly described that as an exercise in power politics (*Machtpolitik*) (Finley 1978: 120).

The symbolic element is clear: Meiggs compared the common use of Athenian coin with the common obligations to the Great Panathenaea, as expressions of the reality of Athenian empire (Meiggs 1972: 173). One wonders whether the Athenians were trying to demonstrate their power to their allies or to themselves.

PERSIA

The situation in the Persian empire was quite different. The Persians took over a gold and silver coinage when they subjected the kingdom of Lydia [27–8]. Before 500 BC they had created a distinctive coinage of their own, consisting of gold darics and silver sigloi [29–30]. The Achaemenid royal coinage appears to be just that: showing the Great King in a variety of warlike poses (Carradice 1987a).

It is possible that the creation of the royal coinage was connected with the reforms by which tribute came to be expressed in gold or silver under Darius. Before that, according to Herodotus (III, 89), there had been no regular tribute, but rather a system of revenue from gifts. The connection between the royal coinage and the imposition of tribute expressed in silver and gold is postulated on the basis that the two developments belonged to the reign of Darius, but it is problematic. First, some form of tribute may have been paid earlier, and even after the reign of Darius much tribute was paid in kind rather than bullion (let alone coinage) (Tuplin 1987: 137–45). Second, the limited circulation of the coinage means that there can have been no practical connection between coinage and tribute throughout much of the empire. The gold does seem to have circulated widely (the evidence is sparse), but the earlier sigloi enjoyed a significant circulation as coin only in Asia Minor. Sigloi are found in hoards elsewhere in the Persian empire, but alongside a variety of Greek coinages and scrap metal, and often broken or test-cut in a way which indicates that they were being treated as bullion. In the fourth century BC sigloi circulated more widely and occur in hoards from Babylonia and Persia (Carradice 1987a: 89–90). This presumably marks a stage in the spread of coin-use to the Persian heartlands.

There is no suggestion that the Persians ever tried to impose exclusive use of the royal coinage in any area. The story of Aryandes, sometimes cited in this connection, has little relevance (Hdt. IV, 166). Herodotus tells how Aryandes as governor of Egypt gave offence to Darius, by producing a fine silver coinage in emulation of the King's fine gold coinage. Darius is said to have concealed the cause of his anger, and to have executed Aryandes on a charge of rebellion. The story is an implausible one: no coinage of Aryandes survives, and no other coinage was produced in Egypt until the fourth century BC. Whatever the truth of the matter, even in the story the striking of coinage was not the charge. Later coining by satraps seems not to have been a problem, and some even struck coins with their own 'portraits' (perhaps 'representations' is a better word, as it does not beg the question of whether an attempt was made to render the features of individuals) (Cahn 1989) [36]. It is actually quite hard to find any reflection of the great satrapal revolt of 362/1 BC in their coinage, as satraps were coining both before and afterwards (Moysey 1989). Quite what lay behind satrapal coinages is difficult to discern. Were they struck from the satrap's own resources, or from bullion in local royal treasuries (and, if so, with or without royal permission) (Briant 1989: 328–31)?

Numismatic evidence demonstrates the freedom of production and circulation of a wide variety of coinages within the empire. In most areas the royal coinage was not even dominant; it was less common than satrapal, dynastic, or civic issues, according to the region concerned. For examples one can cite the satrapal issues of Cilicia [37], the dynastic coinages of Lycia [34–5] and Hekatomnid Caria, and the civic silver of Ionia [33] (Kinns 1989). There may even have been some sort of 'trade-off': in the fourth century BC the small output of sigloi may be explained by the increased production of 'local' coinages in some areas (Carradice 1987a: 93). There were substantial 'local' coinages in gold and electrum, as well as in silver (most notably the gold of Lampsacus, and the electrum of Cyzicus [32] and Phocaea). It is impossible to know the realities behind the production of substantial civic coinages. It is quite possible that the Persians encouraged the coining of money to be paid as tribute, or even made use of civic mints to coin bullion for themselves. 'Greek' coinages may have been more suitable than royal coinage for some external transactions, and Cyzicene electrum seems to have become the accepted coinage for the Black Sea region.

The Persians did not intervene even to standardize weights. In some regions at certain periods local coinages were struck so as to be equivalent to, or compatible with, the daric or siglos – for example Cilician silver or Cypriot gold in the fourth century BC – but such standards were never all-pervasive. The lack of concern may be illustrated by the coinage struck in the name of King Artaxerxes in Egypt after the Persians had put down a revolt there. The silver coins have Athenian types and are on an Attic weight standard, and call the King 'pharaoh' in demotic Egyptian [38]. Coinage thus reflected the cultural and administrative diversity which prevailed within the Persian empire.

PHILIP II AND ALEXANDER

The practice of the Macedonian kings was more in line with that of Persia than with the dramatic measure attempted by Athens. Martin has shown that Philip II did not suppress coinage in Thessaly: the silver drachms of Larissa continued under Alexander, as demonstrated by hoard evidence (Martin 1985). Nor did Philip have any reason to take such action; his political protestation was respect for Thessalian customs and law (*nomos*). Some coinages elsewhere can be shown to have continued after Philip's reign, although the chronologies are not always sufficiently secure to show that coins were produced specifically in his reign. The coinage of the Amphictions at Delphi is securely dated by epigraphic evidence to *c*. 338–333 BC, and the Attic tetradrachms of the Euboean Confederation were struck between 357 and 338 BC (Kinns 1983; Picard 1990). Other cities which continued to coin included Abdera, Thasos, Ambracia, Athens, Corinth, and, after the dissolution of the Euboean Confederation, Chalcis, Carystos, and Hystiaia (Mattingly 1988; Picard 1990). One should perhaps hesitate before moving from the observation that some coinages were not suppressed to the proposition that none was (which numismatic evidence cannot demonstrate, or at any rate has not yet done so). Should a single policy in respect of all cities and areas be attributed to Philip, or might he have acted differently in different circumstances?

A major development under Philip was the exploitation of the gold mines in the territory of Krenides to pay mercenaries and bribe Greeks (Diodorus XVI, 8, 6–7), but the chronology of the gold coinage is problematic (Le Rider 1977; Price 1979a) [43]. Hoard evidence has been taken to imply that Philip's gold did not commence until *c*. 345 BC or even later, by which time much military expansion and bribery had already taken place. It is always dangerous to force coinage to fit a preconceived historical framework in defiance of the material evidence. On the other hand, the numismatic evidence relies heavily on one hoard from Corinth, which may be anomalous. There perhaps remains some scope to push the start of Philip's gold back before 345 BC (Martin 1985: 271–92).

The same hoard tends to indicate that gold in the name of Philip continued to be struck early in the reign of Alexander. Again it is just possible that the hoard is anomalous, and that Philip's gold ended at (or soon after) Alexander's accession. If so, production was intense in the last years of Philip, but that is plausible in the light of his plans to invade Asia (Martin 1985: 271–92). Not everything can be tidied up, however. There certainly were posthumous gold and silver issues in the name of Philip, and not all of them can be argued away as being coinages of Philip III (as the silver continued for several decades after his death) (Le Rider 1993a). What is clear is that the coinage was struck in large numbers. Nearly two centuries later Livy records the parade of gold *philippei* in Roman triumphs (by that time the term may have been extended to embrace the gold in the name of Alexander as well).

The substantial scale of the gold and silver in the name of Philip is pertinent to our theme. Even if, as appears to be the case, it was not intended to be an exclusive coinage, its prevalence had consequences. Picard has made the interesting observation that a number of mints stopped producing large denominations at about this time (Picard 1990; cf. Mørkholm 1991: 88). He sees this development as reflecting an increasing distinction between the large denomination 'hellenic' coinage for international use and smaller denomination coinage for local use. In making this contrast, Picard is echoing the distinction between hellenic and local currency proposed by Plato (*Laws* V, 741 e–742 c), and reflected in the wide acceptability of Athenian coin noted by Xenophon (*Poroi* II, 3 (2)). The distinction never became absolute – for example Athens and Crete continued to produce large denominations – but it does show how local coinages might have been affected by the Macedonian issues other than through suppression or impoverishment.

The 'international' role of Macedonian coinage was spectacularly enhanced under Alexander (Price 1991a). Again the date of introduction of the coinage in his name is problematic. It has already been noted that hoard evidence suggests that gold in the name of Philip may have extended after his death. Quite a strong case has been made on the basis of typology that Alexander's silver did not commence until three years after his accession (it is argued that the Zeus on the reverse was copied from the Baal on coins of Tarsos, and that such an influence makes sense only after Alexander's capture of Cilicia) (Troxell 1991) [42 cf. 37]. Since Philip's latest silver coinage shares symbols with Alexander's earliest, it has been argued that the production of Philip's silver also extended into Alexander's reign [41–2]. A 'posthumous' series is not impossible – that the coinages in the name of Alexander and Lysimachus continued long after their deaths is beyond all doubt – but in the case of Philip's coinage it should not be accepted without some circumspection. If Alexander had to use silver in the name of Philip for the first three years of his reign, why is 'Philip's' silver not found in reasonable quantities in Asia Minor (or is the absence of evidence misleading in this respect: de Callataÿ 1982: 24)?

For our purposes the chronological crux is not of great importance. Whether Alexander struck in his own name before 333 BC or not, it was the capture of Persian treasure between 333 and 330 BC which supported the massive production of his coinage. It is said that 180,000 talents (calculated in silver) were gathered together at Ecbatana in 330 BC, representing the booty of conquest. No such sum changed hands again through conquest until the Spanish exploitation of the New World in the sixteenth and seventeenth centuries. By no means all of the booty from the Persian empire will have been coined, but the coinage was nevertheless massive (de Callataÿ 1989).

Alexander's coinage was geographically extensive, as well as large. Mints were established at satrapal centres and points of communication back to Macedon. Twenty-six mints have been identified during Alexander's lifetime, stretching from Macedon to Egypt and Susa. Heavy minting in a number of areas in the last few years of the reign has been plausibly associated with the paying-off of soldiers sent back from the east from c. 324 BC (Thompson 1984; Troxell 1991; Price 1991a: 453–7). The coining of so much bullion into a standardized coinage of gold, silver, and bronze across such an area was a monetary phenomenon of unparalleled importance.

In the east Alexander's coinage took over the role of an international coinage from the Athenian tetradrachm, and extended its scope. No doubt this was facilitated by Alexander's adoption of the Attic standard for his silver. Areas such as Cilicia, where the Persian (to be exact the double-siglos) standard had prevailed, came to be dominated by Attic weight coins. Coinage in the name of Alexander became so well established that it continued to be produced by kings and cities for up to 250 years [66–7]. The majority of the four thousand varieties were in fact posthumous. Coinage struck in the name of Alexander had the advantages not only of being recognizable and widely accepted, but also of being politically neutral in the shifting sands of hellenistic hegemony. The international role of posthumous Alexanders may be illustrated by a consideration of the coinage struck at Rhodes. The circulation of coins with civic types on the Rhodian standard was largely confined to Rhodes and its territory in Asia Minor, but the 'Alexanders' produced there (with the mintmark of a rose) in *c.* 200–190 BC travelled much more widely [66]. Such 'Alexanders' are perhaps best considered as civic coinages struck for international use (whether for military purposes, trade, or whatever).

The domination of the currency by Alexander coinage came about gradually. A hoard from Babylon buried around the time of Alexander's death still had imitation Athenian tetradrachms as its largest component (it also had local coinages in addition to the 'imperial' issues) (Price 1991b). There was no attempt to impose Alexander's coinage as an exclusive currency. Civic issues continued, as we have seen (p. 48). It is tempting to single out the coins of Hierapolis-Bambyce in Syria which show Alexander on horseback and have his name transliterated into Aramaic [48]. Not only did some cities continue to strike, but some local style coinages even bore the name of Alexander's governors (Balacrus was named on a silver issue from Tarsos, Mazaeus on the lion staters of Babylonia, and Stamenes on the double darics also from Babylonia [47]). The denomination of the double daric was an innovation under Alexander, but otherwise the coinage shows him striking in continuation of the Achaemenid coinage. Five and two shekel pieces were produced with types which honoured Alexander's Indian campaigns [45–6]. The cultural diversity tolerated by the Persians was in a sense continued by Alexander's policy of fusion.

Even more than the coinage of Philip II, that of Alexander functioned as an 'hellenic' currency. In so far as it replaced anything, the losers were primarily the coinage of Athens and its imitations. There may well have been a significant diminution in civic issues, but, if so, the causes were lack of need, desire, or resources, rather than suppression.

SELEUCIDS

The successor kings continued to strike coinage with Alexander's types, sometimes in Alexander's name and sometimes in their own. Under Seleucus I 'Alexanders' were struck at all mints except Bactra. A coinage with new royal types was minted in his reign, but it was left for Antiochus I to put his own portrait on the coins [70]. 'Alexanders' were the dominant currency of the Seleucid empire, and the coinage with royal types was only one among many. In general, coinages not on the Attic weight standard were excluded: thus, for example, Ptolemaic and Rhodian coins did not circulate there, nor did Attalid cistophori. There may well have been regulations enforcing the use of Attic weight coins: without regulation different weight-standards had co-existed under the Achaemenids. If there were regulations they were presumably motivated by practical rather than ideological considerations, and they were not applied in Coele-Syria and Phoenicia after these areas were captured by Antiochus III in 200 BC. The Attic standard co-existed with the Ptolemaic there, and the Seleucids even struck coins on the Ptolemaic standard for the region (Le Rider 1986).

The impression given is that Seleucid policy (if there was any) tended towards the laissez-faire, but that is not the whole story. Under the Persians satraps had struck coins, and some of Alexander's governors had continued the practice. The Seleucids retained the Achaemenid system of satrapies, but did not allow satraps to coin in their own name (Sherwin-White and Kuhrt 1993: 23, 42; perhaps with a few exceptions, 76–7). Some cities did strike their own bronze coinages, but the production of gold and large silver denominations became confined to royal mints (Mørkholm 1984: 103). Moreover, we have already seen that some cities reacted to the gradual withdrawal of Seleucid control in the last decades of the second century BC by producing their own silver coinages, often blazoning their new autonomy (see p. 41). This may be taken to imply some measure of restraint earlier, and that this was considered as an aspect of the limiting of political autonomy. Even the civic bronze coinage cannot be taken as an unequivocal indication of a (restricted) freedom of action by the cities. In the year 169/8 BC nineteen cities in Cilicia, Syria, Phoenicia, and Mesopotamia suddenly issued bronze coins bearing the portrait of Antiochus IV (Mørkholm 1984: 101–2) [72]. Whatever the context, it is hard to imagine that these civic coinages were not produced by royal command.

PTOLEMIES

In stark contrast to the Seleucid laissez-faire was the imposition of an exclusive royal coinage by the Ptolemies (Le Rider 1986; Jenkins 1967). By c. 310 BC Ptolemy I had stopped striking coins with Alexander types and had abandoned the Attic weight standard. Before the end of the century his portrait began to appear on the royal coinage. By c. 290 BC, after a series of reductions, the weight of the

Ptolemaic tetradrachm was established at 14.3g (the Attic standard was 17.2g). The new tetradrachms had the portrait of Ptolemy wearing a diadem on one side, and the dynastic badge of an eagle on a thunderbolt on the other [77]. Hoard evidence shows that already under Ptolemy I the royal coinage became the only currency used within the kingdom. A papyrus of 258/7 BC reveals some of the mechanisms of an exclusive currency: those coming from abroad with foreign gold coinages had to exchange them for (or have them restruck into) Ptolemaic gold at the mint.

In one respect the imposition of a monopoly coinage will not have been problematic in Egypt. Some imitation Athenian silver coins had been produced at Memphis (and perhaps elsewhere) under the Persians [38–9], and some Alexander coinage may be attributed to Memphis or Alexandria. There were, however, no Greek cities with a tradition of coinage to suppress. That said, the monopoly enjoyed by the royal coinage came to apply also to the Ptolemaic dominions in Cyprus and Syria-Phoenicia, and royal coinage was minted in Cyprus, Phoenicia, and Palestine (and occasionally elsewhere). In other areas there was some latitude: Ephesos under Ptolemaic protectorate struck on a Ptolemaic standard, but with both royal and local types (Le Rider 1991: 195). Cyrenaica too produced both royal and local coinages.

In areas where Ptolemaic dominions confronted other kingdoms, such as Cilicia Trachea, one finds hoards in which Ptolemaic coins are mixed with other types of coinage. Such hoards presumably reflect in some way the need for transactions (including trade) across political boundaries. In areas of Ptolemaic 'influence' – sometimes occasional as in the case of temporary garrisons, military interventions, or political subsidies – Ptolemaic coinage in all metals is again found mixed with other coinages. Greece, Crete, and the Aegean fell into this category. Otherwise Ptolemaic coinage was not (as far as we can tell) exported in significant quantities. It is possible (even plausible) that those who wanted to transact business within Ptolemaic dominions had to exchange Attic tetradrachms directly for Ptolemaic, despite the lower weight of the latter. If that was the case it is easy to see why there would have been a disincentive to export the relatively over-valued Ptolemaic coinage to regions where that artificial premium would not be recognized.

The Ptolemaic closed currency system may have had revenue as its prime objective (there may have been a charge for exchange, or just the profit in bullion of exchanging lighter coins for heavier).

It is also possible that the effect of retaining Ptolemaic silver coinage within the kingdom was intended. Egypt did not possess significant sources of silver, and the Ptolemaic realms came to rely more heavily on gold and (heavy) bronze coinage (from the second half of the third century BC) than was the case elsewhere (Mørkholm 1991: 101–11). Whatever the motivation, the currency system was one aspect of royal control over contact with the outside world, and internally the use of a standardized royal coinage was not without a symbolic significance.

ATTALIDS

The Attalid dynasty at Pergamum exploited the weakness of the Seleucid empire to become a major force in Asia Minor in the third and second centuries BC (Le Rider 1989 for the coinage). The dynasty was founded by Philetaerus who had been Lysimachus' treasurer at Pergamum, but made himself independent in 284 BC. Philetaerus struck Attic-weight coins with Alexander types, first in the name of Alexander, then in that of Seleucus. Afterwards he struck in his own name, but seemingly with a portrait of Seleucus. Later kings put the head of Philetaerus himself on their coins [58]. As was the case in the Seleucid empire, this royal coinage never played more than a subordinate role in the currency even within the Pergamene kingdom. The kingdom seems to have been open to all Attic-weight coinages, and the 'philetaeri' travelled abroad.

A major change took place with the introduction of the cistophoric coinage at some time between the late 190s and the late 170s BC. The coinage was named after its type, the sacred chest (cista) [59]. Issues were produced by a number of cities, perhaps with some degree of centralized minting (there are a small number of die links between cities, and Tralles seems to have been responsible for most of the fractional coinage). As with the Ptolemaic system, the cistophoric tetradrachm was lighter than the Attic (by 25 per cent), and it appears to have been an exclusive currency within Attalid territory.

The Attalid situation was more complicated than the Ptolemaic in one respect: some Attic-weight coinages continued to be produced within the kingdom. The last issue of 'philetaeri' was (almost certainly) struck after the introduction of the cistophori, as may have been two other rare types of tetradrachm, one with the portrait of Eumenes II, the other showing Athena Nikephoros. Civic coinages on the Attic standard also continued: Tralles and Ephesos both struck gold, and

Ephesos minted a substantial series of drachms [65]. The interpretation of the cistophori as the basis for a closed currency system on
the Ptolemaic model rests on the assumption that all these Attic-
weight coinages were struck for export. When the findspots are known
they do indeed prove to be outside the kingdom. The Ephesian
drachms, for example, are found in Syria and Phoenicia, and at Susa,
and were imitated at Arados.

The same explanation may lie behind the sizeable issues of
stephanephoroi (Attic tetradrachms, termed stephanephoroi because
the reverse design appears within a wreath), struck by eight cities in
Aeolis and Ionia *c.* 155–145 BC [64]. Two features in particular need
explaining. First, the relative size of issues does not seem to have
reflected the importance of the cities (for example the issues of Cyme
and Myrina were very substantial, that of Smyrna small). Second,
great hoards of stephanephoroi have been discovered in Cilicia and
Syria. Both these aspects would be explained if the stephanephoroi
were produced (at least in part) for the Attalid kingdom as a currency
for external purposes (whether for trade or for military subsidies)
(Kinns 1987: 106–7). Some, at least, of the mint cities had been
declared free after the peace of Apamea (for example Cyme, Smyrna,
and Heraclea) (Jones 1971: 52–3), but that does not exclude the possibility that Attalus II had coins struck there by arrangement.

By contrast with the Attic-weight coinages discussed so far,
cistophori circulated largely within the Pergamene kingdom. That is
understandable if they were over-valued in a similar manner to
Ptolemaic coinage, and there is reason to think that they were. Soon
after the introduction of the cistophori a number of Attic-weight
tetradrachms were stamped with cistophoric countermarks (the bow
case from the reverse of the cistophori, and letters indicating the mint)
[68]. The most plausible explanation is that early in the new monetary regime the Attic tetradrachms were being equated with
cistophori, despite the fact that the latter were lighter by a quarter.
If cistophori were overvalued it is easy to understand why it was
preferable to receive proconsular expenses in denarii (Cic., *Att.* II, 6).

Thus the Attalid system was in some ways similar to the Ptolemaic,
but there were differences. First, Attic-weight coins continued to be
produced for export (it is hard to tell whether civic issues of Attic
weight were merely tolerated, or are themselves really an Attalid
coinage for export). Second, the appearance of the cistophori is not
that of a royal coinage although the types do refer to Dionysus and
Heracles, from whom the Attalids claimed descent [59]. They carried

no royal name or portrait, but were signed by the cities which collab-
orated to produce them. Le Rider (1989) has interpreted the coinage
as royal in character, but in form that of a confederation of cities. It
is possible that the form reflects a certain ambivalence in the status
of cities such as Ephesos and Tralles under the Attalids (as Le Rider
points out, they were given to Eumenes II by the treaty of Apamea,
but in what sense?). It is also possible that the relative neutrality of
the types was part of the rhetoric of the Attalid posture of championing the cause of the Greeks in Asia Minor. Moreover, the lack
of portraits may be taken to reflect the basically civilian model of the
style of rule publicized by the Attalids (cf. Sherwin-White and Kuhrt
1993: 114; Hansen 1971: 187–203). These suggestions bear directly
on our general topic: the use of cistophori was part of the definition
of belonging to the Attalid kingdom, and the visual symbolism of the
coinage arguably reflects the presentation of the kingdom.

ROME

'None of the cities should be allowed to have its own separate coinage
or system of weights and measures; they should all be required
to use ours' (Dio LII, 30, 9). The words put into the mouth of
Maecenas by Dio may be taken to show that there was debate
on the topic when Dio was writing in the early third century AD.
The context within Maecenas' speech is a programme for ordering
the affairs of cities in the Empire, and of constraining unnecessary
expenditure, but also of emphasizing the supremacy of Rome
(LII, 30, 1). The passage thus weaves together some of the principal
strands with which we have been concerned, the more so since
the tone and the juxtaposition of coinage, weights, and measures
is highly reminiscent of the Athenian decree with which we began
(see p. 44).

The story of what happened to coinages as Rome expanded and
consolidated its imperial rule is too complex to tell in detail here
(Crawford 1985; Burnett and Crawford 1987; *RPC* I). An important
part of the context, but one which is difficult to link to the ending
of particular local coinages, is the siphoning off to Rome of vast
quantities of precious metals from around the Mediterranean
(Crawford 1985; Howgego 1992: 4–5). It has already been noted
that there were tendencies for civic or regional coinages to persist
longer in the east than in the west, and for coinages in base metal
to last longer than those in silver (see p. 11). When local coinages

persisted there was also a trend towards systems of denominations becoming assimilated to, or easily convertible into, the Roman (Howgego 1985: 52–60; *RPC* I: 26–37). This process will have been in part the result of a multiplicity of decisions taken in particular circumstances. We happen to know that in Thessaly reckoning in denarii was imposed by an edict of Augustus, and that Germanicus in Syria in AD 18–19 stipulated that taxes should be reckoned in Italian asses (*RPC* I: 28, 31).

Rome took over and continued a great variety of coinages, including the Seleucid, Ptolemaic, and Attalid currencies which we have already discussed. The continuity of form means that it may be hard to decide when (or to what extent) such coinages should be considered Roman (struck on Roman orders, perhaps from Roman bullion, perhaps for the purposes of the Roman state). For example, after Asia was bequeathed to Rome in 133 BC cistophori continued to be struck [60–2]. Some Roman involvement is suggested by the way in which the cost of Lucullus' campaigns against Mithridates in 70–67 BC seems to be reflected in the increased size and complexity of the Ephesian cistophoric issues of these years (Kinns 1987: 111). When cistophori began to bear the names of proconsuls in 58 BC [60], or ruler-portraits from the time of Mark Antony [61], were these changes of substance or merely of presentation? In a similar vein, it is a matter for debate how the Athenian 'New Style' coinage, probably inaugurated after Rome put an end to the kingdom of Macedonia in 167 BC, and struck in substantial quantities until the 40s BC, came to be an important regional coinage in southern Greece and beyond (Crawford 1985: 125; Price 1987a) [53]. To what extent, and in what ways, were the Romans involved? One can, and should, ask such questions of all the regional silver coinages which continued after annexation.

The gradual process of the Romanization of the coinage is hard to illustrate directly from the coinage, because it largely consisted in the ending of the production of local series. It does, however, seem poignant that the last issue struck at Locri in south Italy, after the Pyrrhic War, had a clear reference to the city's *deditio in fidem* to Rome [86]. After that, no coinage. Assimilation to the Roman system of denominations may be illustrated by the civic bronze of Chios: a coinage of obols and chalcoi was gradually replaced by one of multiples and fractions of assaria (Roman asses) in the first and second centuries AD [161].

The apparent inevitability of the process of Romanization masks a long process of *ad hoc*, and sometimes contrary, decisions. In the early years of expansion the effect of Roman control was unequivocal. By the end of the Second Punic War not only had all the cities in Italy and Sicily ceased to mint silver coinage, but the 'local' silver had virtually disappeared from circulation. (By contrast some civic bronzes continued to be struck until the reign of Tiberius.)

The later Republic was a period of greater ambiguity. It is not surprising that the gold and silver of Carthage ceased to circulate after its destruction in 146 BC. In Spain, on the other hand, although Roman denarii did arrive during the Second Punic War and again from the last quarter of the second century BC, local style coinages in silver and bronze were actually introduced under the Romans in the second century BC [87]. These 'Iberian' coinages were modelled on Roman denominations, but had different (although fairly standardized) types, and inscriptions in Iberian and Celtic. Whether one sees these coinages as a Roman institution or as a local initiative is a matter of debate. Such 'Iberian' coinage ended c. 50 BC, although civic bronzes flowered in Spain in the early principate. Elsewhere in the west local tribal ('Celtic') coinages tended to come to an end soon after annexation [149–52]. In the east, regional silver coinages were continued under the Romans. Denarii were slow to arrive in the east, and finally displaced the regional systems only in the third century AD.

In the west civic bronze coinages gradually petered out, and none was struck after the reign of Claudius. In the east they showed great vitality, until themselves petering out in the third quarter of the third century AD. The reason for the ending of the civic bronzes is unclear in both cases. In neither west nor east does the gradual ending suggest a single Roman measure banning local coinage, although some more subtle form of discouragement is possible. The fact that civic bronze coinages lasted more than two centuries longer in the east than in the west also needs explaining. It is possible that the phenomenon reflects a cultural difference. The citizens of the western provinces came to see themselves as Romans: there were no local histories, and civic architecture was very much on the Roman model. In the east, despite some degree of assimilation and identification with Rome, Greek traditions were consciously maintained, renewed, and even created. The production of local coinage by a community in the east became an indication (although not a defining characteristic) of its claim to the status of a *polis* (see pp. 42–3). This cultural dichotomy may help to explain why the western provinces came to use standardized Roman coin exclusively from the early principate, but in the east that development had to wait until the later third century AD.

It was with the ending of the 'Ptolemaic' closed currency system in Egypt under Diocletian [173] that the Empire finally came to have a unified currency based on a standardized coinage in all metals produced at mints throughout the provinces. Such a uniformity had been attempted by Athens, and achieved by the Ptolemies, but for much more confined areas. In the light of the debate reflected in Dio (see p. 56) there can be little doubt that there was a measure of intention behind the imposition of uniformity, but not all the steps along the way will have been taken consciously towards that end. That does not weaken the case for considering coinage systems in the context of imperialism. It has been persuasively argued that the true driving forces behind the development of Roman imperialism in general were Rome's political, military, and cultural systems, of which conscious motives were merely one superficial aspect (North 1981).

CONCLUSION

The strongest impression gained from this selective review of the impact of empires on monetary systems may be one of variety and complexity. Approaches ranged from the totally laissez-faire, to the imposition of a single currency. Individual empires might change their approach over time (for example, the Attalids, or Rome), or adopt different policies in different regions (thus there is a contrast between core and periphery within Ptolemaic domains, and between east and west under the Roman Empire). It may, therefore, be worth drawing attention to some general points which do emerge.

It does seem that a connection was felt to exist at one time or another between the act of coining and the assertion of autonomy, independence, and political or cultural identity. The political status symbolized by the act of minting changed as the role of cities evolved. Imperial coinages for their part may be seen as a manifestation and assertion of power and belonging. The effectiveness of the propagation of ideology through coinage will be addressed in the next chapter.

Between the poles of laissez-faire and the imposition of an imperial currency, a wide range of possibilities and nuances existed. Some imperial coinages were never dominant in a numerical sense (for example the sigloi of Persia, or the royal portrait coinages of the

Seleucids and Attalids). 'Royal' coinages might show a representation of the founder of the dynasty rather than the current king, and sometimes even avoided both (the posthumous Alexander coinage, and the Attalid cistophori). On the other hand, civic coinages might be the object of interference by the imperial power (for example, through the granting of permission to coin, the coordination of the introduction of royal portraits, and the standardization of denominational systems). Local bronze coinages might be tolerated longer than those of silver or gold. Moreover, some apparently civic or local coinages can be understood only as imperial coinages in disguise (see under Persia, the Attalids, and Rome). The very existence within empires of cities with some degree of independence posed questions to which different solutions were found.

Why different arrangements were adopted in different circumstances must remain to some degree conjectural, but monetary systems do seem to fit the character of particular empires (or perhaps one should say their presentation of power). To caricature brutally, coinages reflect the power politics of Athens, laissez-faire under the Persians, the fusion of Alexander, central control by the Ptolemies, the looser royal prerogatives of the Seleucids, the civilian style of rule and the championing of Greek cities by the Attalids, and the *ad hoc* but seemingly inevitable imperialism of Rome.

Imperial ideology was not the only factor at work. The differences between the east and west of the Roman Empire may be explained most easily in cultural terms. These were also hard economic and financial realities. The dominant international role of the coinages of Athens, Philip and Alexander, and Rome depended upon the minting of vast quantities of bullion from the mines, or tribute, or booty. The need to collect tribute may well have coloured the monetary policies of Persia (under Darius), Athens, and Rome among others. The closed currency systems of the Ptolemies and Attalids may have been motived by profit, or by the need to control the movement of silver coin. Ideology is not to be underestimated, however. The extraordinary attempt by Athens to impose its own civic coinage on its allies is indeed suggestive of how Athenians may have come to conceive of their empire as a *polis* writ large, with themselves holding a monopoly of political and judicial power, and of prestige.

As a final observation, the apparent neatness with which monetary systems fit the character of empires should cause us to question whether coinage has to some extent determined our own typology of empires. Has the lack of a coherent coinage system contributed to our confusion about the nature of the Carthaginian 'empire' (cf. Whittaker 1978)? Have the prohibition against the ownership of coinage by Spartiates, and the fact that Sparta produced no coinage of its own until the third century BC, coloured our approach to Spartan activities abroad? And has the lack of an imperial coinage informed our view of other regional hegemonies?

Chapter 4

Politics

COIN TYPES AND POLITICS

The symbolic significance of the varied emblems found on early electrum coinage is seldom apparent. Most types may be no more than decorative means of identification drawn from a stock repertoire, although a few do appear to be civic or regal badges (Spier 1990). Most subsequent coin types are political in that they assert the identity of the *polis*, kingdom, or state which produced them, or of the individual responsible for the coinage. It might be a matter of pride for the badge of the city to be current, and the act of coining itself might be an affirmation of the status or autonomy of a *polis*, or of the legitimacy of a ruler (see pp. 39–44). This chapter confines itself to coin types which are more specifically political in content, and which bear on the realities and presentation of power, or on achievements and aspirations.

Coins cannot compare with literary sources in revealing the complexity of intentions and shifting sands of allegiance which make up political life, but they do have several advantages for the historian. First, in periods of autocracy they generally present the official line, and hence provide an important supplement to an often meagre body of surviving official literature and monuments. Second, while literary sources may illuminate brilliantly short periods or episodes, coins offer a much more continuous chronological and geographical coverage. Third, for many periods we may be confident that we have a comparatively complete knowledge of the typology of the coins, in sharp contrast to the low and uneven survival rate of literary sources. Finally, coins are a strictly contemporary source, lacking the disadvantages (and advantages) of the element of retrospect characteristic, for example, of historical writing.

PATTERNS OF POLITICAL REPRESENTATION: GREECE

The history of 'political' representations on coinage is revealing in itself, as regards both what was thought suitable for depiction, and what was not. Coin types of the archaic and classical periods were very rarely 'political' in the narrow sense already defined. They emphasized civic identity, often through religion or mythology, but revealed hardly any trace of war or dominant external powers, of internal struggles between oligarchs and democrats, or of powerful individuals. The only significant exception is the aristocratic pre-occupation with panhellenic competition displayed by some tyrants or kings, and which is readily recognizable from Pindar. Anaxilas, for example, celebrated his Olympic mule car victory of 484 or 480 BC on his coinage at Rhegium and Zancle-Messana (the types earned comment from Aristotle, fr. 578 R) [14].

The clearest case of political symbolism was evoked by the need to choose a coin type which would be suitable for a coordinated issue by seven cities in Asia Minor, apparently in the context of a pro-Spartan alliance after 405 BC. The issues have appropriate civic types on one side, but share the symbolism of the infant Heracles strangling a serpent on the other [10]. The reference appears to be to Lysander, the Spartan naval commander, who was a Heraclid, and who was praised by Ion of Samos for having broken the force of the snake-shaped Kekrops (Athens) (Karwiese 1980). This exceptional use of political symbolism is explicable because it was precisely the political context of the alliance which the seven cities had in common.

A more obvious, but still rare, political use of coin types was the intrusion of extraneous symbols to reflect control by outsiders. Thus the Samians who occupied Zancle in Sicily c. 493–488 BC struck coins with Samian types (see p. 6; Robinson 1946) [13]. When Theron of Acragas took Himera c. 483 BC, the crab of Acragas appeared on the reverses of coins of the occupied city (Kraay 1976: 209). Likewise the 'Syracusan' quadriga on coins of Gela and Leontinoi in the 470s BC was a symbol of control by the Syracusan tyrants (formerly of Gela) (Kraay 1976: 210–11).

Of greater general significance was the development of the representation of individuals on coins. The extent to which recognizable individual characteristics were represented in particular cases, rather than generic types, is important for the history of portraiture, but the fact that individuals were depicted at all is paramount. It implied that the individual was a symbol of the state, and hence demonstrated a claim to rule.

The history of numismatic portraiture leaves the impression that portraiture was an eastern phenomenon, a notion which is at variance with other evidence (Richter 1984; Fittschen 1988). Private representations of individuals in public places in the Greek world date back to the middle of the seventh century BC. Literary and typological evidence reveals the erection of public statues and paintings of individuals in fifth-century BC Athens. The salient point is that portraits could occur on coins only in situations where an individual held power: hence the preponderance of early portraits within the Persian sphere (although the lack of depictions of kings on the coins of Macedon, at least before Philip II, may still be remarked, and cannot be explained away by the no longer tenable idea that the Macedonian monarchy was a limited autocracy; Sherwin-White and Kuhrt 1993: 118). If it is correct to identify the bearded head on coins of Magnesia on the Maeander as a contemporary head of Themistocles (and hence as the earliest numismatic portrait), then arguably we may see an Athenian in exile exporting the idea of portraiture and exploiting it for coinage in a way which would have been impossible at home (Cahn and Gerin 1988) [31]. The identification of the head and the date of the Magnesian coins are far from certain, and perhaps should not be pressed. At any rate, satrapal and dynastic portraits are a well-attested phenomenon in Asia Minor from the last decades of the fifth century BC to the middle of the fourth (Fittschen 1988: 20–1; Cahn 1989) [34–6].

Outside the Persian sphere we have to wait for the bearded figure on horseback on the early silver of Philip II, which is generally taken to be the King himself [40]. Earlier in this tradition, but from within the Persian empire, were the coins from north-west Asia Minor depicting Tissaphernes on horseback, and later the figure of the mounted Alexander on coins from Hierapolis-Bambyce in Syria [48]. Most striking of all is the issue, possibly minted at Susa *c.* 324 BC, which depicts Alexander on horseback fighting against an Indian (presumably Porus) mounted on an elephant, and, on the other side, Alexander dressed as a Greek cavalryman, but holding a thunderbolt and crowned by a flying Nike (Price 1982) [45]. Here we have a foretaste both of the martial and triumphal iconography of imperialism, which came to be characteristic of Roman coinage, and of the intimations of godhead, strictly paralleled by the painting of Alexander as Zeus by Apelles at Ephesos, and which is a feature of hellenistic royal portraiture from the start.

Portrait heads are not found on the coins of Philip II or Alexander, with the possible (if not plausible) exception of the supposed head of Alexander on some small bronze coins from Memphis in Egypt (Price 1981). The origin of hellenistic portraiture on coins lay with Ptolemy in Egypt *c.* 305/4 BC [77], and in Europe with Demetrius Poliorcetes a decade or so later [51]. Kings were shown with a diadem, the white headband which became a royal symbol from the time of Alexander (Smith 1988a: 34–8).

In the early period, and also later in the case of the Ptolemies, royal portraits were adorned with divine attributes (Smith 1988a: 38–45). Ptolemy I was depicted wearing the aegis of Zeus [77]. Demetrius Poliorcetes donned the bull's horns of Dionysus, on whom he modelled himself (Plutarch, *Dem.* 2) [51]. The horns also imitated Alexander's horns of Zeus Ammon (Smith 1988a: 41, 52). Such divine iconography seems in some cases to have antedated the official organization of state ruler cults (cf. Sherwin-White and Kuhrt 1993: 116–18). Later coin inscriptions made the implications of godhead explicit. Thus the Seleucid king Antiochus IV was labelled 'god manifest' [71], and Antiochus VI became more specifically 'the manifest Dionysus' [73]. Claims might be multiplied: on posthumous issues Ptolemy III was depicted with the aegis of Zeus, the trident of Poseidon, and the radiate crown of the sun god Apollo [79].

Nor was the usefulness of portraiture for emphasizing dynastic continuity missed: coins under Ptolemy II showed not only the king and his sister-wife Arsinoe II, but also the deified Ptolemy I and Berenice [78]. Legitimacy might also be claimed by displaying earlier rulers. The invocation of Alexander remained a potent force (Stewart 1993; Sherwin-White and Kuhrt 1993: 115–16). His image, with divine attributes, was to be found on the early coins of Ptolemy I [76], on some issues of Seleucus I, and regularly on the coinage of Lysimachus [56]. In the same vein the coins of the Ptolemies and the early Attalids continued to display portraits of the founders of their dynasties, Ptolemy I and Philetaerus [58] respectively.

The development and spread of portraiture was far and away the most important aspect of political iconography on coinage of the late classical and hellenistic periods. More general political aspirations and references to specific achievements were rare. A claim to be Greek, and to lead the Panhellenic cause, may be seen in the coinage of Philip and Alexander. Philip's gold and silver coinage depicted Zeus and Apollo, the gods of the two great panhellenic centres at Olympia and Delphi, and his reverses showed his Olympic victories in the manner of a true Greek aristocrat (cf. Plutarch, *Alex.* 4, 5) [41, 43]. The head of Athena and the naval victory on Alexander's gold presumably harked back to Salamis, and implied common cause against Persia [44]. The Heracles on the obverse of his silver had precedents under earlier Macedonian kings, and recalled Alexander's claim that he was related to the hero through Temenos of Argos (and hence established his credentials to be Greek) [42]. If the Zeus on the reverse was indeed modelled on the Baal of Tarsos (see p. 49), then the figure perhaps hinted at a wide claim to rule [42 cf. 37]. Such interpretations are necessarily speculative, and intentions and meanings will have been complex even at the time the coins were minted.

Claims to divine origins might be alluded to on the reverses. The adoption of Apollo as a standard Seleucid type under Antiochus I reflected the emphasis placed on the god as founder of the dynasty and father of Seleucus [70]. Antiochus I, unlike Seleucus, placed his own head on the coins. Both the royal portrait and the figure of Apollo on the reverse may be viewed as an attempt by the second Seleucid king to establish a sense of dynasty (Sherwin-White and Kuhrt 1993: 27–8).

Greek coins did not go far beyond this generalized type of political iconography. Alexander's Indian campaign was celebrated on coins from Susa (?), as we have seen [45–6]. There are no other such 'historical' action scenes on Greek coinage before the Roman period, although there are some more oblique references to significant events (cf. Hölscher 1973: 200–2, 218). The prominence of elephants on coins struck at the eastern mint of Seleucus after *c.* 305 BC reflected his acquisition of a huge force of war elephants from Chandragupta (Sherwin-White and Kuhrt 1993: 12; Mørkholm 1991: 71–3) [69]. Demetrius' Nike on a galley and Poseidon referred back to his great sea victory of 306 BC, at a time when he had come to rely heavily on his fleet [50]. The eponymous boy Taras appealing to his father Poseidon on an issue of gold from Taras in Italy *c.* 340 BC may plausibly be understood to symbolize an appeal to Sparta, the parent city of Taras, for help against the Italian tribes (Kraay 1976: 191–2). Various other less vivid coin types from Greek cities in south Italy and Sicily reflected such appeals to champions in mainland Greece, from the Spartan king Archidamus to Alexander the Molossian and Pyrrhus (Kraay 1976: 189–203; Carradice and Price 1988: 120). At the end of this tradition belongs the silver coinage of Locri which represents the city entrusting itself to Rome (its *deditio in fidem*) by a figure of Good Faith (Pistis) crowning Roma [86].

It is very rare for Greek coin types to carry references as specific as these. In marked contrast, Roman coinages came to display a much greater intensity and complexity of political imagery, and raise more acutely questions of intention and reception. For these reasons the discussion in the rest of this chapter will be confined to the Roman period.

PATTERNS OF POLITICAL REPRESENTATION: ROME

The iconography of early Roman coinage was drawn from Greek coins, and shared the tendency to keep types the same over long periods with scarcely any specific reference to political concerns. The types represented the state as a whole, and were thus in line with other forms of public representational art (in which – by contrast with the coins – individuals were depicted, but only in contexts which were significant for the state) (Hölscher 1980: 269–71). All that changed from the 130s BC. Some conservatism persisted, but the overwhelming impression is of a multiplicity of types which came to reflect the individual concerns of the annually changing moneyers, the *triumviri monetales*, or of the other magistrates or supra-legal commanders who from time to time struck coins.

Roman coin designs developed from the repertoire and idiom of hellenistic art (see p. 75), but one is struck most of all by the contrast between Greek and Roman coinage. It is the specific character of subsequent Roman coin types which needs explaining, rather than the more typical conservatism of Greek coinages. The explanation lies in the increasing acceptability of public display as a weapon in the heightened competition within the elite at Rome. The Lex Gabinia of 139 BC, which sought to restrain electoral corruption by introducing a secret ballot, is clearly relevant to this theme, although there is perhaps no need to see a direct link with the increased political content of the coinage (as an alternative means of canvassing, as once argued by Crawford, *RRC* p. 728). The more general context is provided by the sumptuary laws of the second century BC, which are best understood as (vain) attempts to restrain excessive competition within the oligarchy (Harris 1979: 89; cf. Appadurai 1986: 25). The second half of the second century BC saw a move away from the necessary oligarchic conception that there should be some moderation in the pursuit of individual power and glory (Harris 1979: 27).

The choice of personal types by annual officials set the pattern of variable and sometimes highly specific typology which was to persist until the later Roman Empire. The coin types may be considered political from the start, for the ubiquitous references to family and to ancestral achievements were a normal part of political discourse at Rome. Inevitably individual choice of coin types soon led to the reflection of contemporary events and powerful individuals. The Gallic trophy on coins of c. 119 BC commemorated the defeat of the Allobroges and Arverni [92], the Victory and Gallic trophy in c. 101 BC the defeat of the Cimbri and Teutones (*RRC* 326/2). What is even more significant on coinage of the latter year is the depiction of Marius as triumphator [93]. Coins struck in Sulla's lifetime show his two trophies for Chaeronea and assert his double imperatorial acclamation [96], depict Sulla as triumphator crowned by Victory [97], and display his equestrian statue labelled L. SULLA FELIX DIC(TATOR) (*RRC* 381).

A highly abbreviated system of visual symbols was used to glorify the achievements of Pompey. A single coin type struck by Faustus Cornelius Sulla, Pompey's lieutenant in his eastern wars and later his son-in-law, displayed one large and three smaller wreaths, the stern ornament of a ship, an ear of corn, and a globe, with reference respectively to the *corona aurea*, the three triumphs, the command against the pirates, the *cura annonae*, and the claim to have extended the frontiers of the Empire to the ends of the earth [100]. This last claim was made by Pompey in a grandiose inscription, and by the trophy for the 'Oikoumene' represented in his triumphal procession (Diod. XL, 4; Dio XXXVII, 21, 2). This abstract symbolism of power foreshadowed the emphasis placed on the *corona civica*, the *clipeus virtutis*, and the laurel branches under Augustus (Zanker 1988: 89–98) [114].

The introduction of portraiture marked an important stage, as it had done in the hellenistic kingdoms. The implicit identification of the individual portrayed with the state was obviously a problem for the Romans, although it may have been partially mitigated by the tradition that coin types might be private. The portrait of Flamininus on gold coins struck in Greece stood wholly outside the Roman numismatic tradition [52]. It was not until c. 54 BC that portraits of recent ancestors appeared on the coinage of Rome, and when Julius Caesar became the first living individual to be portrayed it was of sufficient significance to be done by senatorial decree (Dio XLIV, 4, 4) [105]. Once adopted, portraiture rapidly became an established feature of the coinage. Given that the first coin portrait belonged in the context of the quasi-regal honours for Caesar in 44 BC, it cannot fail to surprise that within two years the conspirator Brutus was depicted on coins [107]. As hypocritical as this may appear, it at least makes sense in the context of the inevitable drift towards autocracy.

The authority for coinage in the triumviral period was presumably as irregular as other constitutional arrangements, but with the show of a return to Republican legality in 23 BC the *triumviri monetales* were again named on the coins [115–16]. For a while the types of the precious metal coinage reflected the claims of both moneyer and emperor. References to the moneyers' families persisted for no more than a few years, and the names of the moneyers disappeared from the precious metal coinage in 11 BC, and from the base metal *c.* 4 BC. This phenomenon may readily be understood against the background of the increasing monopolization by the emperor and his family of significant forms of public display, particularly at Rome (Wallace-Hadrill 1986). The names of non-imperial individuals continued to appear on Roman provincial coinage, although non-imperial portraits disappeared under Claudius (*RPC* I: 40–1).

This thumbnail sketch of the development of coin types at Rome is sufficient to show that they were a thermometer of the political temperature. An innocent reading of the coins, in total disregard of other sources of evidence, would imply increased competition within the elite from the 130s BC, the emergence of powerful individuals from the time of Marius, the advent of autocracy with Julius Caesar, and the tightening of imperial rule in the last two decades BC. Those are not quite the conventional dates of constitutional history, but the picture has its own validity.

From the reign of Augustus imperial themes dominated the coinage. As the principate progressed the tendency was for greater emphasis to be placed on military aspects, and less on the civilian. The tradition of variability of coin types persisted into the fourth century AD, and may well have influenced the dramatic escalation in the range of types found on Roman provincial coinage in the first three centuries AD (Burnett 1993). The tetrarchic period, with its emphasis on the unity and uniformity of the emperors and their Caesars, ushered in the decline of varied and sometimes specific typology. The monotony might be relieved at dramatic moments. The power struggles between AD 306 and the achievement of sole rule by Constantine evoked a multiplicity of types, and some usurpations still produced notable types (the Christian symbol Chi-Rho of Magnentius [179], or the 'pagan' bull of Julian [180]) (see p. 74; Ehrhardt 1984: 44–5). It is more significant, however, that the reduction in the numismatic repertoire was matched by a decline in sculptural reliefs and portraiture in general. Politics were now at court, there was no longer the same need to appeal to wider groups (Hannestad 1986: 331).

CHOICE AND INTENTION

The fact that for the most part we do not know who chose coin types is a problem more apparent than real for their interpretation.   In periods of autocracy, at any rate, whether coin types were dictated from above to present an official image, or chosen by lower officials to flatter, the result will have been the same. The coins showed what was desirable to the regime. That is what matters.

For what it is worth, it is more than just plausible that the *triumviri monetales* played the major role in choosing coin types for the Roman mint under the Republic, at least from the 130s BC. Otherwise, the significant element of the typology which referred to the achievements and origins of the moneyers' families would be inexplicable. The situation for the imperial coinage under the principate is less clear. There is a scatter of literary references to emperors stipulating coin types of particular significance, but it is quite insufficient to demonstrate the hypothesis that emperors regularly chose or vetted all coin types (Crawford 1983b; S. Price 1979). One may hazard a guess that the *triumviri monetales* still played a role. Depictions of their family types, and subsequently also their names, disappeared from the coinage during the reign of Augustus, but that was simply a reflection of tightening autocracy (see p. 69). We know from career inscriptions that the office continued in existence at least until the reign of Severus Alexander (AD 222–35) (Jones 1970). Given that the mint came to be run by a *procurator monetae*, and that if anyone decided how much coin was minted it was probably the *a rationibus* (Statius, *Silvae* III, 3, 103–5), it is unclear what the *triumviri monetales* actually did, if not select types. As young men making the most prestigious start to a senatorial career in the vigintivirate they would surely have been in a position to know what was required.

The question of who chose coin types would have little importance were it not for the movement to interpret Roman coin types as systematic and deliberate official propaganda (which gained force after the experience of the Second World War), and the subsequent reaction against that movement (e.g. Sutherland 1951; Jones 1974: 61–81). Scholars remain heavily influenced by their own experiences in this area; those from eastern Europe, for example, continue to give greater credence to views of coinages as systematic propaganda (e.g. Polański 1992a; b). The topic is of obvious interest, but the paucity of ancient evidence for intentions behind the choice of coin types has rendered the debate somewhat sterile.

The question may be side-stepped by referring simply to the undoubted 'political themes' on coinage, rather than to 'propaganda' (which carries the implication of a deliberate attempt to persuade, rather than, say, to honour) (Levick 1982). For most purposes that will do, as long as it is remembered that the term evades rather than decides the question.

There is scarcely any evidence that coin types were 'targeted', that is to say aimed at the particular group within the community who would receive the coins. One example would be the coins struck at Rome under Hadrian and depicting Britannia, all of which seem to have been sent to Britain (Walker 1988: 290) [134]. It is not easy to find other issues of imperial coins which were consigned in full to areas or groups for which the types were particularly suitable. Furthermore, the almost complete lack of references in literary sources to coin types being used for political persuasion (and in particular the silence of Cicero) may reasonably be taken to imply that coinage was not considered a potent weapon in the political armoury (Crawford 1983b).

The use of the word 'propaganda' may thus carry anachronistic connotations. On the other hand, some degree of intention beyond the purely honorific, and some care for the impact coins had on those who used them, should not be controversial hypotheses. Dio wrote that Brutus struck a particular coin type *to show* that he, with Cassius, had liberated the fatherland (Dio XLVII, 25, 3) [107]. Dio (who should have known) thought that coin types might be intended to demonstrate something to somebody.

Once in circulation the types of the coins still mattered. The senate thought it worthwhile to withdraw from circulation the coins of Gaius and of Geta after their deaths (Dio LX, 22, 3; LXXVII, 12, 6), and some cities erased the names or portraits of disgraced emperors and others from their coins [164]. In this vein it is significant that coins might be struck to echo the types of old coins in circulation, and in some cases specifically to restore them (*restituit*). In one instance at least (under Trajan), such 'restoration issues' were made in connection with a withdrawal of old coin [129]. This demonstrates some awareness of old types, with their historical resonances, and a desire to preserve them. Such interest in coins in circulation shows that one should not assume *a priori* that the mixing of new coin with old in circulation means that new coin types are unlikely to have been 'persuasive' either in intent or in effect.

There is no doubt that at some periods coins were politically charged, and that considerable care was taken over them. The coinage of Nerva, for example, is programmatic, and in some cases highly specific (it refers *inter alia* to cash handouts to the people, the corn dole for the urban plebs, the remission of the burden of the imperial post for Italy [128], an orphanage scheme in Italy (the *alimenta*), and the removal of abuses relating to the Jewish tax) (Shotter 1983). Most coin types are not so specific, but even apparently anodyne types may have had a point. For example, the first appearance of certain personifications on the coinage correlated with the first recorded use of the associated imperial titles (Providentia and providentissimus for Trajan, Nobilitas and nobilissimus for Commodus etc.: Wallace-Hadrill 1981b: 23–4).

Different themes might be plugged at different times, for example Domitian's building programme in AD 95/6 [127], or the provinces under Hadrian [133–4]. Events might be given the best possible gloss. The accommodation with the Parthians in 20 BC became an outright submission [115], and when Philip was forced to buy off the Persians in AD 244 it was presented as the establishment of peace (PAX FVNDATA CVM PERSIS; Millar 1993: 154) [141]. Care is equally apparent in what was not shown on the coins: there is thus a meaningful contrast to be made between restraint in the presentation of the emperor on official coins, and the excesses of the imperial cameos in the private sphere (Hannestad 1986: 78; Smith 1988a: 12).

Some coin types engage in political debate, and even enter into dialogue with each other. Examples of the former are the types under the Republic which showed the subordination or breaking of symbols of regal power in a topical context. The placing of a sceptre and wreath below a curule chair on coins of 53 BC represented the legal election of consuls and the exclusion of Pompey from sole rule [101]. Similarly, coins of Brutus and Casca Longus, struck after Caesar's murder, showed Victory tearing a diadem and trampling on a broken sceptre (*RRC* 507/2).

Dialogue between coin types may be illustrated by rival appeals to *libertas*. The representation of Libertas on Caesar's denarii of 48 BC reinforced the claim that he had left his province in order to free the Roman people (*BC* I, 22, 5) [102]. The technical term used by Caesar in this passage (*in libertatem vindicare*) was used of the freeing of slaves, and the image was subsequently turned against him. Denarii of Brutus, struck after Caesar's murder, showed two daggers and a *pileus*, the cap of liberty worn by manumitted slaves, one of which had been held aloft by the conspirators after the assassination (Weinstock 1971: 136, 147–8) [107]. The same imagery, two daggers and a cap, was used only once again, and with obvious deliberation, on the coinage of Galba (who marched against Nero with a dagger hung around his neck; Suetonius, *Galba* 11) [120]. The significance of the type is spelled out: the liberty of the Roman people had been restored (LIBERTAS P(OPVLI) R(OMANI) RESTITVTA). Again the type and slogan had a particular point. Nero had instituted a cult of Jupiter Liberator and had been hailed as Zeus Eleutherios following his proclamation of the freedom of Greece (Weinstock 1971: 144) [156]. Galba's coinage implied the opposite: the loss of *libertas* under Nero, and the consequent justification of tyrannicide.

Similar rival claims were laid to *pietas*. Julius Caesar had in this regard used the supposedly ancestral imagery of Aeneas carrying his father Anchises [103]. The same allusion is found on coinage of Octavian as early as 43 BC, and was later to find full expression in the *Aeneid*. What is interesting for us is the rival imagery of Sextus Pompeius 'Pius', who depicted Pietas on his coins, and also the Sicilian legend of the two brothers from Catana with their parents on their shoulders (Weinstock 1971: 253–5) [108]. The latter was clearly a rival to the Caesarian image of Aeneas carrying his father.

Whether one sees such numismatic ripostes as active agents in the political arena, or merely as reflecting dialogues from other media or contexts, is a matter for debate. It is part of the wider issue of whether the term 'propaganda' may be appropriately applied to coin types. At a minimum it should not be controversial that coin types may reflect what we may as well call propaganda.

AUDIENCE AND RECEPTION

As with the intentions behind the choice of coin types, so with their reception, a scatter of literary references to people noticing them will not support generalization (the earliest in the sixth/fifth-century BC poet Simonides, fr. 114 Diehl = Diog. Laertius IV, 45). Scholars hold widely differing views about the degree to which coin types will have been looked at and understood (e.g. Crawford 1983b; Ehrhardt 1984). It is at least possible to establish the minimal proposition that coin types might, on occasion, make an impact. The people of Antioch 'broke out against the emperor (Julian) and shouted . . . that his coinage had a bull, and the world was subverted' (Socrates, *Hist. Eccl.* III, 17; *PG* LXVII, 424–5) [180]. Perhaps they misunderstood the intention: Julian wrote to the people of Antioch berating them for ignorantly deriding his coinage (*Misopogon* 355 d; Kent 1954; Gilliard 1964; Szidat 1981). Coin types were no doubt often 'misunderstood', but there is no doubt that this one at least had an impact.

The literary evidence, such as it is, plausibly suggests that it was the portraiture on the coins which was most likely to be noticed (Crawford 1983b: 54–7). The ubiquity of portraits on coins, together with the rapid and widespread adoption of the imperial cult, and the erection of imperial statues in public places, were probably the most obvious physical manifestations of the transition between Republic and Empire throughout the provinces (see p. 43). It is hard to believe that coinage did not play a major role in spreading knowledge of the imperial image. Imperial portraits were an important aspect of the symbolism of power, and the widespread copying of new imperial hairstyles is one indication of the impact they had (Zanker 1988: 292–5).

If literary sources are inadequate to allow assessment of the impact of coin types, a more productive approach has been to analyse the way in which imperial imagery became embedded in private contexts from the age of Augustus onwards (Hölscher 1984: 20–32; Zanker 1988: 265–95). Victories and trophies, symbols of prosperity and world rule, capricorns and sphinxes, and even highly specific symbols like the *corona civica* and the *clipeus virtutis*, turn up variously on 'jewelry and utensils, furniture, textiles, walls and stuccoed ceilings, door jambs, clay facings, roof tiles, and even on tomb monuments and marble ash urns' (Zanker 1988: 266).

It is thus clear that, in addition to the portraiture, the type of visual imagery found on the reverses of imperial coins was also noticed, and that it influenced taste in both non-imperial public monuments and in domestic settings. Such imagery was propagated through public monuments as well, but it is again hard to believe that coinage did not play a significant role in its diffusion. At a minimum, it cannot be wrong to assert that coinage was one of the means by which imperial imagery penetrated into private contexts.

IMAGERY AND LANGUAGE

Significant insights have been gained by attempts to understand the iconography of the coinage as a form of language (Hölscher 1980). Much of Republican typology is highly recondite, both in its subject matter and in its oblique imagery. The majority of the precise allusions are unlikely to have been understood, except by the elite. Roman Republican coins, like other monuments of the period, were a form of 'insider-art', reflecting the self-image of the great families (Hölscher 1984).

Developments under the Republic were, nevertheless, vital for what was to come. Attempts to convey a great variety of themes led to the development of a complex visual language. Roman art took some of the vocabulary and syntax of that language from hellenistic art, but it adapted them, extended their range, and made them more systematic (Hölscher 1980: 271–81; 1982: 271–3). Of particular significance was the use of personifications and the abstract symbols which came to denote them. The multiplication of such symbols might allow the essence of a political programme to be conveyed on a single small coin. Thus a Caesarian type with rods, a caduceus, a globe, an axe, and clasped hands was able to allude to Republican office, Felicitas, world rule, Pietas, and Concordia [105]. The complexity and obscurity of the images led to coin inscriptions being used to explain, clarify, or extend meanings in a way which had never happened before.

Personifications and explanatory inscriptions are vital components of the typology of the imperial coinage. The impact of the reign of Augustus ensured a widening of appeal of official iconography. After the early principate coin types retained their political content, but tended to become less complex and more explicit, thus reinforcing the wider appeal. The language of the coinage, like that of the monuments, ceased to be 'exclusive'. Coin types and coin inscriptions became standardized (and thus more accessible), and the principal themes remained remarkably static until late antiquity.

Roman imperial coin types and their inscriptions drew their concerns and forms of expression from a highly developed visual and verbal language of imperial ideology. This proposition may easily be justified by comparing coins with official monuments and literature, where they survive. Indeed the most obvious characteristic of the numismatic material is simply the need for drastic abbreviation of both the image and the inscription.

It is remarkable how little 'official' literature survives for comparison. Few imperial speeches have come down to us (but see Levick 1982 on Claudius' speeches). Court poetry and panegyric clearly have value in this context, but there is nothing to compete with the *Res Gestae* of Divus Augustus. The concerns of this document and of the coinage meet at many points: the capture of Egypt [113], the symbolic honours of 28/27 BC [114], the defeat of Armenia and the return of the standards by the Parthians [115], the holding of the saecular games, the title Father of his Country (*pater patriae*), the honours for Gaius and Lucius, the building or restoration of temples and roads, and many other themes (Simon 1993).

Not only the topics depicted but even the language of coin inscriptions may echo the political rhetoric of the literary sources. Good examples may be found by scrutiny of the coinage of the year of four emperors (AD 68/9) and its aftermath (Kraay 1949). For example the slogan 'salvation of the human race' (SALVS GENERIS HVMANI) on coins of Galba [121] strongly recalls the exhortation of Vindex to Galba 'to make himself the liberator and leader of the human race' (*ut humano generi assertorem ducemque se accomodaret*; Suetonius, *Galba* 9, 2). The word *assertor* was also topical for a highly specific reason. Both Julius Caesar and Augustus had claimed to free the Roman people or state (*in libertatem vindicare*: see p. 73; *Res Gestae* 1.1), and Augustus had been called 'champion of the liberty of the Roman people' (*Libertatis P(opuli) R(omani) Vindex*) on coins of 28 BC [62]. The political posture was needed again in AD 68/9, but the word *vindex* had to be avoided because of the dubious role played in events by C. Julius Vindex. The adoption of the word *adsertor* as an alternative to *vindex* is apparent not only from the passage of Suetonius cited above, but also from coins of Vespasian struck in AD 71 with the inscription SPQR ADSERTORI LIBERTATIS PVBLICAE (Kraay 1949: 138–40) [122]. The nexus of coinage and literature is sufficient to show that both shared in the political jargon of the period.

Visual imagery is in effect also a language capable of both general and highly specific reference. Again it is easy to demonstrate that the concerns and visual language of the coins might be shared with other imperial monuments. The arch of Trajan at Benevento, for example, includes commemoration of his Dacian triumph, his new harbour at Ostia, and the orphanage scheme, and stock scenes of Trajan being crowned by Victory, receiving a thunderbolt from Jupiter, and raising up a province, all of which are heavily reminiscent of the coinage (Hannestad 1986: 177–86). The two friezes of the Anaglypha

Hadriani from Rome include depictions of Hadrian addressing the people, a figure of Italia with two children which refers to the orphanage scheme, and a scene of the burning of documents in the context of the cancellation of debts, all of which are coin types (Hannestad 1986: 193–4). Twenty reliefs of the personifications of provinces from the Temple of the Deified Hadrian at Rome nicely parallel the provincial coin series of his reign (Hannestad 1986: 197–200).

Not only might coins share the same concerns and visual language as other monuments, but they might actually depict buildings, triumphal arches, statues, or (more rarely) paintings. That could be a political act in itself. Thus coins show the equestrian statue of Sulla, the first to be erected officially in the Forum at Rome, the gilded equestrian statue of Octavian set up near by in 43 BC, and two statues of Octavian which commemorated in polemical fashion his victory over Sextus Pompeius (Zanker 1988: 37–43) [110, 112].

The visual and verbal languages of imperial ideology were used (deliberately or not) to construct images of the emperor and empire, and need to be understood in the context of other ways in which such concepts became embedded in society, from city planning to ceremonial. The processes involved cannot be analysed here, but will be apparent from the subtle and wide-ranging works of Weinstock (1971) and Zanker (1988). The pervasiveness of imperial iconography, and the extent to which it became insinuated even in private contexts (see p. 74), makes it likely that some groups in society (above all in Rome itself) were well able to 'read' the imagery on coins if they wanted to. A second consequence is that the survival of coins means that we have more or less continuous access to one aspect of the development of imperial ideology.

THEMES OF POWER

The nature and potential force of the ideology found on coinage may become more apparent by tracing the occurrence of certain themes which bear directly on power. To this end, the final section of this chapter explores claims by leaders to divinity, legitimacy and valid succession, expressions of the Roman right to rule, and the benevolent ideology of rule evolved by the provincial elites.

Divinity

We have already seen that divine attributes were a common feature of the depiction of rulers from the time of Alexander. The Roman respect for 'republican' traditions called for greater circumspection in this area, but the pull of divinity as a convenient expression and justification of power proved strong.

One expedient was to claim a close relationship with a particular deity. Both on the coinage and by other means Sulla, Pompey, and Julius Caesar all placed emphasis on Venus (Weinstock 1971: 15–18, 80–90) [e.g. 96, 103]. All three built temples for the goddess at Rome (Zanker 1988: 20–1, 24). Caesar was able to over-trump the others by honouring Venus as the mother of his family (Genetrix), and brought out the ancestral connection by the representation on his coins of Aeneas (the son of Venus and father of Iulus-Ascanius) [103].

Here was an area for competition. On gold coins issued in parallel in 42 BC Octavian was paired with Aeneas, and Antony with Anton, the son of Hercules (*RRC* 494; Zanker 1988: 45). Octavian laid heavy stress on his more immediate claims to divine parentage through his adoptive father, now Divus Julius [110]. Sextus Pompey aspired to Olympian parentage by depicting his father as Neptune, with a trident and the inscription NEPTVNI [106]. The final step was obvious. Antony, who had been hailed as Dionysus at Ephesos, was depicted on Asian cistophori wearing the ivy wreath associated with that god [61]. With greater subtlety but unmistakable intent, a series struck for Octavian around the time of Actium compared him to Jupiter, Neptune, and Apollo. A herm of Jupiter was even given the features of Octavian (Burnett 1983; Zanker 1988: 53–7) [111].

The ideology of the restored Republic called for greater reticence. The status of *divus* came to be accorded to dead emperors unless their memory was repudiated, and was extended after death to close members of the imperial family. This occasionally gave rise to excess, as in the depiction of the deified infant son of Domitian among the firmament [124], but the iconography of deification became largely standardized. As a consequence of the deification of their predecessors, many emperors, from Augustus and Tiberius onwards, were able to claim divine parentage (to be *divi filius*).

It was still possible to make claims to a special relationship with particular deities. Such relationships might be expressed by the devotion of a heavy preponderance of coin types to the deity concerned, as with Minerva under Domitian (cf. Suet., *Dom.* 4, 4; 15,

3; Hannestad 1986: 140–1). The use of the appellations Guardian and Companion (*Conservator* and *Comes*) for gods may be read in the same way. *Conservator* was normally reserved for Jupiter before the third century AD (as for the Jupiter who towers over Trajan) [130], but Elagabalus utilized the concept for his sun god, and Gallienus applied it to a range of gods, possibly in the context of ceremonial propitiation at a time of crisis (Weigel 1990). The term *comes* received its greatest exposure to express the place of Sol Invictus under Constantine [177].

Divine attributes, for all their ambiguity, went somewhat further. Agrippina was shown wearing a corn wreath under Claudius, and Nero adopted the aegis (the goatskin badge of Jupiter and Minerva) and the radiate crown [119]. The latter, which had been, and was to continue to be, a mark of *divi*, came to be used for all emperors as a standard designation of certain denominations (particularly dupondii and the so-called 'antoniniani'). The solar imagery of the radiate crown was, at least in certain contexts, quite deliberate. Some precious metal issues under Septimius Severus depicted the emperor radiate and the empress with a crescent, and thus as the sun and the moon [138]. In the third century AD the same parallelism is apparent on the 'antoniniani', which regularly portrayed the emperor as radiate and the empress as lunate [e.g. 140–3]. It may be that to some extent the iconography had become devalued, rather than that all emperors were staking a claim to godhead. Even if this is so, it is still note-worthy that divine iconography might become banal.

Suetonius alleges that Nero had himself shown on the coinage as Apollo (Suet., *Nero* 25, 2), but, as far as the imperial coinage is concerned, the allegation seems unfounded. It is true that Apollo is depicted on coins of Nero, and that an identification of the lyre-playing emperor with Apollo might have been understood by some [118]. However, there is no element of iconography, facial characteristic, or inscription on the coins to indicate that Nero is intended. The coins simply show Apollo. On the imperial coinage it is from the reign of Domitian that we can trace a trend towards a more specific identification of emperors and gods.

One of a series of coins depicting Domitian shows the emperor holding a thunderbolt and crowned by Victory, a combination of iconography which invites comparison with Alexander [126 cf. 45]. The thunderbolt chimes well with contemporary poetry, in which Jupiter is the god to whom Domitian is most frequently likened (Carradice 1983: 144). The iconography was continued for Trajan.

The representation of Hercules Gaditanus also under Trajan was not an overt identification, but there was surely an implied comparison between the Spanish emperor and the Spanish Hercules. The coinage of Antoninus Pius with the figure of Romulus and the dedication ROMVLO AVGVSTO came close to the mark, but full identification had to await the last year of Commodus' reign. On the obverse the portrait of the emperor was adorned with Hercules' lion skin, on some reverses Commodus was shown as Hercules in the act of refounding Rome, and coin types were dedicated to HERCVLI ROMANO AVGVSTO [136]. The posturing of Commodus as Hercules is well known from other evidence, and marks a pronounced anomaly on the imperial coinage (Speidel 1993).

That a degree of restraint was (normally) exercised on the imperial coinage can be seen from one case in which it went out of control. For some reason, which we do not know, a highly anomalous series of coins was struck at the mint of Serdica under Aurelian, which includes in the imperial titulature the description of the emperor as Invictus (implying comparison with Sol) or as god and lord incarnate (DEO ET DOMINO NATO). These issues are interesting because they show us what might have happened (but did not) on the normal imperial coinage. Roman provincial coinage is revealing in the same way (see p. 85). The coinage fits the broader picture of the imperial cult, which reveals greater flexibility and excess in the provinces.

Legitimation and succession

The legitimacy conferred on an emperor by his descent, character, and achievements was a frequent theme of Roman imperial coinage in all periods. Personifications of imperial 'virtues', scarce and sporadic under the Julio-Claudians, came to be a major feature of the typology. They portrayed the charismatic nature of the emperor through his moral qualities and powers, and also the benefits of autocracy (Wallace-Hadrill 1981a; Hölscher 1980). Some types placed emphasis on the emperor's relationship to the army, others on his care for, and generosity to, the people. This section will focus, by way of example, on the narrower but vital issue of the transfer of imperial power.

Succession, like divinity, was a topic which required careful handling in the constitutional fiction of the early principate. The early reticence of the imperial coinages (note the absence of depictions of Marcellus, the first intended heir of Augustus) gave way at just the time when imperial monopolization of coin types suggests a more open display of autocracy (see p. 69). In 13/12 BC denarii were struck with the portrait of Augustus on one side and that of Agrippa on the other [116]. The implication of giving the portrait of Agrippa equal weight with that of Augustus was reinforced by another type which showed the two seated side by side on the rostra. The dynastic message was spelled out by a third type which showed a portrait of Julia beneath a *corona civica*, and flanked by portraits of Augustus' grandsons, Gaius and Lucius (Zanker 1988: 216; Wallace-Hadrill 1986).

The imperial coinage again remained more reticent and controlled than some provincial coinages. For example, the issues from Corinth *c.* AD 4–5, with portraits of Tiberius, Agrippa Postumus, Germanicus, and Drusus Minor, had no parallel on the imperial series (*RPC* I: nos 1139–43). Portraiture on the imperial coinage was more significant. Tiberius appeared on the opposite side of the coin from Augustus (just as Agrippa had done) but with head bare on the gold and silver of AD 13/14, and alone and laureate on the base metal coinage from AD 9–11 [117]. Such coins carried an easy message about the realities of power and succession. It is impossible, when looking at them, not to share Tacitus' scepticism about the proceedings in the senate which followed Augustus' death. It had been clear for some years that Tiberius would succeed to the position of Augustus.

The use of portraits remained potent. The mainstream imperial coinage of Claudius portrayed Nero, his adopted son and successor, but not Britannicus, younger than Nero but Claudius' natural son. The efforts of the new emperor Vespasian to establish a dynasty were bolstered by the depiction of his sons (Metcalf 1982: 333). His coinage reveals a new twist in the designation of succession: the elder son, Titus, shared reverse types with his father, but the younger, Domitian, did not (Buttrey 1972: 107). It became standard to issue coins in the name of the heir-apparent as Caesar. The need to foster the sense of a new dynasty is again manifest in the coinage of Septimius Severus. The situation evoked a heavy emphasis on the family (Julia Domna, Caracalla, and Geta) [138–9], and also the highly unusual and blatant description of Caracalla as the emperor to be (DESTINATO IMPERAT). When Caracalla married Plautilla they were depicted clasping hands with a caption which indicated that the future of the Empire would grow from them (PROPAGO IMPERI).

A more standard iconography of succession was developed around the concept of *providentia*, and served to emphasize legitimacy after the event. Titus received a globe from Vespasian PROVIDENT. AVGVST. [123]; Nerva received it from the Genius of the Senate

PROVIDENTIA SENATVS (*RIC* 90); Hadrian received it from Trajan (*RIC* 2) and also from Jupiter (*RIC* 109), and an eagle brought him a sceptre through the forethought of the gods (PROVIDENTIA DEORVM) (Strack 1931–7 II: 43–5). One cannot help wondering whether the coins of Hadrian were protesting too much. The official version of the suspicious circumstances surrounding his accession is clear from the scene of Trajan and Hadrian clasping hands, with its unambiguous label ADOPTIO [132].

At times of civil war the claim to avenge a predecessor was also a claim to legitimacy. Thus Septimius Severus struck coins for the murdered Pertinax as Divus, and the Mars Ultor (Mars the Avenger) type issued by Pescennius Niger presumably made the same claim (Buttrey 1992: xi–xiii).

Usurpation raised the question of legitimacy in an acute form. That the issuing of coinage in itself represented a claim to be emperor is something of a leitmotif in the *Historia Augusta*, but it is also found in earlier authors (Crawford 1983b: 48, 51; e.g. Herodian I, 9, 7; II, 15, 5). In the same vein it is noteworthy that no usurper ever adopted a separatist or 'nationalistic' posture, with the exception of 'Simeon, prince of Israel' during the Second Jewish Revolt (cf. p. 41) [159]. The coinage of usurpers presents them simply as emperors, usually without reference to their rivals [144]. More rarely they might claim that other emperors were colleagues. Carausius, who used his naval command to declare himself emperor in Britain in AD 287, provides the most blatant example [147–8]. Not only did he strike coins for Diocletian and Maximianus, but he even issued some with the portraits of all three side by side, described as brothers (CARAVSIVS ET FRATRES SVI). In the east *c.* AD 269/70 Vabalathus took the unusual titles of King and Leader of the Romans (*Rex* and *Dux Romanorum*) as well as *Imperator*, which is the nearest one gets to a 'usurper' being presented as somehow different from an emperor [146]. Initially, however, he acknowledged Aurelian by putting the latter's portrait and titles on the other side of the coin. The latest issues dropped the unusual titles and the portrait of Aurelian, and presented Vabalathus as emperor and his mother Zenobia as empress (Augusta) (Millar 1993: 171–2, 221, 334–5).

Imperial imagery

The imagery on coins speaks not only of the rights of individuals to rule the Romans, but also of the right of the Romans to rule the world. A range of martial, triumphal, and other types bear on this theme, and only a few of the more pertinent may be noticed here. Peoples and regions are shown as defeated, and kings kneel before Romans, or are recognized and crowned by them. Thus Jugurtha surrenders to Sulla, Vespasian towers over the defeated Judaea, Trajan dominates the recently annexed Armenia and the rivers of Mesopotamia (ARMENIA ET MESOPOTAMIA IN POTES-TATEM P.R. REDACTAE), and presents a king to the kneeling figure of Parthia, REX PARTHIS DATVS [131] (cf. Weinstock 1971: 337–8). In a different vision, which was expressed most extensively on the coinage of Hadrian, provinces might be shown not as defeated, but unbowed as constituents of the Roman Empire [133–4]. Sculptural sequences had depicted provinces without any icono-graphic hint of defeat before, but only in contexts which commemorated Roman victories (Smith 1988b; cf. Hannestad 1986: 197). The unambiguous presentation of a range of provinces as peaceful partners was a new development under Hadrian, as far as we can tell from the surviving evidence. Paternalism also had its place. Emperors raise up the *Res Publica*, Roma, and (under Hadrian) a wide range of individual provinces, and even the whole world (RESTITV-TORI ORBIS TERRARVM).

It is with the imagery of the world, often represented as a globe, that the right of the Romans to universal rule is most clearly expressed. The iconography illustrates the concept, expressed first by Polybius in the surviving literary sources, that the whole world had come under Roman dominion (Brunt 1978). Rome had a mission and a right to rule. In the context of the war against the rebel Sertorius in Spain the Genius of the Roman people was associated with symbols of domination by land and sea (sceptre with wreath, globe, and rudder) [98], and shown crowned by Victory with his foot on a globe (*RRC* 397). In a coin type of *c.* 70 BC, which commemorated the eventual enfranchisement of Italians after the Social War, Roma clasps hands with Italia, but Roma has her foot on a globe [99]. The claims of both Pompey and Caesar to have extended the boundaries of empire to be coterminous with the *orbis terrarum* are reflected in globes on their coinage (see p. 68; *RRC* 464/3) [100]. Under Caesar, Roma was depicted seated on a pile of arms, crowned by Victory, with a sceptre in hand, and her foot on a globe [102]. That about said it all. As we have already seen, in the imperial period the handing over of a globe became a standard element in the iconography of succession.

Benevolent ideology of rule

The ideology of empire propagated at Rome was to some extent taken up on the civic coinages of the provinces, but the local elites (who presumably were responsible for the coin types) also formulated their own attitudes to empire (Harl 1987). They were themselves increasingly incorporated into the Roman governing class, and virtually all free inhabitants of the Empire became Roman citizens by the universal grant of AD 212. To a significant degree the civic coinages reflected the beneficial ideology of rule developed by the provincial elites in response to Roman power, and to their own participation in it.

The civic coinages belonged to a tradition which did not share Rome's proclivity for variable and topical types, and they were slow to copy the Roman model. Thus the impact of annexation was little noticed on provincial coin types (Burnett 1987: 52, 80). The figure or head of Roma was rare, and is often readily explicable when it did occur: for example on the coinage of Gortyn after the Romans won Crete back from Mithridates [55], or on the standardized coinages organized for the cities of Bithynia and Pontus as part of the ordering of the new province (see p. 42) [63]. For the most part only the very rare intrusion of the name of a Roman magistrate gives any indication of the subject status of the cities under the Republic. Portraits of Romans were likewise very uncommon. In the east Julius Caesar was depicted at no more than three cities, and there were hardly any portraits of Antony, except in areas controlled by Cleopatra, where he appeared as her consort.

All that changed under Augustus (*RPC* I: 38–51). Suddenly, more than two hundred cities struck coins with the imperial portrait. The dramatic nature of that change tends to mask some uncertainty about how to react to the new reality of power. Portraiture was not adopted everywhere at once: the dates on coins produced in Syria, for example, show that the phenomenon was not common there before the last two decades of Augustus' reign. Hesitation was not the only sign of uncertainty. It took time for a pattern to emerge, and various ways in which cities tried to formulate their relationship to the new order may be seen with retrospect to have been anomalous. The enthusiasm for portraits encouraged the depiction by some cities of a far wider range of members of the imperial family than was to be found on the imperial coinage (see p. 81). At first, some provincial governors were also honoured with portraits [153]. This was not an awkward survival from the Republic, but a new phenomenon, albeit perhaps an inappropriate one. It did not outlive the reign of Claudius. For a short while some cities honoured emperors in the hellenistic tradition as founder, saviour, or benefactor (*ktistēs, sōtēr,* or *euergetēs*). Others identified empresses as specific goddesses, for example Livia as Hera, or Julia the elder as Aphrodite (someone must have been embarrassed about that after she was banished for adultery) [154]. Curiously emperors were not honoured in the same way, until Nero became Zeus Eleutherios and Apollo in the context of his proclamation of the freedom of Greece (see p. 73) [156].

By contrast with the obverses, the reverses continued to be dominated by local themes and competing claims to status, although there was a clear tendency over the first three centuries AD towards greater variety, topicality, and reference to the emperor. The reverses of the Roman imperial coinage were not much copied in the east, and the personifications of imperial 'virtues', common on the imperial coinage, never became a major theme in the provinces. Imperial 'events' scarcely impinged on the coinage in the Julio-Claudian period: there were, for example, only a few direct references to Actium. Even Nero's visit to Greece, 'the first systematic allusion to an event' (*RPC* I: 45), was noticed, outside mainland Greece, only at Alexandria, where the emperor was mistakenly expected to arrive [157].

Such specific allusions to imperial events remained exceptional. The references to emperors on the reverses of provincial coinage were usually either generic, or bore on the relationship of the emperor to the city or kingdom concerned. The ratification of client kings by Rome (a part of Rome's imperial ideology; see p. 83) was, not surprisingly, echoed by some of the kings: by Rhoemetalces III of Thrace, Agrippa I of Judaea and Herod of Chalcis, and even as late as the reign of Gordian III (AD 238–44) by a king of Edessa in Mesopotamia [167].

Patronage was at the core of the relationship between emperor and city. Cities sought material advantages, and also the titles of prestige which became the focus of intense inter-city rivalry (Robert 1977). The words *dōrea/donatio* became used of both types of imperial benefaction: for example of the building of a bridge [170], or of the diversion of Egyptian corn to meet local needs, or of the right to call local games sacred or world-wide (oecumenical) (Harl 1987: index p. 231). The presence of an emperor was a great opportunity for patronage. The best numismatic illustration is the series of types at Pergamum which commemorated the visit of Caracalla in AD 214, and which culminated in the bestowal on the city of its third neo-corate (temple of the imperial cult, and (presumably) the right to hold associated games) (Harl 1987: pll 23–4) [165].

Such civic honours suited both local aspirations and imperial ideology. An additional neocorate allowed a city to gain an advantage in prestige over a local rival, but it was also an extension of the imperial cult, a focus of loyalty to the emperor and Rome. The same applies to the imperial titles given to some of the games, which became an important part of the typology of civic coins from the late second century AD onwards. For example, the appellation 'Philadelphian' applied to a number of games in the Severan period drew attention to the supposed fraternal harmony of Caracalla and Geta [163]. This type of patronage was a two-way street (Mitchell 1993 I: 221).

From the second century AD the conception of the emperor displayed on provincial coinage became in some cases more sophisticated than it had been in the Julio-Claudian period. At Smyrna the subtle pairing of obverses of Antoninus Pius with a reverse of Pelops [162], and of the young Marcus Aurelius with a scene of the dream of Alexander, seemed to liken the emperor to the original (mythological) founder of the city, and Marcus to Alexander, the re-founder (Klose 1987: 36). Such antiquarianism was a feature of the Second Sophistic, and had been largely absent from the coinage in the Julio-Claudian period (*RPC* I: 43). One further example may suffice to illustrate how the role of emperor might be formulated. Coins from Laodicea under Caracalla depicted the emperor as the Sun (with radiate crown), raised aloft by Land and Sea, above an imperial eagle and wreath [166]. Such imagery is reminiscent of panegyric inscriptions, and also of the sculptural depiction of Augustus with Land and Sea in the Sebasteion at Aphrodisias (Smith 1987: 104–6; 1988b: 77).

The emperor was increasingly shown in martial and triumphal guise (Harl 1987: 38–51) [164]. This may reflect the hope that the emperor would protect the cities of the east against the Parthian/Persian menace. It may also mirror the significant shift in Roman military activity from the west to the east, and the increasing tendency for emperors to campaign in person. These developments brought the emperor into ever greater contact with the cities of the east.

After some false starts in the Julio-Claudian period the beneficial ideology of rule developed in certain well-defined ways, although in a rich variety of expressions. The role of the emperor was formulated through the imperial cult, and by less official comparisons with particular deities or mythological figures. The cities looked for dynastic stability, and for an emperor who would be victorious in war against external enemies and a fount of patronage, a source of both material benefactions and honorific titles.

CONCLUSION

The early part of this chapter sketched the evolution of political representations, and tried to indicate the historical relevance of important developments such as the introduction of portraiture, the escalation of personal types at Rome under the Republic, and the subsequent imperial monopolization of coin designs. The central sections discussed the fundamental questions of the intention behind the choice of themes, of the manner in which they were expressed, and of how they were received. Finally, four aspects of the typology of power were considered in somewhat greater detail, to give an impression of what may be gained by asking more specific questions of the material.

One is left with the impression that contemporary concerns have unlocked much of value in the subject, from the emphasis on propaganda and the attempt to understand how that concept might apply to antiquity, to the fashion for semiotics and the analysis of imagery as a form of language. A clear lesson is that both approaches have proved most fruitful when the coinage has been viewed in the context of the other relevant material and literary evidence.

Chapter 5

Circulation

THE EVIDENCE AND ITS LIMITATIONS

It is necessary to begin with an emphasis on what we cannot know, and on the complexities of interpreting the evidence we do have. This may seem rather discouraging, but it should become clear from the examples discussed later that simplistic approaches to coin circulation are unlikely to prove genuinely fruitful. Approached with due caution, coin circulation has much of value to offer the historian. Some of the evidence is spectacular, from the significant movement of silver around the Mediterranean in the archaic period, to the dramatic export of Roman coinage to Dacia, India, and Scandinavia. But let us look before we leap.

First, the absolute number of coins retrieved from a site is heavily dependent on local factors, both in antiquity and nowadays (cf. Howgego 1992: 3–4 with references). As regards antiquity, the most significant factor is that the hoards left in the ground are the ones that were not recovered in antiquity. Concentrations of coin hoards tend to reflect not prosperity or heavily monetized contexts, but rather the insecurity (particularly warfare) which resulted in owners not recovering their treasure (Crawford 1969; Duncan-Jones 1994: 85). This is a vital consideration, because the vast majority of precious metal coins known to us come from hoards. Since it was normally the precious metal coinages which were used for medium and long distance exchange, patterns of hoarding may give a distorted picture of how coins circulated in antiquity, and hence of trade patterns or whatever. Small change makes up the bulk of casual losses and hence to a significant degree evades the problems relating to hoarding, but is itself prey to the variables of modern recovery, including the extent and nature of archaeological excavation, and the use of metal detectors. All categories of evidence available to scholars are heavily dependent on patterns of recording and publication.

Absolute numbers of coin finds thus require wary treatment, although dramatic differences between areas and periods certainly call for attention. It is generally more fruitful to look at the composition of coin finds in terms of percentages. The pattern of the contents of hoards and site finds may be compared to others from the same region to detect anomalies, and may then be considered in their own right, or contrasted with the patterns in other regions. It is not difficult to see the historical interest in this. If, for example, a significant proportion of coins found in a region were struck elsewhere, it is clearly worth asking how they got there.

Even so, there will be systematic blind-spots in our evidence. If coins were transported to an area where they could not be used, perhaps because they were of the wrong weight standard or fineness, or because of a policy of using only one type of coin in the area, that movement may have left no trace. The coins may all have been traded back again or, probably more often, melted down or re-struck into local coin. Where coins were 'overstruck' without being melted down, the original type of the coin may still be visible underneath the new type to supplement our knowledge of how coins moved (Le Rider 1975) [e.g. 54].

Much original movement thus goes undetected. It is notable, for example, that the transport to Rome of vast quantities of hellenistic gold and silver coin, and its parade in the Roman triumphs recorded by Livy, has left virtually no material trace (except perhaps in the output of Roman coinage, and in the increased use of precious metals at Rome). If the tenor of these comments seems unduly sceptical, it is worth reflecting that shipwrecks have not as yet revealed any evidence for the transport of gold and silver ingots from Spain, the principal mining area of the Roman Empire (Domergue 1990: 371). Such gaps in the evidence are to be expected.

The mention of ingots serves to remind us that when money did move it was not necessarily in the form of coin. From the earliest archaic hoards to the end of antiquity (although more so in some periods than in others) bullion is found alongside coin in hoards. Bullion might be stamped, at least in some contexts (e.g. Arnold-Biucchi, Beer-Tobey, and Waggoner 1988; Baratte 1976; 1978) [183–4]. It might certainly be used to make payments (Howgego 1990: 13–15). By way of example we are told that in 415 BC the Athenians brought 60 talents of uncoined silver from Egesta in Sicily (a month's pay for sixty ships) (Th. VI, 8), and it is recorded that 50 pounds of uncoined silver was delivered to a Roman legion in Egypt in AD 300 (*P. Panop. Beatty* 2, 298–304). If taxes in gold coin were regularly melted into bars before being despatched to the imperial *comitatus* mint for recoining following the reforms of AD 366–9, then we have an example of one major category of money flow which in one period is systematically excluded from the numismatic evidence (Hendy 1985: 386–94; for reservations Howgego 1994: 18–20). Bullion behaved to some degree like coinage (cf. Howgego 1992: 9–10), and thus represents one type of movement of money which could not be reflected in coin circulation.

Another such category consists of the various mechanisms found to allow money to be transferred from one place to another without the cost, inconvenience, and insecurity involved in the transport of coin or bullion. The surviving evidence for classical Athens, which is better than that for any other Greek state, reveals only three known instances of arrangements to circumvent the physical movement of coin (see p. 20; Millett 1991: 8). It is likely that the practice grew under the Roman Empire, facilitated by relative peace and the universality of Roman law (Howgego 1992: 28–9). The *publicani* had a system of debits and credits to transfer tax revenues back to Rome, and on occasion this *publica permutatio* might be used by individuals. Private contacts might provide the same service at least to rich friends, by providing funds in one area against receipts in another. Further, maritime loans taken out in one place might be repaid in another (*Dig.* XLV, 1, 122 (Scaevola) for a hypothetical loan at Berytus in Syria which might be repaid in Italy; Casson 1990 for an actual loan contracted in India and repaid at Alexandria). Here again is a possibly important flow of money, this time in trade, which numismatic evidence cannot reveal (see also p. 22). That said, such mechanisms for the transfer of money were never anything like as important as the bill of exchange was to be from the fourteenth century onwards (Spufford 1988: 254).

Our view, then, is partial. Some movements of coin will appear distorted through the vagaries of loss and recovery, some will not appear at all. Some movements of money were never reflected in movements of coin. There remains, importantly, the movements we can see, particularly as measured by the proportions of different types of coin in circulation. Patterns may be defined and tested against new evidence, but can we make sense of them?

REASONS FOR THE MOVEMENT OF COIN

The interpretation of circulation patterns requires some under-standing of how and why coins moved. Thucydides' account of the departure of the Athenian expedition to Sicily in 415 BC is useful as a warning against simplistic approaches (VI, 31, 3–5). Many talents were taken out of Athens. Over and above their pay everyone took money for private expenses, and soldiers and traders took money for the purposes of exchange. Without these comments it would be tempting to interpret the small groups of Athenian 'owls' in Sicilian hoards from the last decade of the fifth century BC as a purely mili-tary phenomenon (Mattingly 1969: 221). There is justice in this, but Thucydides' picture is more nuanced. Traders had a role, as had private expenses.

In theoretical terms categories of movement of coin may be con-sidered separately, even if, as we have just seen, they shaded into each other in practice. One of the great areas of debate about coin circu-lation (and about the ancient economy more generally) is the balance between state (redistributive) and private (market) activity. Most of the discussion which has taken place has concerned the Roman Empire, under which some scholars believe that the role of the state in the interregional movement of coin was paramount. There will be more to say about this later (see pp. 107–10), but it is worth reflecting that the evidence for earlier periods casts some doubt on this view. Already in the archaic period silver coin moved in quantity from one part of the Mediterranean to the other. In the politically circumscribed world of the archaic city state, it is hard to imagine that external state payments can account for this. Within the Persian empire the system of tribute in silver may have played a role, elsewhere states will have purchased food and materials from abroad, and military activity is to be reckoned with everywhere, but it is impossible not to take private trade seriously. Is it really plausible that trade was less important under the *pax Romana*? Here Greek numismatics perhaps has a lesson for Roman history.

If, as argued above (see pp. 33–8), state expenditure was the dominant mode by which coins were put into circulation, it follows that the state had the most important role in the initial distribution of coin. For an empire or kingdom that distribution might be geographically extensive; in the case of city states it would not be, other than in respect of some military and external payments (forced or voluntary). 'External' military payments might include mercenaries as well as state troops while on campaign, in addition to sums spent on equipment and supplies. Other external payments ranged from the purchase of food and materials (*inter alia* for building projects) to booty and indemnities, subsidies and ransoms, and gifts and bribes. In some cases there were also loans between states. 'Old' coin flowed back to the state, principally through tribute or taxes, rents of public land, fines, confiscations, gifts, and bequests. The state might then put that 'old' coin back into circulation through expenditure, if it did not choose to restrike it. All of this activity may conveniently be considered as redistribution.

Once coin was in circulation, it became subject to influences within the private sphere. When individuals moved around – as traders, soldiers, tourists, or whatever – they carried coin to cover travel expenses, or simply to move their accrued wealth to where it was required. Private rents and loans, too, might result in the movement of coin.

Precious metal coinages were most suitable for substantial inter-regional transfers, and their patterns of circulation are likely to have been dominated by state factors and dominant trading rhythms. The circulation of small change will have been much more influenced by the way in which people moved around, carrying small change with them. The connection between the circulation of small change and the mobility of individuals has been suggested or explored in a number of contexts, including the empire of Alexander (Price 1991a: 65–6), contact across the Adriatic in the hellenistic period (Crawford 1978), between the east and Italy under the Roman Republic (Crawford 1985: 178–9, 319–20), within Asia Minor under the Roman Empire (see pp. 101–2), and, in relation to transfers of personnel, for north Gaul in the mid-fourth century AD (Wigg 1991: 210–12).

Trade on a significant scale will normally have involved precious metal coinages rather than small change, in so far as it was monetized at all. The relationship between coin circulation and trade is an important topic, but a complex one (cf. Howgego 1994: 7–8).

Clearly flows of money will not have matched the flow of traded goods in any precise way. Trade by barter avoided the use of coin entirely. Even when cargoes were sold for money, it will have been preferable in most circumstances to purchase another cargo for the return journey, on which a profit could also be made. Thus monetized trade took place, but no coin moved. According to Xenophon, writing in the 350s BC, the coins of Athens were exceptional in that they were profitable to export:

But on the other hand also, in the majority of *poleis* it is necessary for traders to convey goods of some kind away, since they have coins which are useless elsewhere; but in Athens more useful things are to be found to export than anywhere else, and if they do not wish to convey any goods away, even if they export coins, they will be exporting a marvellous object of trade. For wherever they dispose of it they will everywhere get much more than their outlay.

(Xen., *Poroi* III, 2)

What seems to be at issue is the wide acceptability of Athenian coin rather than any putative low price of silver in a mining region, although no doubt the variable availability of precious metals (and hence presumably its 'price') caused them to be traded, sometimes in the form of coin. Coin will also have moved in trade when it was not possible to obtain goods which could be traded profitably. Sometimes, therefore, coins will have been traded on the same routes as other goods, but in the opposite direction. It would not be surprising if merchants often carried a mixture of money and goods.

If coin did not always move in trade, it certainly did sometimes. A variety of literary evidence makes this clear, and goes beyond specific instances. A law of 375/4 BC appointed an official to check coin in the Peiraeus for the benefit of (ship) owners and merchants (Austin and Vidal-Naquet 1977: no. 102). A decree of the mid-fourth century BC from Olbia on the Black Sea stipulated that the import and export of any amount of coined gold and silver was to be free of duty (Austin and Vidal-Naquet 1977: no. 103). A Ptolemaic papyrus of 258 BC reveals that the mint of Alexandria normally restruck foreign gold coin into Ptolemaic coin for 'the foreigners who came here by sea, the merchants, the forwarding agents and others' (Austin 1981: no. 238). There is no need to multiply examples, and evidence from the Roman period can be found (Howgego 1994: 8 n. 23).

In addition to money for the purchase or from the sale of goods, traders would have carried coin for travel expenses, harbour dues, road tolls (in some contexts), and, importantly, to pay customs duties. Customs duties were a substantial phenomenon. In 401/400 BC the right to collect the two per cent duty on imports and exports at Athens was sold for no less than thirty-six talents. The potential revenue was presumably higher, as the contractor aimed to make a profit, and is particularly impressive as it did not include the duty on grain, which was leased separately (Isager and Hansen 1975: 51–2). In the hellenistic period Rhodes grew rich on trade, obtaining most of its revenues from merchants sailing to Egypt (Diodorus XX, 81, 4). Her annual harbour revenues fell from a million to 150,000 drachmas after Rome declared Delos a free port in 167 BC. Rome itself had an elaborate organization for customs (de Laet 1949). Charges were generally low in antiquity, but the Ptolemies imposed a rate of 50 per cent on some categories of merchandise, and Rome levied 25 per cent on her eastern frontier (Jones 1974: 171–2). The existence of customs duties gave rise to a systematic need for the movement of money in trade.

A further need for money to move may be held to arise when there is an imbalance in the value of goods (apart from coin) traded between two regions. In the short term such imbalances may in principle be dealt with by mechanisms for the transfer of money without the movement of coin, a role performed by the bill of exchange in the later Middle Ages (Spufford 1988: 254). There must, however, be considerable doubts about whether mechanisms of this sort played an important role in antiquity (see p. 90). Medievalists are accustomed to argue that in the long term such imbalances had to be settled by the physical movement of coin or bullion. That is presumably true of many periods of antiquity as well, including periods characterized by independent city states. In the context of empires, however, flows of wealth of a different nature might offset any imbalance in trade. Net outflows in trade might in principle be balanced by inflows in taxes or rents, or by transfers in the ownership of land.

So it is clear that trade will sometimes have given rise to the movement of coin, but not always. Two features of the evidence further complicate the link between coin circulation and trade. First, when coins moved in trade one cannot tell from the coins themselves who carried them. The trader was not necessarily attached in any way to the state which minted the coins. Second, the type of the coin did not necessarily reflect the origin of the silver. It is a safe bet that the majority of the Athenian owls were produced from Laurion silver, but most Greek states did not possess their own silver mines. A significant part of the interest in the study of coin circulation is what it reveals about the flow of precious metals between states. It is therefore something of a handicap not to know the ultimate origin of the metals, which scientific techniques have only begun to overcome in very limited contexts (see pp. 24–6).

It is thus not much of a surprise that patterns of coin circulation often fail to match closely other evidence for trade. The movement of Athenian silver in the classical period only partially maps onto the literary, epigraphic, and other material evidence. Athenian coin is not found in significant quantities along the Black Sea and Adriatic coasts, or in Macedon and Thrace, or in Thrace and northern and western Asia Minor, to match known imports of grain, timber, and slaves respectively (Isager and Hansen 1975: 42–9, 214–24). Coin circulation is often at considerable variance with pottery distribution, the principal source of material evidence for trade. The archaic coins of Chios, unlike its amphorae, are not found in the Black Sea and North Africa (Hardwick 1991: 110). Rhodian coinage, perhaps because of its particular weight standard, is much more restricted in circulation than Rhodian amphorae. Early Roman silver coinage spectacularly fails to match the movements of Roman fine pottery (Burnett 1989: 51–2). These examples are not intended as a counsel of despair, but as a warning against simplistic approaches.

We have reviewed the principal categories of movement of coin, and noted that in practice they will have shaded into each other. An attempt has been made to draw some distinction between state and private activity for the purposes of analysis. It has been noted that there is reason to consider precious metal coinage and small change separately, and that the aggregate movements of individuals are likely to have played a larger role in the circulation of the latter. The complex relationship between coin circulation and trade has been examined. It remains to illustrate from selected contexts what actual patterns of circulation have to say to the historian.

ARCHAIC PERIOD

The extent of the movement of silver coin in the archaic period is impressive, and its interpretation involves many of the issues already discussed. There can be no pretence of a systematic treatment here, but for our purposes it will be sufficient to consider the circulation of coins from the Thraco-Macedonian region, Athens, Aegina, and Corinth, as revealed by selected hoards from the Levant, Egypt, and Sicily.

Let us begin with a few hoards from within the Persian empire, which illustrate the import of silver coin from the north Aegean. A hoard of 39 coins from Ras Shamra, south of Al Mina on the Syrian coast, buried *c.* 510–500 BC, included 32 (82 per cent) from Thraco-Macedonian mints. Two hoards from the Nile Delta, found at Demanhur and Sakha and buried *c.* 500–490 BC, contained 38 per cent and 27 per cent respectively from the same area. The great

hoard from Asyut, about two hundred miles south of Cairo, originally of about 900 coins and dating to *c.* 475 BC, contained 24 per
cent (Price and Waggoner 1975).

Numismatics has little to reveal about how the coins from the
northern Aegean got to Syria and Egypt. The coins in the Ras Shamra
hoard display much internal die-linking, which indicates that they had
stayed together as a parcel from their area of origin, and had not
been repeatedly mixed with other coins. We may imagine a relatively
direct journey to Syria, in the sense that the coins were not trans-
mitted by multiple small transactions (Rutter 1981: 3). Some of the
coins which were exported from the Thraco-Macedonian region to
the Persian empire were of large denominations, up to twelve drachm
pieces [26]. This has suggested to some scholars that they were like
ingots. Certainly they, like other types of coin, were treated as bullion
in the Persian empire, and are frequently found tested with cut marks
or broken up.

The historical reality which lies behind this movement of coin is
the location of important silver mines in the Thraco-Macedonian
region. However, it is hard to explain why the silver was coined before
being despatched, if it was a simple matter of the export of silver
from a mining region. Guarantees of quality or origin, the ease of
handling small and reasonably fixed weights, and even a cultural or
economic requirement for coin-like objects in the exporting or
importing regions may have played a part.

Egypt had no significant silver source of its own. Thus the distribution of silver resources provides one answer to why the coins moved,
but it is far from a complete one. First, what type of 'payments' were
involved? There are three serious candidates: tribute, plunder in 490
and 480 BC, and trade (Price and Waggoner 1975: 124–5). The
Persian advance into Thrace and Macedonia in *c.* 513 BC and the
assessment of tribute in silver within the Persian empire under Darius
(521–486 BC) (see p. 46) coincide with the early movements of coin,
and thus the mechanism of tribute must be taken seriously. But if
tribute was the principal mechanism, why are the coins found in the
Levant and Egypt, and not in the Persian heartlands? Moreover, it
is now clear that the production of large denomination coinage in
northern Greece and its export continued after the Persian withdrawal
in 480/479 BC (Kagan 1987; Price 1987b). So trade played a part
too. Perhaps it is inappropriate to look for a single answer.

Trade raises further questions. The Persian empire had a long
history of using silver as money (see p. 9), and the demand must

have increased in so far as tribute was exacted in silver after the reforms of Darius. What was exported in return? Egyptian corn, papyrus, linen? Also, who carried the silver? Perhaps the East Greek or Aeginetan traders, who alone were represented at the Greek trading settlement in Egypt (Hdt. II, 178)? It is important to be forced to ask such questions.

The owls of Athens are another example of a significant export coinage which depended on local mineral resources [20–1]. Athenian coins are not found abroad in significant numbers before the exploitation of Laurion from c. 500 BC (see p. 25). Between then and the time of Alexander they became the dominant currency of the eastern Mediterranean, and were extensively imitated in some regions of the Persian empire (Phoenicia, Egypt, Babylonia) [38–9]. Already in the Egyptian Asyut hoard of c. 475 BC Athens was the largest single mint, with 19 per cent of the total. It does not, of course, follow that Athens imported corn in quantity from Egypt as early as this, and recent work has been sceptical on the matter (Garnsey 1988: 107–13). Likewise the movement of Athenian coin to Sicily, especially between c. 500 and c. 480 BC, may or may not have been connected with the export of Sicilian grain. At any rate, the presence of 187 owls (22 per cent) in a hoard from Gela buried c. 480 BC needs explaining somehow (Rutter 1981: 4; Price and Waggoner 1975: 20).

It used to be postulated that it was only the coins of mining regions which travelled abroad in quantity (Kraay 1964). We can now see that this is not the case. A hoard of c. 510–500 BC from Selinus in south-western Sicily supports and extends what was learnt from the Asyut hoard in Egypt (Arnold-Biucchi, Beer-Tobey, and Waggoner 1988). The coinage of Aegina accounted for no less than 49 per cent of the Selinus hoard, and 15 per cent of Asyut [cf. 16]. The coinage of Corinth made up 24 per cent of Selinus and 5 per cent of Asyut [cf. 17]. These were not mining cities, but both the Aeginetans and the Corinthians were famous as traders.

It is obvious that nothing proves that Aeginetan and Corinthian coin was carried by traders from these cities, but the numismatic evidence marks a real, if ambiguous, advance in our knowledge. Ceramics make up the bulk of our material evidence for trade, but the Aeginetans produced no distinctive pottery, and Corinthian pots were displaced in the west by Athenian in the middle of the sixth century BC. Clearly there is no need to assume that pottery, any more than coinage, was carried by traders attached to the state which produced them. And one can postulate that Corinthian perfume, for example, continued to be exported, but in Athenian vases. Nonetheless, apart from trademarks on some pots (Johnston 1979), it is hard to find material evidence for the activities of these great trading peoples of the late archaic period. Now we at least know that silver was carried in quantity from Aegina and Corinth by someone, and we can ask how it came about that Aegina and Corinth produced significant export coinages when they possessed no local sources of silver.

LATE CLASSICAL AND HELLENISTIC PERIODS

As we move later in time it becomes easier to identify movements of coin which were military or politico-military in nature. A good example is the arrival in Sicily of substantial quantities of Corinthian pegasi, and of similar coins produced at a number of mints in north-west Greece, shortly after the middle of the fourth century BC (Salmon 1993). For about fifty years pegasi accounted for about 70 per cent of the coins in Sicilian hoards, the majority of them from Corinth itself [cf. 18]. It seems clear that the initial impetus for the pro-duction and movement of the pegasi was the financing of the Corinthian expedition to Sicily under Timoleon in 344 BC. The need to pay and supply the task force and its reinforcements cannot be the whole answer, however. Pegasi continued to arrive in Sicily until about the end of the century. Some coins may have been brought by the colonists to whom Timoleon subsequently offered plots in Sicily, but it is unlikely that this movement would have continued until the end of the century. Trade has always seemed the most likely explanation for the continuing pattern. The situation is reminiscent of the complex motivation for the movement of coin described by Thucydides in connection with the Athenian expedition to Sicily some seventy years earlier.

The activities of mercenaries have also been seen behind the changing patterns of coin imported into Crete. Both foreign and local coins were routinely overstruck, but the operation was often done carelessly so that the undertypes reveal the origin of the money. In the fourth century down to *c.* 320 BC most of the overstruck coins were Cretan, with a few from Aegina. After that date, the great majority were foreign, most coming from Cyrenaica [54], with a few from Boeotia and Sicyon. The change has plausibly been explained as marking the involvement of Crete with the wider hellenistic world, as mercenaries repatriated their earnings (Kraay 1976: 51; based on

Le Rider 1966). The same explanation may help to account for the dramatic increase in the production of silver coinage in Crete between *c.* 330 and 280/270 BC (Mørkholm 1991: 89).

In terms of coin circulation far and away the most important aspect of the transition to the hellenistic period was the replacement of Athenian coin and its imitations by Alexander coinage as the dominant currency of the eastern Mediterranean. Gold and silver in the name of Alexander had a wide circulation from the start, even reaching Italy and Sicily. The gold in particular was exported in large quantities to the 'Celtic' tribal areas of the north Balkans (Price 1991a: 65–6, 142; de Callataÿ 1994: 32–5). Military movements and the use and subsequent dispersal of mercenary troops will have had an important role to play in the circulation of coin. It seems clear that patterns of production were heavily influenced by the need to pay off Alexander's troops returning from the east (see p. 50). Careful analysis of circulation by mint and denomination should have much to offer in the future (de Callataÿ 1994). What has long been clear is the spectacular scale of the movement of the standardized coinage. Of the nearly six thousand coins recorded in detail from the hoard of *c.* 320–317 BC from Demanhur in Egypt more than a third came from mints in Macedonia, a quarter from Asia Minor (including Cyprus and the Gulf of Issus), and a seventh each from Phoenicia and Babylonia (Zervos 1980: 187).

Some of the military and diplomatic interventions of the hellenistic period have likewise left clear traces in the numismatic evidence. Ptolemaic coinage was normally confined within the core areas of the kingdom, but may also reflect temporary garrisons, such as those in Corinth *c.* 308–306 BC, or in Attica during the Chremonidean War (268–261 BC) (see p. 53). As we have already seen, Pergamene subsidies to the Seleucid pretender Alexander Balas may lie behind the movement of large numbers of stephanephoroi from Aeolis and Ionia to Cilicia and Syria *c.* 155–145 BC, although again we should not totally discount trade as an explanation (see p. 55) [64].

The booty carried off to Rome and the indemnities imposed on defeated enemies by the Romans gave rise to massive movements of coin which have left little direct trace, presumably because the coins were melted down (see p. 89). It is clear that some indemnities were, at least in part, actually paid in coin, although sometimes it may have been a matter merely of reckoning in coin. In the treaty of Apamea in 188 BC the Romans defined the indemnity imposed on Antiochus III in terms of coins of the highest fineness on the Attic weight standard (Polybius XXI, 42, 19). The indemnity imposed on the Aetolians in 189 BC specified payment in silver coin of a quality not inferior to the Attic, but also terms under which a third of the sum could be paid in gold coin (Polybius XXI, 32, 8). In these cases it would be against the natural reading of the texts to assume that uncoined metals were involved in the payments to any significant degree (cf. Le Rider 1993b: 50–2).

Even if we would not expect such movements to be reflected in hoard evidence from Italy, their indirect effects may be seen in changing patterns of circulation and minting elsewhere. Was the disappearance of large denomination (Attic tetradrachm) silver coinage from Greece *c.* 200 BC connected with the need for Macedonia to find silver to pay the indemnity to Rome after the Second Macedonian War (Crawford 1985: 124)? If silver was sucked into Macedonia, what was the mechanism involved? Trade? Was the imposition of a closed currency system by Eumenes in the Attalid kingdom intended to prevent Pergamene silver being 'sucked into' the Seleucid kingdom to pay the indemnity imposed on Antiochus III (Kinns 1987: 106)? In the same vein, did the movement of silver from Lycia and Pamphylia to the Seleucid kingdom *c.* 200–160 BC somehow fill a gap left by the payment of this indemnity (Crawford 1985: 155; cf. Mørkholm 1991: 143)? If so, what were the mechanisms involved? Again, is it merely a coincidence that Rome began to produce a plentiful coinage in gold from 46 BC onwards, only after the other principal gold coinages of the hellenistic world had ceased to circulate, or was the withdrawal of those coinages more directly connected with minting at Rome (Howgego 1992: 5)?

The imprecise chronologies of many hellenistic coinages do not make it easy to answer such questions, but it marks an advance in hellenistic numismatics that they are being asked.

ROMAN PERIOD

The unparalleled degree to which coin production was centralized under the Roman Empire requires different strategies for the recognition and interpretation of circulation patterns. To the extent that the same coins were in circulation everywhere it is impossible to detect interregional movements. Centralization should not be over-stated: some civic and regional coinages persisted until the production of the imperial coinage itself became devolved from the middle of the third century AD (see p. 11). The fact remains that until then Rome, and, for part of the first century AD, the Roman imperial mint at Lugdunum, provided virtually all the gold coinage for the Empire, a silver coinage which came increasingly to dominate first the west and then the east, and, from early in the principate, a base metal coinage for the western half of the Empire. That such a degree of central-ization was maintained is a dramatic testimony to the scale of transfers of bullion and coin possible within the Roman economy (Millar 1991).

Given the nature of the evidence five approaches to Roman coin circulation have proved the most profitable. First, one may evade the problem by studying the circulation of such civic or regional coinages as were still minted. Second, Roman imperial coin found outside the Empire is clear evidence for export by some means. Third, the chrono-logical profile of coins found on a site or in a region may reveal something about relative patterns of supply of coinage to the area, which may be compared with patterns from elsewhere. Fourth, the centrally minted imperial coinage may be analysed by individual type to see whether particular issues were despatched to particular regions, and to consider to what extent the coins in circulation really were homogeneous throughout the Empire. Fifth, the imperial coinage comes to provide fertile ground because it was increasingly produced on a decentralized basis at identifiable mints.

Civic and regional coinages

Civic bronze coinages did not (with one minor exception) survive the reign of Gaius (AD 37–41) in the west, but they continued to flourish until the middle or second half of the third century AD in the east. The circulation of small change such as this cannot tell us much about the grander economic issues of trade and state finance, but it has been suggested that it may reveal something about the aggregate movements of people (see p. 92). This is a topic of real interest, and it is hard to think of other types of evidence better able to throw light upon it.

The regional circulation patterns of civic bronzes in Asia Minor under the Roman Empire have been interpreted in this light (Howgego 1985: 32–51). Other evidence for how people moved around, where it exists, normally coincides with the patterns derived from the circulation of small change. This strongly suggests that it is appropriate to use the numismatic evidence in this way. The speeches of Dio Chrysostom, for example, confirm the close connections between Nicomedia and Nicaea, so apparent from coin circulation, and the road running east along the Maeander valley from Ephesos, which had a strong influence on the movement of coin, was described by Strabo as the common road used by all who travel from Ephesos towards the east (XIV, 2, 29). By contrast with such movement within natural geographical regions, long-distance interregional movement of small change was exceptional. In the case of the eastern half of the Roman Empire, at least, the few major movements of bronze coin outside a natural geographical area of circulation may all be tied to specific military occasions. This suggests that the army was in terms of numbers the most significant mobile body of population within the Empire.

The circulation patterns of civic and regional silver coinages prove to be less revealing than one might hope, because more often than not their distinctive patterns of denomination and fineness confined them to the regions where their use was traditional. We do not normally know whether restricted circulation was a matter of custom or regulation, although in the case of Egypt it is clear that the Romans continued the closed monetary system of the Ptolemies. In a few cases, however, the coins looked sufficiently like denarii to circulate along-side them. Thus, for example, the silver coins of Numidia struck under Juba I (60–46 BC) and the drachms of Lycia minted under Trajan in AD 98–9 [160] were widely dispersed. Both, for example, are found in Britain. This type of evidence is important in showing that they, and by implication denarii, might move widely subsequent to, and for reasons not connected with, their initial issue. That observation is not surprising, but in most periods it is hard to demonstrate from the evidence of the denarii themselves (Howgego 1994).

Export

The earliest of the dramatic movements of Roman coin beyond the frontiers was to the basin of the Lower Danube. Crawford has rightly drawn attention to the massive import of denarii to this region in the late Republic, which is in marked contrast to the surrounding areas (Crawford 1985: 226–36).

The reasons for the export of Roman coin to Dacia will have been complex, but that does not preclude one explanation being para-mount. Crawford argued that the dominant cause was the slave trade, which was forced to look elsewhere after Pompey cleared the eastern Mediterranean of pirates. This bold theory is attractive, but has not gone unchallenged (e.g. Fulford 1985). The evidence for the slave trade at all periods is slight, so that the general paucity of attestations of slaves from Dacia in this period need not be a problem, but the theory may underestimate the significance of old and new supplies of slaves from elsewhere (for example, Gaul from the 50s BC).

It is always a problem to date the export of coinage. Old coin continued to circulate, and thus may in principle have been exported long after it was struck. The Republican coins from the Lower Danube range in date from the second century BC onwards. Hoards from the area, dated by the latest coin in them, suggest that the massive penetration did not take place until the 60s BC, and continued down to the end of the Republic and beyond. The apparent chronology of the movement thus helps to underpin Crawford's view, but is not unproblematic. It is possible that the pattern of hoarding reflects not so much the chronology of the import of the coins, but rather the insecurity associated with the campaigns of Burebista to unite the Dacian tribes from c. 60 BC, and their aftermath (cf. p. 88). The activities of Burebista are relevant not only to chronology, but may also suggest alternative models for the export of coin in the first place (plunder, ransoms, 'protection money'?).

Whatever the case, the Roman denarii in the area must be seen in a broader context. Large numbers of drachms of Apollonia and Dyrrhachium are also found in the south and south-east of the Carpathian Basin and throughout Dacia (Crawford 1985: 224–5). The import of the majority of these coins has been dated to a relatively short period, c. 75–60 BC, which tends to favour an explanation connected with military activity rather than trade (although it is not formally inconsistent with the slave theory) (Torbagyi forthcoming). Finds of tetradrachms from Thasos in the region also need to be taken into account.

Some, perhaps the majority, of the tetradrachms of Thasos on the lower Danube were local imitations. This is true to some extent of the 'Roman' denarii also. Some denarii were certainly produced locally, and dies have been found in the region. The question of scale is still very much a matter of debate, but local imitations may have led us to overestimate the quantity of true Roman imports.

Finally, both Crawford and Fulford have discussed what need the Dacians and other peoples of the region had for coin. Coin had been drawn into the area from the time of Philip II and Alexander, no doubt in the first instance as mercenary payments, and had been imitated locally [49]. It is more plausible that coin was required as a form of prestige goods to define rank, rather than to meet the needs of a monetized market economy, which is unlikely to have developed significantly prior to annexation by Rome.

In many ways less problematic is the impressive movement of Roman gold and silver coin to India, for which trade is the only sensible explanation (Turner 1989). Pliny tells us that luxuries from India, China, and Arabia cost the Empire 100 million sestertii every year, and that India alone drained half that sum (*HN* XII, 41 (84); VI, 26 (101)). The *Periplus*, a trading handbook of the first century AD, emphasizes the quantity of Roman coin taken to Indian markets (Casson 1989: 29–31). The gold and silver were imported as bullion. It has been suggested that they may have been required, among other purposes, for the production of two new coinages, the silver of Nahapana, the Saka satrap of western India, and the gold of the Kushan king Vima Kadphises (MacDowall 1990a: 59).

In drawing inferences about Roman trade with India two points in particular should be remembered. First, the movement of gold and silver coin is an index of the movement of bullion, rather than of trade in general. Specific needs, and perhaps the relative values of bullion in the Roman Empire and in India, gave rise to the movements of coin at certain times. Trade may have been conducted without coin at other periods. Second, as we have already noted, coins may be exported some time after they were struck. The evidence of hoards and coin wear strongly indicates that significant movements of Roman gold and silver to India began only in the Flavian period and continued during the first half of the second century AD. The lateness of the movements is of great interest, as it casts light upon the motivation for the export of coin. The vast majority of the silver coins found in India were struck before Nero's coinage reform of AD 64. It thus appears that pre-reform coins were deliberately selected for export later. Indeed, many of the Republican denarii seem to have been exported after Trajan's debasement in AD 107, and thus at a time when they were disappearing (or had virtually disappeared) from circulation within the Empire. It makes sense that old coins, which contained more precious metal, were chosen for export to a region where they would be valued as bullion. This practice may help to explain a reference to 'old aurei' (*chrysa palaia denaria*) in an inscription from Palmyra of AD 193 (*pace* Buttrey 1963). Thus the pattern of export of coin to India was driven in part by Roman coinage reforms (MacDowall 1990a; 1990b; 1991).

This last observation has relevance for the interpretation of the final pattern of export which will be discussed here, namely that of the Roman coins found in substantial numbers in much of Europe to the north and east of the Roman Empire (Lind 1981). The vast majority of the silver coinage found in 'Barbaricum' was struck between the reign of Vespasian and the debasement under Septimius Severus in AD 194/5. Again it is quite possible that much of the coinage left the Empire later, but that the better quality pre-reform coins were selected, although some scholars believe that the export ceased suddenly at that date. By what direct or indirect routes the coins reached 'Barbaricum', after what delay, and whether as a result of trade, political gifts and subsidies, booty, ransoms, payments to those serving in Roman armies, or whatever, are hotly debated topics (e.g. Wielowiejski 1980; Kolendo 1980; Bursche 1989; Duncan-Jones 1994: 92–4).

Particularly striking is the density of hoards from the Baltic, and especially the island of Gotland, where the pattern is repeated in the fifth and sixth centuries AD by gold solidi, and later by German, Anglo-Saxon, and Islamic coins. There is thus good reason to suppose a culturally defined need for the possession and prestige-burial of precious metal in the region.

Taken as a whole the finds in 'Barbaricum' seem to fall into two categories. A 'buffer zone', loosely conceived as extending 200 km from the Roman frontier, is characterized by finds of bronze coins. This may reflect trade and other contacts with the Roman Empire, and perhaps the extension of some degree of monetization. The zone beyond is characterized by finds of silver coin and other prestige goods, where we may assume that their symbolic value was paramount (Fulford 1985).

Chronological patterns

Movements outside the Empire may be problematic to interpret, but at least one can see what they are. As regards the imperial coinage within the Empire one knows only that the coins have moved from the mint to where they are found by some manner of means, direct or indirect. Analysis of chronological patterns (percentages by period) has proved a fruitful approach, and is perhaps at its most developed in work on Britain (Reece 1987).

The pitfalls of the approach have often been listed. It is necessary to use site finds, as hoarding tends to reflect patterns of insecurity rather than patterns of supply of coinage (see p. 88). Thus this type of work is largely confined to the patterns of small change, as finds of gold and silver are comparatively rare outside hoards. Site finds will tend to give an exaggerated sample of small coins (easier to lose, harder to find), low-value coins (not worth looking for), coins which circulated for long periods (which had longer to get lost), and forgeries, foreign, and demonetized coins (deliberately thrown away). Demonetization is a particular concern since it may lead to large numbers of a particular type of coin being discarded, and hence give a mistaken impression of abundant supply. Further, it must be remembered that the date at which an individual coin was lost (as opposed to struck) is usually unknown, although the normal maximum circulation period of particular types of coin may be revealed by the evidence of hoards.

For any region there will be something like a normal pattern. Individual sites may be compared and contrasted with that norm to illuminate individual site histories. For example, the fort at Richborough in Kent displays a relatively normal pattern for Britain, except for a high representation in the last period (AD 388–402) (Reece 1987: 80–8). It is thus relative rather than absolute patterns which pose the most interesting questions for the archaeologist.

Norms for different sub-regions may be contrasted. A distinction between the east and west of Britain has been demonstrated. Relative to each other the east has a higher proportion of coins of AD 260–96, and the west has a better representation of coins of AD 330–402. This may show greater resilience of monetized exchange in the west towards the end of the Empire, although other explanations are possible (Reece forthcoming). Another approach is to compare town and country sites to see whether money-use took longer to penetrate the countryside (Reece 1987: 71–97).

Contrasts between different regions may be very marked (Reece 1987: 98–113). Italy, for example, has a fairly even loss rate throughout the imperial period, but Britain has dramatically more coins from *c.* AD 260 onwards than from earlier periods. The British pattern may well have been affected by demonetization, particularly of coins of the 'Gallic' and 'British' empires in the second half of the third century AD, which may have led to large numbers of coins being discarded (and thus to an increased 'loss' rate for that period). No doubt the presumed lower level of monetization in Britain in the earlier period by comparison with Italy is also a significant factor in explaining the lower percentage of pre-AD 260 coins in Britain. Relative patterns are always susceptible to more than one explanation. Should we be seeking to explain an 'abnormally' low representation of coins in

Britain before AD 260, or a high representation after 260, or both? Or is the whole British pattern 'normal', and Italy's even loss rate 'anomalous'. The material evidence is at least verifiable by repetition, and raises interesting questions.

Analysis by individual type

Differences in chronological patterns between regions resulted from variations over time in the proportions of the total output of coin which reached each region (by whatever means) and stayed there. Analysis of particular issues, whether by individual type or by year of issue, may likewise reveal unevenness in the distribution of coin from the mint which was not eradicated by subsequent circulation.

Work on the twelve and a half thousand Roman coins from the Sacred Spring at Bath led to important conclusions concerning the base metal coinage (Walker 1988). Some issues, including the Britannia types of Hadrian and Antoninus Pius [134–5], were virtually confined to Britain. Once they had arrived the coins did not leave the province to any great extent. Furthermore, analysis of the base metal coinage of Domitian (AD 81–96) showed that only the issues of AD 86–7 reached Britain in any quantity, in marked contrast to a much more even supply throughout the reign on the Continent. This shows that small change did not drift into Britain in the ordinary course of circulation, and strongly implies that official consignments largely dictated what base metal coinage did enter the province.

Walker's work produced another interesting observation. The issues of AD 153–5 which are largely confined to Britain differ from the normal run of imperial coinage in their technique of manufacture. There is thus the distinct possibility that they were actually minted in Britain. This revelation is unlikely to undermine our perception that production was predominantly centralized, but it would not be surprising if some other cases of local minting are identified in the future.

Work on the coins found at Vindonissa in Switzerland has also produced interesting conclusions (Peter forthcoming). The series of *aes* coinage there ends in AD 100 with the abandonment of the legionary fort. That is not surprising, but the paucity of small change in the years after AD 100 affected the surrounding region as well. It follows that the official supply of *aes* to the fort dictated to a significant degree what was available locally.

In considering circulation it is vital to distinguish between small change and the precious metal coinages. We have seen that some types of imperial base metal coinage from the Rome mint are largely confined to one province. That is not the case with individual types of imperial gold or silver coin from Rome, or at least no such case has been identified. Precious metal coinage was despatched more evenly, or circulated more widely, or (most probably) both. Hopkins (1980) put the topic right at the heart of the debate about the nature of the Roman economy. His argument is that provinces which paid in tax and rent more money than they received through government expenditure (principally military pay) and the inflow of rents had to earn back that money through trade, in order to be able to continue to pay their taxes and rents on a sustainable basis. Taxes and rents stimulated trade.

Hopkins adduced in support of his view that it explained the homogeneity of silver coin in circulation throughout the Roman Empire between AD 50 and AD 200. In this period the proportions of coins of different emperors are broadly similar in all provinces, but why is this so if at some periods expenditure was higher in some areas than in others? His answer is that the process of returning coin in tax and rents to the centre and earning coin back by trade thoroughly mixed coins in circulation.

In an important critique, Duncan-Jones read the evidence differently and drew different conclusions (Duncan-Jones 1990: 30–47). The coins could have been mixed prior to despatch from Rome, old as well as new coin was sent out for expenditure, homogeneity does not need to be explained by mixing through taxes, rents, and trade. He further observed that gold coin will have been of great importance in the flow of money between regions, but that we have insufficient information to know whether the mix of gold coin was of the same kind everywhere. As regards silver Duncan-Jones showed, by the analysis of coin hoards, that the proportions of a few types of silver coin struck from Trajan to Commodus varied from province to province. The coin in circulation was thus not homogeneous, coin was despatched to certain areas and stayed within regional economies, the Roman economy as a whole was not integrated.

It has been argued elsewhere that neither of these contrasting models of the Roman monetary economy is entirely satisfactory (Howgego 1994). Neither gives due consideration to the monetary or political factors, other than the lack of economic integration, which may have limited the physical circulation of coin. Neither addresses the timescales involved in the mixing of coin. Moreover, a possibly significant omission from both models is the role of army movements in the transfer of coin between regions (as opposed to the despatch of army pay which is central to both views).

Both models have, in addition, their own particular flaws. The Hopkins model needs modification because it is unlikely that the currency was ever exactly the same in all regions. The problem with Duncan-Jones' view is that the lack of complete homogeneity does not mean that an economy is not integrated in meaningful ways. The test is too severe: coin can move about significantly in an area without totally eradicating local differences.

What both approaches have shown is that in principle numismatic evidence may be of great use in testing important theories about the structure of the economy. Further light may be shed on the debate by turning to our final category of numismatic evidence.

Decentralized minting

It is much easier to discuss patterns of circulation within the Empire in periods when more than one mint was involved in the production of the imperial coinage. One can then investigate the extent to which coinage from the various mints became mixed in circulation, and learn something about how long that process took. The decisive steps towards decentralized minting were taken in the 250s AD, but even before that, during some periods of military activity in the east, imperial coinage was struck in Syria as well as at Rome.

It is a feature of the eastern issues of the first half of the third century AD that in hoards from Britain they continued to rise as a proportion of all contemporary issues for some decades after they were struck (Howgego forthcoming). In Britain the eastern denarii of Septimius Severus struck between AD 193 and 196 [e.g. 137] are not represented among denarii of the period AD 193–196/7 in hoards buried c. AD 210, but rise by stages to account for about 50 per cent by the early 260s. A rising trend of eastern material in British hoards, admittedly less clear, is seen also for the coins of Gordian III (AD 238–44).

The reason for these trends must be that the eastern coins did not all travel to the west soon after they were struck, but moved over a period of time. The result of repeated movements was an increasing presence of eastern coins in the west. The delay between the minting of the coins in Syria and their transport to the west makes it virtually certain that the movements were of a secondary nature, not envisaged at the time of striking. It is, in any case, hard to believe that coin was struck in the east, principally at Antioch, in order to make payments in, or otherwise supply currency to, the west. The demonstration of such secondary movement is important because it renders untenable, at least for the early third century AD, any model of the Roman economy which posits that new silver coin was despatched from the mint to different regions, and that coin subsequently stayed in the region to which it was sent.

Secondary movement between regions can thus be demonstrated for silver, and is plausible *a fortiori* for gold coinage, which is more suitable than silver for interregional exchange. The precise mixture of reasons for such secondary movements – multiple transfers of military personnel, taxes, rents, or trade – may be unknowable, but the fact that they can be shown to have taken place at all marks an advance in our understanding of the Roman monetary economy.

CONCLUSION

The litany of problems and alternative explanations which runs through studies of coin circulation is bound to be discouraging. An understanding of the complexities of the subject helps to explain why it has not produced the easy answers to economic questions which some have expected from it. But caution is not to be mistaken for pessimism. At a theoretical level much can be learned from asking questions such as why coin moved, and what was the relationship between circulation and trade. At an empirical level, the movement of coins provides verifiable evidence for economic activity of a kind which is so often missing in the literary sources. This chapter has tried to indicate how studies of coin circulation have been used to address a wide range of topics, including trade, the movement of people, the economic effects of military activity and empires, individual site histories, regional levels of monetization, the distribution of coin by the state, and models of the Roman economy. So perhaps, after all, there is achievement and promise.

Chapter 6

Crisis

CRISIS AT ATHENS AND ROME

Given that the need to make state payments was an important cause of the production of coins in antiquity, it is not surprising that the effects of crises in state finances may be observed in the coinage. An impoverished state might simply spend less, but at times the needs for expenditure were paramount (particularly, but not only, at times of war), and other expedients had to be found. Some of the possibilities may be examined by comparing the coinage of Athens at the end of the Peloponnesian War and of Rome during the war against Hannibal.

The Spartan occupation of Decelea from 413 BC onwards cut Athens off from her silver mines, and, as the tide of war changed, tribute no longer flowed in as once it had. Two new monetary stratagems were tried. First there was an exceptional issue of gold coinage [23]. Eight statues of Nike on the Acropolis had been clad with two talents of gold each, to be removed in case of emergency. In 407/406 BC the gold was struck into coin. One statue survived, and the tools used to produce the coins were subsequently dedicated in the Treasury of Athena. Apparently in the following year Athens resorted to the second stratagem of issuing a copper coinage, not as small change (Athens did not produce small change in base metal until the second half of the fourth century BC), but as a replacement for silver coinage. It is a modern inference, based on surviving specimens, that the emergency coinage was of copper plated with silver. At any rate, by 392 BC the 'copper' coinage had been demonetized (Robinson 1960; Thompson 1970). Both the gold and the 'copper' were emergency measures only.

The financial difficulties of Rome during the Second Punic War, and particularly during Hannibal's invasion of Italy, are well known

(Crawford 1985: 52–74; Nicolet 1963). Financial expedients included a loan from Hieron of Syracuse, a doubling of tribute, and borrowing from her own citizens (the only time Rome ever resorted to credit to fund state expenditure). The coinage was not immune. A gold coinage was struck for the first time [88], the silver coinage was debased from *c.* 97 per cent fine down to *c.* 89 per cent, and the bronze fell in weight dramatically. At the outbreak of the war the bronze As had weighed ten Roman ounces, or a little less (it had drifted down from the full weight of one Roman pound of twelve ounces). In the six years which followed the invasion of Italy in 218 BC the As lost by stages a total of 80 per cent of its weight [85 cf. 84]. When a new system of coinage based on the denarius was instituted *c.* 212 BC the As weighed only two ounces, and the Italic tradition of full-weight bronze money had been broken.

The creation of the new denarius coinage marked a return to stability, which seems all the more impressive in hindsight, as the denarius was to remain the standard silver coin for four hundred and fifty years [90]. It is true that Rome's fortunes took a turn for the better from about the time of its introduction, but there were still signs of stress. The striking of a gold coinage in parallel with the denarius may be seen as one indication of continuing difficulty [89]. Although the new gold coinage began a few years earlier, it was presumably in part funded by the contributions from Roman citizens of all levels in 210 BC, and by the recourse in 209 BC to the gold in the *aerarium sanctius*, which had been set aside for use in emergencies. Further, alongside the relatively pure silver denarius at *c.* 96 per cent, another silver denomination, the victoriatus, was struck at an average of only *c.* 84 per cent pure (Walker 1980) [91]. The debased victoriati continued to be produced in significant numbers until the series was ended *c.* 170 BC. The precise function of the victoriatus is uncertain, and it seems to have circulated initially in the south of Italy. Whatever the explanation, the continued production of a significant debased coinage is noteworthy.

It is not difficult to trace certain common strands in the situations at Athens and Rome. Both were under dire pressure from enemy invasions. Both had resort to coining gold set aside for emergencies. Both eked out their supplies of silver by substituting base metal, Athens unusually by creating a token emergency currency, Rome by what was to become the much more common expedient of debasement. Rome, in addition, reduced weight standards.

COINAGE UNDER PRESSURE (EXCLUDING ROME)

The two contexts discussed so far are comparatively well documented, so that the relationship between crisis and response is apparent. The numismatic phenomena are more widespread, but the background is not always so clear.

Except in periods when gold coinage became a normal part of the monetary system, the striking of gold may sometimes be seen to be a reaction to specific crises (see pp. 8–9). There is a danger that when chronologies are vague the coinages are dated by known crises, so that the argument becomes circular. Nevertheless, plausible examples may be found, including the gold coinages struck in Sicily at Syracuse, Gela, Acragas [15], and Camarina at the end of the fifth century BC, which were presumably evoked by the Carthaginian attacks of 406/405 BC (cf. Kraay 1984).

The Athenian resort to a token currency was not a common expedient. It is possible that some such measure lay behind the electrum plated lead coins from Samos, which Herodotus places in the context of a Spartan attack c. 525/524 BC (Hdt. III, 56, 2; Barron 1966: 17). A closer parallel is provided by the story that the Athenian commander Timotheus devised a token bronze coinage in order to pay his troops on his expedition against Olynthos in 363–359 BC (Ps. Aristotle, *Oeconomica* II, 2, 23, 1; Robinson and Price 1967). The presumably widespread substitution of bronze for lower silver denominations as it took over the role of a fractional coinage is a rather different phenomenon (cf. Picard 1989).

Even straightforward debasement was not common in Greek coinages of the archaic and classical periods (Kraay 1976: 11), although it became more widespread in the face of Roman expansion. In the first century BC both the Seleucid and Ptolemaic silver coinages were significantly debased, the latter apparently in the context of Roman exactions after the restoration of Ptolemy Auletes in 55 BC (Walker 1976–8 I: 151).

Carthaginian coinage, by contrast, seems to have been systematically debased, with the 'electrum' falling from 98 per cent gold early in the fourth century BC [81] to 30 per cent in the Second Punic War (Jenkins and Lewis 1963). Conflict with Rome again provides one of the contexts for debasement. Carthaginian silver fell to c. 33 per cent in the First Punic War, and again to 15–23 per cent, perhaps in the period of the Libyan revolt (241–238 BC). The silver coinage struck either by or in the name of the Libyans themselves was only 25–43 per cent pure, although it was made to look more silver by the use of arsenical copper (perhaps a hint of Carthaginian sophistication) (Carradice and La Niece 1988) [82]. Carthaginian silver coinage of the Second Punic War fell as low as 18 per cent pure (Jenkins 1984: 135) [83].

The other type of coinage to show a significant debasement was the 'Celtic'. The native coinages of Gaul and Britain, among others, were heavily debased in the periods leading up to annexation by Rome (Cowell 1992; Northover 1992) [149–52]. A significant debasement of Gallo-Belgic gold has been attributed to the period of Caesar's Gallic Wars, so it is likely that direct pressure from Rome again had a part to play [149]. The general context was presumably one of a series of societies which had acquired a need (whether 'cultural' or 'economic') for precious metal coinages, but without adequate supplies of the metals. Shortages may have been the result of the drying-up of mercenary pay (Rome did not use mercenaries), the draining of gold and silver to Rome, and the lack of mines and mining technology adequate to make good the shortfall.

Within the Greek world the lowering of weight standards was a more common expedient than debasement. There was perhaps a natural tendency for standards to drift downwards, as worn (and hence lighter) coins were received back by states and then recoined. More noticeable reductions in weight may sometimes be linked with specific pressures. For example Taras, Croton, Heraclea, Thurii, and Metapontum all reduced their standard silver coin from 7.9g to c. 6.6g in the context of the Pyrrhic War, and the subsequent issue from Taras was debased by 5 per cent (Burnett 1977; Burnett and Hook 1989). At the time of the final Macedonian war against Rome (172–168 BC) the coinage of Perseus was reduced in weight by 7–8 per cent to 15.5g (Price 1989: 237). At virtually the same time, in 172 BC, the Seleucid tetradrachm at Antioch was reduced by 2 per cent to 16.8g (Mørkholm 1982a; 1984). Some have seen behind this synchronism a general scarcity of silver in the eastern Mediterranean as a result of Roman depredations (Carradice and Price 1988: 128–9).

It should be apparent from the selection of debasements and weight reductions noted so far that financial pressures on states, particularly at times of actual or incipient warfare, were a significant cause of such monetary manipulations. A major role seems to have been played by military expenditures to counter the expansion of Rome, and by shortages caused by Rome's acquisition of precious metals through plunder, indemnity, and annexation.

Monetary change may also be motivated by considerations of an entirely different nature. For example, the impositions of closed monetary systems by the Ptolemies and Attalids were both marked by a significant reduction in the weight of the silver coinage for internal use (see pp. 52–6). In these cases, a variety of alternative motives are possible – profit, control of external exchange, the retention of silver coinage within the kingdom – so that we cannot be certain that financial pressures lie behind them.

The Roman world was itself no stranger to monetary manipulations. The (comparatively) fuller historical narrative and the extensive modern debates about Roman monetary affairs make the Roman Empire a good context for assessing causation.

REASONS FOR MONETARY MANIPULATIONS IN THE ROMAN WORLD

The imperial coinage of Rome suffered no major collapse between the Second Punic War and the middle of the third century AD, although there were periodic, and sometimes quite sharp, declines in standards, and occasional innovations (see p. 11). From the reign of Nero (and to some extent earlier) the silver denarius declined through reductions in weight or fineness (Fig. 2), and the gold, at first, through reductions in weight only. The 'brass' sestertius also declined in weight and zinc content, at a rate broadly comparable with the decline of the denarius (Duncan-Jones 1994: 189, 235–7). A new silver denomination (the 'antoninianus' or 'radiate') was introduced in AD 215, which was to become the dominant 'silver' denomination of the Empire [140]. It contained as much silver as 1.6 denarii and was probably (but not certainly) tariffed at two denarii.

The collapse of the imperial coinage system in the third century AD was palpable (Figs 2–3). The gold coinage was struck at lower and more erratic weights, and in small quantities, and after AD 253 it was debased (Bland forthcoming; Morrisson *et al.* 1985: 80). The fineness of the silver fell below 2 per cent. The base metal coinage was virtually abandoned for a while. The third quarter of the century saw the end of the provincial and civic coinages which had continued to provide a base metal coinage and a significant part of the silver coinage for the eastern provinces. There will be more

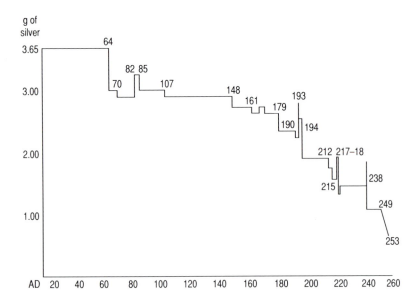

Figure 2 Amount of silver in the denarius of the mint of Rome, on
the assumption that an 'antoninianus' was worth two denarii (after
Walker 1976–8 III: 141)

to say about the numismatic aspects of the third-century 'crisis' later
(see pp. 136–40).

Attempts were made to reform and stabilize the currency under
Aurelian and Diocletian. These proved more successful for the relatively pure precious metal coinages, in that subsequent changes were
less dramatic than for the billon. For the gold, lasting stability was
achieved under Constantine, with the establishment of the solidus at
seventy-two to the pound in place of Diocletian's sixty [176]. The
standard silver coin was stable from the early 290s AD until *c.* 355–60
at ninety-six to the pound [175]. It then fell to 144 to the pound
[181], and subsequently under Honorius (AD 395–423) to 216 to the
pound (King 1993a: 13–14). The billon coinage continued to be prey
to more serious decline, reform, and retariffing throughout the fourth
century AD. Our understanding of all these coinage reforms is greatly
hampered by the lack of evidence for how specific types of coin were
tariffed at various stages. Our only secure viewpoints are provided by

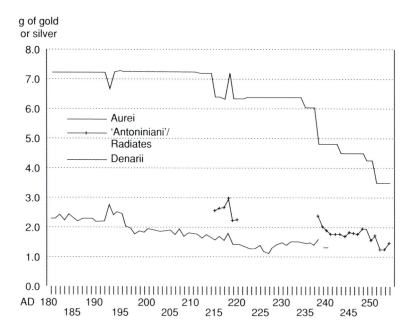

Figure 3 Weight of gold or silver in aurei, 'antoniniani', and denarii
(after Bland forthcoming)

the unfortunately fragmentary inscription of the Currency Edict of
AD 301 (Erim *et al.* 1971), the very occasional marks of value on the
coins themselves, and the names of some denominations in legal
sources which may only tentatively be associated with particular coins
(Bagnall 1985: 9–18; King 1993a). It is clear, however, that there was
a tendency for the silver content of the billon coinage to decline
progressively, despite periodic attempts to re-establish coinage of a
better quality, and for the coins to be tariffed in ever higher numbers
of denarii.

One of the major questions which lies behind the pattern of decline
and reform of the Roman coinage in all periods is whether it was
entirely driven by fiscal pressures, with stabilization or even improvement a goal when possible, or whether other considerations played a
part. That inadequacies in state finances were a major cause of the
lowering of standards cannot be doubted. The nearest we get to a
Roman view of debasement and weight reduction is Pliny the Elder's

comments on what he supposed to be the monetary changes of the First and Second Punic Wars, where the context is clearly understood to be one of financial pressure (Pliny, *HN* XXXIII, 13 (44–6)). The erroneous nature of much of Pliny's account does not matter here, what counts is what he considered a plausible motive. It is perhaps also relevant that when the denarius was retariffed from ten to sixteen asses in the 140s BC the change was made by a law to reduce expenditure (*lex minus solvendi*) (*RRC* pp. 613–14). For the most part, however, we are left to divine motives from the nature and context of the coinage reforms themselves.

Debasement of the silver coinage in the late Republic was rare. The two known debasements – of the coinage of Rome at the end of the Social War and of Mark Antony in the build-up to Actium [109] – were very obviously in contexts of high military expenditure (Walker 1980).

Walker's penetrating study of the Roman imperial silver coinage to AD 253 against the background of state finances gives decisive support to the impression gained so far, notwithstanding the fact that the accuracy of Walker's analyses of silver content is increasingly being questioned (Walker 1976–8). It appears that his sampling technique did not make adequate allowances for the surface enrichment of silver coinage, both through deliberate processing in antiquity and through subsequent differential erosion of the base metal. As a consequence some of his results now seem to have indicated a silver content higher than the real one, and the composition of individual issues seems to have been controlled to a greater degree of accuracy than his analyses implied (Butcher and Ponting forthcoming). Fortunately for our purposes the general pattern of development is not thereby called into question.

Walker has made a strong case that every debasement in the period he treated belonged in the context of particularly high state expenditure, whether for war, cash handouts on imperial accessions or anniversaries, or for various types of 'extravagance' (Walker 1976–8 III: 138). Debasement thus helped to balance income and expenditure. It is a considerable support to his interpretation that during the first century AD, when the financial situation is best documented, the debasements at Rome occurred precisely when we would have expected, namely under Nero in AD 64 after the Great Fire, and in AD 70 when Vespasian was faced by financial crisis after the civil wars. For the period after Walker's work ends it is not hard to conjecture that the debasements in the two decades after AD 253 took place in the context of financial difficulties. In the fourth century AD too, at least some of the declines occurred in periods of high expenditure, for example while Constantine was building up his forces against Maxentius, or while Constantius II had to pay for his campaigns against Magnentius (Hendy 1985: 232–3).

The connection between debasement and high state expenditure under the principate is strengthened by the observations that debasement tended to be accompanied by increased mint activity, and that there was sometimes a temporary drop in fineness at the start of reigns, when there would have been pressure to produce more coins (whether for cash handouts or for 'propaganda' reasons) (Duncan-Jones 1994: 104–5, 238–9).

The problem with finding secure counter-examples is that our knowledge of state finance is rarely sufficient to exclude the possibility that a reduction in standards was motivated by financial stringency or excessive expenditure. For the imperial period the best case is probably Trajan's debasement of AD 107, which occurred at what had been presumed to be the time of the influx of great quantities of booty from the conquest of Dacia. Even this can be rejected on the grounds that the source for the sums involved is late and exaggerated (Walker 1976–8 III: 121–2). Credence had been given to a substantial influx of gold at this time because a papyrus of *c.* AD 108 (?) appeared to show a drop in the gold price. This evidence has been somewhat undermined by the discovery that the gold price in another papyrus of AD 113 was normal (Foraboschi 1984). The debasement may thus be linked with the costs rather than the rewards of the war.

Nevertheless it is as well not to be blind to possible influences on monetary change other than fiscal stringency. Attempts to improve the coinage demand explanation. Here Walker's masterly exposition of the moral dimension to Roman 'economic policy' is entirely persuasive (Walker 1976–8 III: 106–48). The improvements of Domitian, Pertinax, Macrinus, and Gordian I and II (continued under Balbinus and Pupienus) all belonged in a broader context of 'conservative' attempts to restore ancient standards, or of the repudiation of the (mis)deeds of predecessors following a dynastic change. In none of the cases was the financial situation at all propitious, and all the improvements were short-lived. An effective restoration of a pure silver coinage had to await Diocletian, and the cost was the official recognition that his debased silver (billon) issues formed a category of coinage quite separate from the silver [174–5]. Diocletian's pure argenteus was equivalent in silver to a Neronian denarius, but was tariffed at one hundred denarii (at least after AD 301, when its value is known from the Currency Edict).

The suggestion that traditional moral values played a part in Roman economic thinking should not be controversial. Much more debatable is whether rudimentary economic notions also affected monetary policy (Lo Cascio 1981). If the prices of gold and silver fluctuated, as they appear to have done, was it necessary to modify the coinage from time to time to maintain the official relationship of one gold aureus to twenty-five silver denarii? If the price of gold or silver bullion went up, might the standards of the coinage have been reduced to prevent coins from disappearing into the melting pot or being exported as bullion? Such questions are not ludicrous. In some pre-modern contexts where the motivation behind monetary policy is better documented these are real issues (e.g. Cipolla 1989; Challis 1992). It is a classic problem of how to use comparative material, as the Roman evidence is quite inadequate to prove or disprove the proposition that such issues were a consideration. It would help if we had a better idea of the extent to which coin was overvalued against bullion (see pp. 128–30). The greater the degree of overvaluation the more flexibility there was for bullion values to alter without forcing a change in the coinage.

One reason for allowing the possibility that considerations other than purely fiscal ones played a part in monetary reforms is that the gold coinage was not always altered at the same time as the silver, and not always to the same degree. In the first two centuries AD the gold content of the aureus declined by only 8 per cent, while the silver content of the denarius was virtually halved. In the first half of the third century AD the gold and silver coinage declined much more closely in parallel (cf. Fig. 3 on p. 117; Walker 1976–8 III: 154; Bland forthcoming). Perhaps too much should not be read into this. If standards were reduced to increase the spending power of the state, it does not follow that all elements of the coinage would be reduced equally and simultaneously. It is noteworthy that when imperial silver coinages were struck in Syria in the late second and third centuries AD it was not unusual for their silver content to differ somewhat from that of imperial silver of the mint of Rome (Howgego 1994: 12 n. 46). Likewise changes to the silver at the mint of Rome were not always matched, or not at the same time or to the same degree, by changes to Roman provincial silver coinages (e.g. *RPC* I: 52–3 on Nero). In the long run the imperial and provincial silver coinages and the gold coinage all tended to decline (Walker 1976–8). Complex explanations are possible, but the facts can also be accommodated within a simple view of change through fiscal pressure.

One is left with the impression that by far the most significant causes of monetary reform at Rome were a shortage of state funds in relation to expenditure, and a conservative moral desire to return to older and better standards. In the current state of evidence other possibilities should be left open. It remains possible that one of the reasons for wanting to reduce standards was a desire to compensate for price rises, but the causes of 'inflation' in the Roman world require more detailed consideration in their own right.

CAUSES OF INFLATION

The analysis of price rises in antiquity is a most inexact science owing to the poor quality of the evidence for price levels. Our information is not such as to permit the construction of an index of the cost of living from a basket of prices. Comparing prices for the same commodity or service is fraught with danger. Prices naturally varied according to quantity, quality, season, and location. One example will suffice to make the point. A sequence of standard prices, probably compiled from declarations by guilds, survives from the Oxyrhynchite nome in Egypt in about AD 340 (*P. Oxy.* LIV, 3773). The declarations were presumably for standard qualities and quantities from the same location, and yet individual commodities varied by up to 77 per cent within a year. A further problem is that part of our evidence is for official prices in transactions concerning the state, which may be set at artificial rather than market levels. The charting of subtle changes in the level of prices is thus beyond our evidence.

A further fundamental problem is that Egypt is the only area from which a substantial body of prices survives over a long period (Drexhage 1991). From Ptolemy I to Diocletian Egypt had a closed monetary system and so might in principle have gone its own way, but under the Roman principate it was tied to the rest of the Empire by trade and other forms of exchange, and by the notional equivalence between the Egyptian tetradrachm and the denarius. There is thus some uncertainty about whether we should try to compare Egyptian prices with the silver content of the Egyptian tetradrachm or with that of the denarius. The major problem, however, is that we are largely deprived of the possibility of seeing regional variations in price levels and the timing of changes. It is unwise and unhelpful to assume that Egypt was in general more 'untypical' than any other area (Rathbone 1989), but Diocletian's Prices Edict is explicit about the existence of regional variations in price levels and inflation.

We do know something about prices outside Egypt (e.g. Duncan-Jones 1982), and the extent of the problem of inflation under Diocletian is clear from his Prices Edict and its ranting preamble (although there is debate about whether it applied to the west, as all the surviving inscribed copies of the Edict come from the eastern half of the Empire). Moreover, the coins themselves provide evidence for the generality of the phenomenon by the way in which smaller denominations dropped out of the system, presumably in response to rising prices. In the imperial series the quadrans replaced the sextans as the smallest denomination in *c.* 91/90 BC; the quadrans itself was last struck under Antoninus Pius [cf. 125], and after Hadrian (or possibly Antoninus Pius) the semis appeared only as a brief revival under Trajan Decius (AD 249–51).

It is clear that the same process affected the civic and provincial coinages which provided the small change for the east until the second half of the third century AD, although the precise denominations in use are hard to identify. By way of example, plausible reconstructions show that at Aphrodisias the smallest hellenistic denomination disappeared under Augustus, and the half assarion was struck for the last time in the 240s AD (Johnston forthcoming a). At Smyrna the quarter assarion did not outlive Trajan (Johnston forthcoming b). After AD 253 the face values of civic coins in many areas were doubled by the application of countermarks (Howgego 1985: 52–73; Johnston forthcoming b) [171]. In Egypt the production of base metal small change below the billon tetradrachm diminished rapidly after the reign of Marcus Aurelius. Of the five regular base metal denominations of the end of the first century AD only the largest, the drachm, was struck after the death of Elagabalus, and that only very rarely (Milne 1971: xvii) [172]. The progressive pattern of the abandonment of small denominations throughout the Roman world does suggest a general, but not necessarily continuous, tendency for nominal prices to rise from the second century BC onwards throughout the imperial period.

Attempts to explain price inflation fall into three main categories: the quantity of money, debasement, and monetary reform.

Quantity of money

The Fisher equation is a classic formulation of the quantity theory of money: the quantity of money multiplied by how hard it works (velocity) equals the number of monetized transactions multiplied by the prices at which they occur (MV = PT). It is wrong to doubt that the equation can apply to the ancient economy because it is simply a truism (*pace* Hendy 1985: 3–5). It is perfectly valid, however, to refute simplistic assumptions about its explanatory power (as, entertainingly, Veyne 1979: 220–3). If it is assumed that velocity and the totality of monetized transactions are constant, then an increase in the money supply will lead to a rise in prices. There are, however, good reasons to question the validity of that assumption (cf. Corbier 1976–7).

A greater supply of coinage might lead to increased hoarding (thus decreasing V). It might also lead to increased production for the monetized market (thus increasing T). This second possibility is easy to envisage, for example, in the context of an increase in demand created by army pay in frontier zones. Further, more money might lead to a greater proportion of exchange being monetized (again increasing T, which in the Fisher equation must refer to the monetized transactions only).

Change may also be driven by other elements in the equation. The propensity to save and the nature and extent of credit will have affected how hard the coinage in circulation could work (V) (Howgego 1992: 12–16). The demand for goods to buy (which has a direct bearing on the PT side of the equation) is affected by many variables. The size of the population is relevant, particularly at times of rapid change. It is also highly relevant that demand is to some extent a cultural construct (cf. Appadurai 1986: 29ff.). Cultural changes are likely to have had a significant effect on the demand for goods to buy, not least the dramatic increase in urbanization during the Empire, the decline in civic euergetism in the third century AD, and changes in the nature, size, disposition, and remuneration of the army.

The foregoing considerations are sufficient to make one cautious about theories which imply a simple relationship between the coin supply and prices. They are no more than particular aspects of a more systematic critique of the dynamics of the quantity theory of money by Keynes and other economists (de Cecco 1985). A complicating factor in antiquity is that coinage was not just a currency with the sole function of mediating exchange. Coins were made of metals which had alternative uses. The demand for gold and silver for prestige goods and decorative purposes may have helped to underpin the value of the precious metal currencies, and to limit possible variations.

To some extent changes in the supply of precious metals may have led to changes in prices expressed in terms of gold or silver coin. The observation of long-term changes in prices expressed in silver in societies before the introduction of coinage, in which monetary reform can have played no part, gives some credibility to such a mechanism (e.g. Renger 1984: 95–9 on Babylonia in the early second millennium BC). The Romans themselves had some empirical awareness that in specific contexts the quantity of money might affect prices (Nicolet 1971). The evidence, however, appears to be confined to short-term effects. Thus, after Augustus brought back to Rome the royal treasure from Egypt, he made money so abundant that the price of land rose (Suetonius, *Div. Aug.* 41). Short-term variation is apparent also from a law of *c.* AD 371–3 which opines that on account of the reduction in value of the (gold) solidus, the price of all commodities ought to reduce (*C.J.* XI, 11, 2; Hendy 1985: 473). This evidence cuts both ways. While it reveals that prices had risen in terms of gold, it also suggests the expectation that gold and other commodities would march together, and thus the force of traditional pricing. Short-term variations in prices expressed in gold cannot normally be detected owing to the poor quality of our evidence. In the long run they tended to be stable (Whittaker 1980: 4; Bagnall 1985: 49; 1993: 215–16; Depeyrot 1991: 127).[1] This makes it most unlikely that variations in the supply of precious metal were a principal cause of the dramatic rises in price expressed in units of account seen in the Roman world.

A more purely monetarist view is that it was not the supply of precious metals as such but the quantity actually coined which affected prices. Our inability to make accurate estimates of the quantity of coinage is a severe disadvantage in evaluating this approach (see pp. 30–3). However, in the light of the apparent long-term stability of prices expressed in gold it is hard to see how a putative increase in the quantity of gold coin can have been the principal agent of nominal inflation in the fourth century AD (*pace* Depeyrot 1991).

It would be rash to deny that the quantity of precious metals, or more specifically of precious metal coinage, was a cause of price changes. In the later Middle Ages, for which the evidence is a great deal better, it has proved possible to link increases in the supply of coinage to rising prices, and declines to falling prices (Mayhew 1974; 1987; Cipolla 1989: 115). The problem for the Roman world is that our evidence is not sufficiently good to reveal moderate changes in price levels, such as may well have been caused by fluctuations in the money supply. Nor is our evidence for the quantity of coinage adequate to establish links with moderate changes in price. What we can see is dramatic, and finds more obvious explanations in debasement and monetary reform. To the extent that debasement may have allowed more coins to be produced (rather than allowing the government to maintain production from diminishing resources), and that monetary reforms increased the nominal value of the money supply by raising the face value of the coins (which they sometimes did), the link between these phenomena and inflation is readily explicable in terms of the Fisher equation. Debasement and monetary reform are, however, rather special cases, and deserve separate treatment.

Debasement

We have already seen the use of debasements at Rome as a technique to allow the government to spend more than it could otherwise have done (see pp. 117–21). What is at issue now is whether debasements caused prices to rise. The argument, simply stated, is that people knew and cared how much precious metal was in their coinage. When the coinage was debased they demanded more coins for any given transaction to compensate for the debasement. Not only is there no consensus on this issue, but studies based on Egyptian prices have reached very different conclusions for the periods before and after Aurelian's reform of the coinage in AD 274. It has been argued that prices were not affected by the debasement of the coinage before AD 274/5, notwithstanding the fact that the imperial silver declined from nearly pure to under 2 per cent silver, and the Egyptian tetradrachm, which was notionally equal in value with the denarius, also suffered very marked debasement, from c. 32 per cent down to below 3 per cent (Duncan-Jones 1994: 232–5; Rathbone forthcoming). Both types of coin also declined in weight. By contrast, we are asked to believe that in the fourth century prices reacted almost instantly to compensate in full for debasements, and that silver content was still watched even when the coins had fallen to only 0.2 per cent pure (Bagnall 1985; 1989; 1993). It is somewhat uncomfortable to accept two such radically different hypotheses. Both could be right, but only if one assumes a change in the principal mechanism of inflation c. AD 274/5 (after which prices do seem to have reacted to changes in the coinage).

The only serious explanation for such a change, if change there was, is that the relationship of gold coinage to the rest of the monetary system was altered by Aurelian's reform. Before it other types of coin were tied to the aureus at official rates (25 denarii or 25 Egyptian tetradrachms to the aureus, and so on). Afterwards the gold coinage floated in value like any other commodity, and the rest of the coinage system fell in value owing to debasement, being no longer pegged by its relationship to gold. Since the unit of account was notionally in silver (the denarius, or in Egypt the drachm), prices rose as the coinage fell. Such an explanation is possible, for all its anachronistic echoes of 'coming off the gold standard', but is it right? Unfortunately the state of our evidence does not permit an unequivocal answer.

It is clear that the official value of gold coin ceased to be fixed in terms of denarii at some time. The official change seems to have been after *c.* AD 215–25, as for Dio the aureus was still a coin worth 25 denarii (Dio LV, 12, 5; Buttrey 1961). The value of the gold solidus floated by AD 301, otherwise there would have been no point in quoting a maximum price for it in the Prices Edict. The change is confirmed by the declaration of prices from Oxyrhynchus of *c.* AD 340 which shows the value of the solidus fluctuating month by month (*P. Oxy.* LIV, 3773).

The hypothesis of a single and dramatic change under Aurelian is, however, called into question by a variety of documentary evidence which seems to imply some variation in the value of gold coin already before AD 274.[2] The hypothesis might just be saved by assuming that such evidence demonstrates a variability of the value of gold coin in private transactions which was not officially recognized until 274. But would official rates have been strong enough to restrain prices if the market was in fact already using its own rates for gold coin?

It is worth adding a purely numismatic perspective. Before the reign of Severus Alexander (AD 222–35) gold coin was produced to very consistent weights. From then weights became increasingly variable, so that after AD 253 no consistent standard can be recognized at all. This might indicate official recognition that gold coin in fact passed by weight (Bland forthcoming). If gold coin was valued by weight earlier in the third century, there would have been no fixed relationship for Aurelian to abandon.

It is hard to see what in the discussion so far could prove decisive. What does seem to emerge from the current debates is an increasing awareness that Aurelian's reform may have been crucial. This has an implication for our estimation of the extent of change under Diocletian. It was under Aurelian, not Diocletian, that the gold coinage returned to full purity. Further it was Aurelian who first struck an improved billon coin with an indication of its purity (XXI = twenty parts base metal to one part silver) [145]. The XXI mark anticipated that on Diocletian's nummi [174], its meaning being made virtually certain by the existence of rare issues marked XI which are twice as pure (Callu *et al.* 1979).

The increased focus on Aurelian is an advance, but does not meet the main point of our discussion, namely the extent to which debasement caused inflation. The evidence for prices in Egypt makes it tolerably clear that prices did not proceed *pari passu* with debasement at least until after Aurelian's reform. Some connection is possible, as the structural doubling of prices *c.* AD 160–91 is asking to be linked with the halving of the silver content of the Egyptian tetradrachm in AD 176/7. An attempt to blame this price rise on the plague of 166/7 is not very convincing, as the new price level endured for about a century. Nevertheless apparent price stability between *c.* 160–91 and 274 demonstrates that it was not inevitable that prices reacted swiftly to debasement. The silver content of the Alexandrian tetradrachm has not been much investigated, particularly for the third century AD, but it is clear that it suffered significant declines in the 250s and 260s, which do not seem to have been matched by immediate price rises.

Our current understanding of changes in basic rates of military pay gives some cause to doubt the general applicability of the pattern of price changes in Egypt. In addition to their pay, soldiers might receive donations in cash and subsidies in kind. On the assumption that these tended to increase over time, rises in basic pay should provide a minimum estimate of increases in remuneration. As a rough approximation Egyptian prices seem to have been static at least from *c.* AD 45 until they doubled *c.* AD 160–91. Prices again remained level until a more than tenfold increase *c.* AD 274/5, which was followed by stability until Diocletian's reform of the coinage (Rathbone forthcoming). On the other hand the basic pay of a legionary foot-soldier rose by a third in AD 84, doubled in 197, rose by one half in 212, and doubled again in AD 235. Later in the third century the stipendium was not increased, but donatives and *annona* rose such that by AD 300 they overshadowed basic pay (Speidel 1992). The eight-fold rise between Domitian and Maximinus makes something of a contrast with the mere doubling of prices seen in Egypt during the same period. Military pay also outstripped debasement, which saw the silver in the denarius decline from 3.65g to 1.4g in the same period (a decline of 62 per cent). So there is cause for hesitation here, but again no reason to suppose that prices closely mirrored the metal content of the coins.

So was the fourth century AD different? Did price rises automatically follow debasement? As always our evidence for prices is scarcely adequate (see p. 121). It has been shown that it is consistent with the view that prices rose in pronounced steps in line with the debasement of the coinage or its retariffing (which might effectively amount to the same thing) (Bagnall 1985). Unfortunately the evidence is sufficiently flexible to allow different views about the timing even of the most dramatic rise (forty to fifty fold) which occurred sometime around the middle of the century (Bagnall 1985: 44; Callu 1978: 114), and to leave others with the impression that prices rose steadily rather than in steps (Depeyrot 1991: 124, 138).

In one sense the situation is simpler than before. The closed currency system of Egypt had been ended under Diocletian [173], so that there is no longer the ambiguity about whether we should be comparing prices in Egypt with the Egyptian tetradrachm or with the imperial coinage. The imperial coinage was now ubiquitous. Unfortunately we are largely ignorant about how the billon coinage was tariffed in the fourth century (see pp. 116–17). To explain a marked increase in prices by an otherwise unrecorded or undated retariffing may be along the right lines, but is completely circular if what one is trying to prove is that prices marched along with the coinage (as Bagnall 1985: 33–4 dating Licinius' reform and the introduction of the centenionalis from prices; 45 inferring the existence of a myriad coin from prices). Thus the view that prices simply and quickly followed alterations in the coinage in the fourth century remains an hypothesis, neither proven nor refuted.

In the face of ambiguous evidence about what actually happened, it is perhaps worth asking whether it is likely that prices would have been dictated in an immediate way by the precious metal content of the coinage. If a coin is merely a token there is no necessity that a decline in its metal content should lead to a rise in prices. Its face value was simply what the government said it was. If, on the other hand, a coin is like a certified ingot, worth its metal content, then a decline in its metallic value might lead directly to a rise in prices. Roman coinage probably fell somewhere between these two extremes.

There is no evidence that any element of the Roman monetary system apart from the gold coinage floated on the market (for the date at which this occurred see p. 126). For the rest the government set the face value, and required acceptance of good coin (Lo Cascio forthcoming: n. 23). A somewhat arbitrary attitude to face values in the early fourth century is clearly demonstrated by Diocletian's doubling of the value of some types of coin in AD 301, and by Licinius' halving of the value of the nummus *c.* AD 320–4. Such actions, which seem to have affected coins already in circulation as well as new ones (cf. *P. Ryl.* 607), clearly imply that face values were to an extent artificial, rather than dictated by metal content. The Romans viewed their coinage as a fixed measure of value (*pretium*), not as a commodity (*merx*) (Nicolet 1984). On the other hand the value of the gold and silver coinage at least was clearly backed to a significant extent by its metal content.

The export of Roman gold and silver coins beyond the frontiers does suggest that the face value of the coins was close enough to their metallic value that they could be treated as bullion. It is notable that older coins with a higher precious metal content were sometimes deliberately selected for export (see pp. 102–5). The tendency for Roman gold and silver coins in India to be earlier than Nero's weight reduction and debasement in AD 64, and for silver coins found beyond the northern frontiers to antedate the debasement under Septimius Severus in AD 194, suggests that these reforms may have marked significant moves away from the idea of a full value silver currency.

Fluctuations in the market value of gold and silver must have meant that the degree of overvaluation (or undervaluation) of the coinage was subject to change even in the absence of debasements. Calculation of overvaluation is made difficult by the poverty of evidence for bullion prices, and by our ignorance of whether such prices as we do have are 'typical', or reflect local or temporary circumstances (cf. Howgego 1990: 18–19). For the fourth century after AD 301 we do not know the face value of the silver coinage so that calculation of the overvaluation of silver is impossible.

The best evidence for any period may be derived from a comparison of the maximum prices for bullion given in Diocletian's Prices Edict of 301 with the coins themselves, the face value of which is known from the imperial letter concerning a revaluation of the coinage which accompanied the Edict (Hendy 1985: 450–8). Gold was not overvalued, as we would expect of a coin which floated on the market. The silver argenteus [175] and billon nummus [174], however, seem to have been valued at 1.6 and 2.85 times their bullion contents respectively (i.e. were overvalued by 60 per cent and 185 per cent). The principal problem with this evidence is that it is possible that the maximum prices for precious metals in the Edict may have been kept artificially low, perhaps as an aid to compulsory purchases of bullion by the state (Bagnall 1989: 70). If so, we may have overstated the degree of overvaluation in market terms. On the other hand the coins seem from the start to have been struck at lower than the theoretical standards of weight and fineness, which means that in this respect the calculations underestimate the actual overvaluation (King 1993a). The evidence is, however, sufficient to suggest that in AD 301 silver coin was overvalued, and billon coinage to a greater degree.

The general applicability of these observations is not guaranteed, but there is some reason to suspect that the imperial silver had long been overvalued. If the denarius was always worth its weight in silver, how could one explain the occasional attempts to improve its fineness (see p. 119)? Would the improved coins really have been issued at a cost in excess of their face value? Further, one can see from the evidence of hoards that declining standards did not necessarily drive older and better coins out of circulation. Coins of the same denomination but with different metal contents might circulate together for long periods, unless the government withdrew the older coins (Duncan-Jones 1994: 106, 194–200). For example old denarii containing c. 2.85g of silver were still circulating in the 220s AD alongside recent denarii with only c. 1.50g (Walker 1976–8 III: 139–40). On the reasonable assumption that denarii could therefore purchase at least 2.85g of silver (or the old coins would have been melted for bullion) the overvaluation of the more recent denarii is patent.

If Roman silver and billon were overvalued, but it was still felt that they should contain a 'reasonable amount' of precious metal, then a compromise position becomes possible on the relationship between debasement and inflation. Debasement could be tolerated without price rises, but only up to a certain point.

Perhaps, therefore, prices tended to follow the metal content of the coins in the long run, but not in any immediate or accurate way, and with a degree of local variation. People were aware that even very base billon coins contained silver, and were prepared to take matters into their own hands in certain circumstances. That much is clear from a law of AD 349 against the purifying of the maiorina coin and the extraction of its silver (C. Th. IX, 21, 6; Hendy 1985: 470). However, the idea that prices reacted instantly and exactly to changes in the coinage smacks a little too much of an effective economic rationalism. It is as well to recall some of the irrational attitudes to coinage in the fourth and fifth centuries AD (Hendy 1985: 363–8). Laws were passed against valuing the solidus according to the size of the portrait, and against the refusal or lower valuation of coins with the portraits of former emperors, or of relatives of the emperor. There is not much trace of a strictly rational approach to metal content here!

Monetary reform

We have already had occasion to notice that a monetary reform which alters the face value of an existing coinage, or creates a new style of coinage, may be in effect a debasement. If the value of a coin is doubled without a change in its metal content that is equivalent to a debasement by fifty per cent. A new style of coinage, even if it is finer or heavier than the old one, may also mark an effective debasement, if its face value is higher than the old coinage by more than the improvement in its metal content.

Such reforms did take place. A clear example of the first category occurred in AD 301, when the value of some types of coin was doubled (*geminata potentia*). Cogent examples of the second type are harder to find, because often we are not sure about the face value of the coinage both before and after a reform. Better or heavier coins which may in fact have masked debasements include Caracalla's radiate in AD 215 [140], Aurelian's reformed radiate in 274 [145], Diocletian's new silver and billon coinages *c.* 293–6 [174–5], and the FEL. TEMP. REPARATIO billon coinages of 348 [178]. The general drift of what was going on is clear from such evidence for denominations as we do have. Diocletian's silver coin was on the standard of the Neronian denarius but was, at least by AD 301, tariffed at 100 denarii. His billon coin at first probably had a face value of $12\frac{1}{2}$ denarii (hence the value of the follis, or standard bag of coins, at 12,500 denarii was originally equivalent to 1,000 of these nummi). The value of the billon coin was doubled to 25 denarii in AD 301. At some stage before AD 354 (presumably) billon coins were struck with a value of 100 denarii (*centenionales communes*: C. Th. IX, 23, 1). By shortly after the middle of the century it is possible, although not certain, that billon coins were being tariffed as a myriad (10,000 denarii) or a follis (12,500 denarii) (Bagnall 1985: 12, 17–18, 45; Callu 1980: 103). Thus, despite immense uncertainties at almost every stage, the tendency for face values to rise is clear, and at times dramatic.

Monetary reforms of one type or the other do seem to be connected with the most dramatic price rises which we know about. For reasons which we do not understand properly (perhaps because the decline in standards went beyond what the public could tolerate?) some reforms seem to have caused the inflation. In other cases the chronology is sufficiently uncertain to allow the possibility that the reforms were a response to, rather than the cause of, the rises in price. In some cases both could be true.

Ptolemaic Egypt provides a plausible precedent (Reekmans 1948; 1951). The production of silver coin in Egypt declined from *c.* 240 BC (Mørkholm 1991: 109). From *c.* 210 BC accounts were normallykept in terms of the copper drachm, rather than the earlier silver. Prices seem to have doubled on a number of distinct occasions (*c.* 221–216, 183–182, 173, and 130–128 BC?). An increasing scarcity of silver may have had some role to play in this process (see p. 114), but the rapid and dramatic price rises are much more suggestive of monetary reform. The precise details are unclear as we do not know the face value of the Ptolemaic copper coinage in most periods, but the general hypothesis is supported by the existence of bronze coins of Cleopatra marked with values of 80 and 40 (*RPC* I: 480) [80]. If these values are expressed in copper drachmas then it is easy to imagine that the copper currency had been subject to a number of nominal revaluations since the introduction of a heavy copper currency *c.* 260 BC (Mørkholm 1991: 105). The analogy with what happened in Egypt under the Romans seems quite close.

After the doubling of prices *c.* AD 160–191 (see p. 127), price levels seem to have remained reasonably static until *c.* 274/5. There was then a more than tenfold increase, followed by another period of stability. It is thus attractive to posit some connection between the major price increase and Aurelian's coinage reform of AD 274. It is at first sight surprising that a reform of the imperial coinage, which did not circulate in Egypt, should have had such an impact on prices in Egypt. It is possible that the notional equivalence of the Egyptian tetradrachm with the imperial denarius is a sufficient explanation. Thus if the denarius lost its fixed relationship to gold coin (if that is what happened; see pp. 125–6) the tetradrachm also ceased to be pegged to gold (whether or not gold coinage actually circulated in Egypt) (Howgego 1992: 11). At any rate a reform of the coinage affected Egypt at this date in some way, as the weight of the Egyptian tetradrachm was reduced in AD 274/5, and hoard evidence shows that earlier tetradrachms were withdrawn *c.* 273/4, presumably to be recoined (Metcalf 1987).

The price rises which provoked the Edict on Maximum Prices of AD 301 were characterized in the ranting preamble as not simply fourfold or eightfold, but such as to render the name of price indescribable (Lauffer 1971). Again the proximity to reforms of the coinage is suggestive, as it is not unreasonable to assume that the price rises in question were a recent phenomenon. Some scholars have put the blame on the doubling in value of some elements in the coinage in the Currency Edict which took effect in September of the same year (Lo Cascio forthcoming). It is, however, rather difficult to see why a doubling of value should give rise to the scale of price increases castigated in the Edict. The Currency Edict and Prices Edict are perhaps more naturally understood as combined measures in the face of the same problem. The combination of a doubling in the value of the coinage and the fixing of maximum prices looks like a concerted attempt to restore the purchasing power of the coinage, and not least of soldiers' pay (the preamble to the Prices Edict complains that a single purchase may strip a soldier of his donative and pay) (Hendy 1993: 332). In that case we may suspect that Diocletian's earlier reform of the coinage c. AD 294/5 had been the significant factor causing the price inflation.

About the fourth century something has been said already (see p. 128). It can be argued that prices were dictated by a combination of debasement and monetary reform. Unfortunately we are faced by an almost complete lack of certain evidence about the face values of the billon (and silver) coinages following particular reforms (see pp. 116–17). The only exception is the halving in value of the nummus from 25 to 12½ denarii under Licinius c. AD 320–24 (Bagnall 1985: 32–3; King 1993a: 25). This apparent improvement in the standard in fact masked a very significant debasement. Our ignorance about the precise nature of other reforms makes a correlation with prices no more than hypothetical. It is, however, hard not to believe that the most substantial price rise of forty to fifty fold around the middle of the century was not connected with the new FEL. TEMP. REPARATIO series of AD 348, or possibly with one of the stages of its rapid demise (Bagnall 1985: 41–6; King 1993a: 26–30) [178].

The coincidence between monetary reforms and marked rises in prices is striking. The causal link might run in either direction. Diocletian's revaluation of AD 301 looks like a reaction to rising prices. On the other hand, the timing of price rises suggests that Aurelian's reform was in some way responsible for the inflation from c. 274/5.

Where a monetary reform causes inflation one still needs to ask what motivated the reform. Possibilities include a shortage of state funds making a reform necessary to mask an effective reduction in standards, a feeling that the physical characteristics of the existing coinage were too poor to tolerate, and a miscalculated attempt to stem a rise in prices.

Conclusion

Despite much modern scholarship the causes of inflation in the Roman world still leave a lot of room for debate. It has at least proved possible to isolate some of the key issues. Those who are most adept at handling the papyrological evidence in all periods see prices rising not continuously but in sudden and often very pronounced steps. It may be that the poor quality of our evidence does not permit us to detect gradual or more modest changes, but we may as well concentrate on explaining what we can see. Sharp rises are not likely to be dictated by increases in the quantity of money in the absence of nominal revaluation or (possibly) increased output through debasement.

Debasement seems to have been predominantly the result of inadequacies in state finance. The complex relationship between debasement, monetary reform, and price rises is still not properly understood. Interpretations depend crucially upon a possible change in the nature of the gold coinage from a fixed face value to a floating one, and upon the varying degrees of overvaluation of the coinage. We must not miss what is obvious. The periods of greatest inflation in the Roman world, roughly the 270s to the 380s AD, are characterized by repeated debasements and monetary reforms.

Some have seen a connection between inflation and attempts to maintain a heavily debased silver (billon) currency. There may be some truth in this, as the 'billon' coinage declined to the point where it ceased to have any significant silver content by *c.* AD 364, after which the Roman coinage became once again a system of gold, silver, and bronze (King 1993a: 30). It may thereafter have been easier to maintain a stable relationship between the different elements in the monetary system (Carrié 1993: 151). The apparent stability of prices from the 380s onwards may, however, be a consequence of the increasing tendency to express prices in terms of gold, in which prices had always tended to be stable (see p. 124; Callu 1993: 101; Depeyrot 1991: 129).

A final question we should ask is whether inflation in the Roman world was a purely technical matter, or whether it was indicative of, or even responsible for, economic change and even crisis. This is not a subject to which justice can be done here, for it involves an analysis of the nature and causes of the transformation of the Roman world from the principate into late antiquity. It is certainly possible to hold minimalist views of the importance of inflation (Whittaker 1980; Bagnall 1985: 54–5). Land, as the principal form of wealth and source of production, remained unaffected. The Roman economy was not characterized by potentially vulnerable intangible obligations expressed in money. Ways could be found to protect debts even in periods of the highest inflation (Bowman 1980: 33). Prices expressed in gold remained reasonably stable. Nominal inflation simply meant a readjustment of prices, remuneration (including, for the army, donatives and allowances in kind), and the like.

This is to overstate the case. Stability in terms of gold was of less use to those with no access to gold (Bowman 1980: 32). Access to information will also have been of importance. A revealing papyrus which probably relates to Licinius' reform shows a government official writing to someone who may have been his steward urging him to hurry to spend all the official's 'Italian silver' on goods of any kind at whatever price, as the value of the coinage had been halved (*P. Ryl.* 607). But there was surely more to inflation than just differential advantage.

If debasement is held to reflect a chronic inadequacy in state finance then it would be surprising if there were not a broader nexus of effects. One may have been an increased reliance on transactions in kind, both by the government and in the wider economy. This is not uncontroversial for, although such a transformation is part of the classic picture of the late third and fourth centuries, it has proved hard to verify in the detailed evidence from Egypt (the only province from which adequate evidence survives) (Carrié 1993: 131–9; Bowman 1980: 27, 29). Increasing scepticism about the reality of the supposed change is also being expressed in relation to other areas (e.g. Mitchell 1993 I: 245–53 on Asia Minor). Not controversial is the increase in the tendency of the government to exact monetary obligations in gold in the fourth century. Less wealthy individuals might still pay their taxes in billon coinage to collectors who would then purchase solidi (Bowman 1980; Bagnall 1993: 214; Carrié 1993: 139–50). It is, however, not unlikely that access to gold was one of the factors in defining the more pronounced social hierarchies of late antiquity (Depeyrot 1991: 174–5; Banaji 1994). So one can see how inflation might in principle have been linked to economic and social change.

THE THIRD-CENTURY CRISIS

To end, let us set aside the question of causation and try another perspective. On any account the Roman Empire in the third century AD endured military crisis, internal instability, and political and social transformation. It is often thought that there was economic crisis as well, although the precise characteristics are hard to pin down. The period thus offers a good opportunity to examine some of the ways in which stress and change may be revealed in the behaviour of the coinage, and thus to define some aspects of the crisis in concrete terms. The interest of the topic extends beyond a demonstration that the coinage reflects crisis and transformation. Numismatics has tended to shape historical approaches to the third century, partly because the picture derived from the coinage is dramatic, and partly because of the dearth of contemporary historical narrative.

Debasement of the imperial silver has had a significant influence on our picture of what the third-century crisis was. Signs of what was to come in the Severan period, accelerating decline particularly from AD 253, the nadir between 260 and 274, restoration under Aurelian, and reform under Diocletian is a pattern which pervades more than just the coinage. The impression left by a coinage which declined to a mere 2 per cent silver between AD 260 and 268 and fell still further is a strong one. The link with inadequacies in state finance seems inescapable.

The relationship between state finance, the economy, and social and political change is a complex one. Transformation in these areas may be a very slow process, rather than a response to particular events. The pattern of the silver coinage may thus be helpful in giving a sense of the *longue durée*. Progressive debasement in fact began under Nero. The seeds of the third and fourth centuries were sown early.

Rather than dwell further upon the debasement of the silver which has had a part to play in many historical accounts of the third century, it is worth looking at some of the other numismatic features of the period. It has already been noted that the gold coinage did not remain unaffected. The weight of the aureus was more than halved between AD 215 and 253. After 253 the gold was also debased, in some cases to as low as 66 per cent fine. Purity was restored under Aurelian, but possibly at the expense of an official recognition that the gold coinage no longer had a fixed face value, but floated like a commodity (see p. 126). The production and circulation of gold coinage seems to have been at a low level in the third century (Burnett 1987: 112–13; Callu and Loriot 1990: 86, 106; King 1993b).

The problems in the gold and silver coinage in the third century were in the first instance a reflection of the weakness of state finances. Behind that may lie a more general decline in the quantities of precious metal available in the Roman world as a whole (Howgego 1992: 4–12). A comparative scarcity may explain why *in the long run* the state was not able to make up a shortfall in finances by increased exactions, and had to resort to savage debasement.

There were increasing problems too with the production of small change. The striking of a double sestertius and the production of the semis for the first time since the second century AD under Trajan Decius (AD 249–51), and a substantial recoining of old bronze coins into sestertii and double sestertii under Postumus (AD 260–9) in the 'Gallic empire' [144], look like short-lived attempts to stem the tide. By *c.* 270 even the sestertius had ceased to be part of the normal currency (Howgego 1985: 67).

In a very obvious way political instability was reflected by the number of individuals claiming to be emperor on their coinage (forty in the fifty years after AD 235). Imperial style coinages were struck for Postumus and his successors in the 'Gallic empire' (AD 260–74) [144], by Carausius and Allectus in the 'British empire' (AD 286–96) [147–8], and by Vabalathus in the east (AD 270–2) [146]. Such 'breakaway' emperors did not present themselves as leading separatist movements, but as legitimate emperors or co-emperors (see p. 82). What was at issue was the increasing impossibility of maintaining imperial control from the centre, which led ultimately to the division of imperial power under the tetrarchy. The decisive steps towards the decentralization of minting of imperial coinage taken in the 250s AD, and the systematization under Diocletian with roughly (but not exactly) one mint in each diocese, likewise mark stages in a more general devolvement of imperial government (cf. Hendy 1985: 378–80).

The impression of disintegration is strengthened by the evidence of coin circulation, although it is hard to decide whether we should be talking about a decline in the imperial distribution system or in economic integration more generally. There is a case for both. The provision of coinage for the Empire, whether from Rome or from a series of decentralized mints, may certainly be viewed as a supply system. Problems in supply were not new in the third century. For example the inadequacy of the provision of small change to the north-western provinces led to the widespread production of local imitations before the mint of Lugdunum was reopened under Nero (Boon 1988; Giard 1970). It is, however, very striking that throughout the third century Britain and Gaul had to rely heavily upon worn second-century sestertii until they were restruck under Postumus (by contrast sestertii of the first half of the third century are common in Italy and Africa) (Callu 1969: 111–30; Howgego 1985: 67). There were problems too with the supply of notionally silver currency. In the period *c.* AD 275–95 reformed radiates were common in some areas (including Italy) but penetrated others (especially, but not only, the north-western provinces) only in small quantities (King 1981; Burnett 1987: 124–6). It is thus reasonable to assume some degree of breakdown in the system of distribution, and to compare the way in which, for example, the state system of stone supply broke down in the third century (Greene 1986: 152).

For evidence of a more general decline in economic integration we can look again at periods of parallel production of imperial-style silver coinage at Rome and in Syria. We have already seen that coins might move between east and west in both directions for reasons unconnected with initial dispatch by the state (see pp. 109–10). The initial tendency for coins of Septimius Severus in Britain to be exclusively derived from Rome was broken down by subsequent circulation, so that by the early 260s AD about half came from the east. The mixing of coin between east and west declined progressively in the third century. The coins produced in Syria during the sole reign of Gallienus (AD 260–8) never reached Britain in any quantity, and no coins from elsewhere reached Syria. Marked fragmentation in circulation patterns persisted throughout the third century. It is not unreasonable to assume that economic disruption was a significant cause of the increasing heterogeneity of coin populations (Howgego 1994; forthcoming).

A further numismatic phenomenon which deserves to be seen against a wider background is the decline and demise of the civic coinages, which had throughout the principate provided the base metal currencies of the east. The weight standards suffered intermittent declines, which differed in timing and extent between regions. The earliest evidence for weight reductions is in the 160s AD, but the first widespread change appears to have been a halving of standards sometime after 253 (in some places certainly after 260). Sometimes this took the form of a doubling in face values of existing coins by the application of countermarks (Howgego 1985: 60–73; Johnston forthcoming b) [171]. There was regional variation also in the date at which the city coinages ended. The number of cities striking had reached its peak in the reign of Septimius Severus, after which there had been a tendency for fewer cities to strike larger issues. City coinages had ceased virtually everywhere by AD 268. The principal exceptions were some cities in Pamphylia and Pisidia, where weight standards held up better and minting did not finally cease until the reign of Tacitus (AD 275–6) (Howgego 1985: 65, 70–1).

It would be wrong to see the civic coinages of the principate as the death throes to a great tradition of minting by cities, in inevitable decline after the loss of political independence. As we saw earlier, the *polis* under the Roman Empire should be seen as a cultural and administrative body, rather than in political terms. Minting had almost become part of the active definition of what it was to be a city in the eastern half of the Roman Empire (see pp. 42–3). In the first two and a half centuries of the principate both the cities and their coinages showed great vitality.

A more useful perspective is that the ending of city coinages was broadly contemporary with the interruption in the imperial bronze coinages in the west. It cannot have helped that the debasement of the silver coinage meant that the imperial radiate became more overvalued (more of a token) than the base metal currency (Howgego 1985: 69). General disruptions, and not least invasion from outside the Empire, may have made small change less of a priority in east and west.

There is, however, a more important point. Civic coinage did not re-emerge after the crisis. The explanation for this lies in the transformation of the *polis* and the decline of its elite (Garnsey 1974). The preponderance of private over public wealth meant that much of what we would regard as public service and expense in cities was in fact undertaken by rich individuals through the holding of magistracies, the undertaking of other duties (*munera*, liturgies), and benefactions. The elite displayed and justified their rank through euergetism. All this fell apart. The rich increasingly escaped from civic duty and expense by entering imperial service (decisive steps towards lifetime exemptions from civic obligations for those in imperial service were taken in the tetrarchic period: Millar 1983). The less rich were forced to shoulder a greater burden. The habit of civic euergetism was either broken, or ultimately redirected towards the Church and Christian charity to the poor (Mitchell 1993 II: 82). The period from *c.* AD 225 to the reign of Constantine was marked by a pronounced rarity of new public buildings in the cities, with the exception of defensive walls (Mitchell 1993 I: 198, 214; Duncan-Jones 1982: 350–7 on Africa). The production of civic coinage had likewise been a task for rich individuals to undertake and to subsidize; there was no place for it in the new world (Howgego 1985: 71–2, 98–9).

The tendency for fewer cities to strike larger issues, apparent from early in the third century, was part of a more general trend towards concentration in prosperity (Howgego 1985: 98). In the long run this led to the decline and demise of the smaller cities. The sparkle of the successful cities was increasingly due to the initiative of imperial officials (Mitchell 1993 II: 89, 120–1). There was already a clue to this pattern in the greater resilience of the civic coinages of Pamphylia and Pisidia. This will have been due in part to the fact that the area was sheltered from external invasions, but also to the (consequential) imperial interest in the area. It is no mere coincidence that Side and Perge were important headquarters for imperial troops from the early 260s AD, that Perge was the headquarters of the emperor Tacitus, and that the south was the only part of Asia Minor to see a significant amount of new civic buildings (apart from defensive walls) in the third century after *c.* 225 (Mitchell 1993 I: 216, 238).

The shift of initiative in the public affairs of successful cities away from local elites and towards imperial officials was part of a broad nexus of development. Hand in hand with the decline of local elites went a greater decentralization of imperial control. The age of Diocletian and Constantine saw a multiplication of state officials, as the cities lost their earlier administrative responsibilities. The trend was apparent already under the Severans, with the increasing intervention of soldiers or other officials to collect military supplies and money dues (Mitchell 1993 I: 232–3). The numismatic corollary was the demise of civic coinages, and the decentralization and eventual regional organization of imperial minting. The process entailed standardization. The reign of Diocletian saw the end of the last provincial coinage, with the extension of the imperial coinage to Egypt in AD 296/7, and the ending of the closed monetary system which had endured since Ptolemy I (Metcalf 1987) [173].

It is something of a comfort in writing a book on ancient history and coins that the numismatic evidence both reflects and illuminates periods of crisis and change in such a multifaceted way. The causes of the eventual demise of coinage by cities, and of the initial spread of coinage with which this book began, may both be found in radical transformations of the *polis* eight hundred years apart.

Notes

1 MONEY

1 Even here numismatic arguments have been used to move the date of the deposits from *c.* 515 BC into the early fifth century (Stronach 1985). However, the chronology of Cypriot coinage, which was the basis of the numismatic challenge, is itself in need of revision, and the earlier date may be allowed to stand (Kagan 1994). On the other hand the epigraphic evidence for the date of the building is inconclusive (Briant 1989: 324–5).

2 'Peer polity interaction designates the full range of interchanges taking place (including imitation and emulation, competition, warfare, and the exchange of material goods and of information) between autonomous (i.e. self-governing and in that sense politically independent) socio-political units which are situated beside or close to each other within a single geographical region, or in some cases more widely' (Renfrew 1986: 1).

2 MINTING

1 Another coinage for which attempts have been made to calculate the output per die is the gold produced at Athens in 407/6 BC (Thompson 1961: 709–10). The situation is promising at first sight because we have records of some of the bullion coined (14 talents) and of the number of dies employed for the largest denomination (four anvil and twenty-two punch dies). Unfortunately we do not know the quantity of coins produced from the same bullion in the five smaller denominations [23], nor how much other bullion was used (Thompson 1970), nor whether the dies were used until they wore out or broke. Since the dies were dedicated on the Acropolis it may well be that they were still usable. For these reasons little weight can be given to Thompson's calculation that each stater obverse die produced 5,000 coins.

6 CRISIS

1 *P. Oxy.* 3773 (*c.* AD 340) may indicate a (somewhat surprising) increase in the purchasing power of gold since the Prices Edict of AD 301. In 340 a

solidus would have bought approximately twice as much barley or wheat as it had done in 301 (*P. Oxy.* vol. 54: 239 n. 3). On the other hand, the value given for gold in the Prices Edict may have been artificially low (Bagnall 1989: 69–70).

2 An Egyptian papyrus clearly demonstrates that the value of gold coin was fluctuating already in *c.* AD 108 (?) (*P. Sarap.* 90 = *P. Bad.* 37 where the meaning of values is unclear). Two records of priestly expenses from Nubia under Philip I imply a relationship of the Egyptian tetradrachm to the aureus of over forty to one, instead of the supposed twenty-five (*CIG* 5008, 5010; Crawford 1975: 569; but the reading of the numerals is uncertain). It is possible that the aureus had always floated in Egypt, as we do not know whether it was part of the normal currency there (Howgego 1992: 11), but there is also somewhat similar evidence from elsewhere. From Palmyra in AD 193 there is a reference to a sum in old aurei (*chrysa palaia denaria*), which implies that old aurei were tariffed at a level different from new ones (Buttrey 1963; although his explanation is not necessarily correct: see p. 104). An inscription from Thorigny in France boasts of the grant to an officer *c.* AD 220 of the right to have a salary paid in gold (Pflaum 1948: 26). This should mean that there was some advantage in being paid in gold, perhaps because it was worth more than official rates implied. Likewise in a distribution of money in an unknown municipium perhaps in the (early) third century AD a gold coin was given to those ranking higher in the pecking order than those who received 25 denarii (*CIL* VI, 29700; Mrozek 1978: 85, or does the use of the word *solidus* imply a later date?).

Bibliography

Alföldi, M.R. (1958–9) 'Epigraphische Beiträge zur römischen Münztechnik bis auf Konstantin den Grossen', *SNR* 39: 35–48.

Amandry, M. (1991) 'Les coins monétaires et les monnaies', in F. Beck and H. Chew (eds) *Masques de fer: Un officier romain du temps de Caligula*, Paris: Réunion des musées nationaux, 88–104.

Amyx, D.A. (1958) 'The Attic stelai, part III', *Hesperia* 27: 163–310.

Anderlini, L. and Sabourian, H. (1992) 'Some notes on the economics of barter, money and credit', in C. Humphrey and S. Hugh-Jones (eds) *Barter, Exchange and Value: An Anthropological Approach*, Cambridge: Cambridge University Press, 75–106.

Andreau, J. (1987) *La vie financière dans le monde romain: Les métiers de manieurs d'argent (IVe siècle av. J.-C. – IIIe siècle ap. J.-C.*, Rome: Bibl. des Écoles françaises d'Athènes et de Rome 265.

Appadurai, A. (1986) *The Social Life of Things: Commodities in Cultural Perspective*, Cambridge: Cambridge University Press.

Arnold-Biucchi, C., Beer-Tobey, L., and Waggoner, N.M. (1988) 'A Greek archaic silver hoard from Selinus', *MN* 33: 1–35.

Austin, M.M. (1981) *The Hellenistic World from Alexander to the Roman Conquest*, Cambridge: Cambridge University Press.

Austin, M.M. and Vidal-Naquet, P. (1977) *Economic and Social History of Ancient Greece*, London: Batsford.

Bagnall, R. (1985) *Currency and Inflation in Fourth Century Egypt*, Bulletin of the American Society of Papyrologists suppl. 5: Scholars Press.

—— (1989) 'Fourth-century prices: new evidence and further thoughts', *ZPE* 76: 69–76.

—— (1993) 'Discussione', in L. Camilli and S. Sorda (eds) *L''Inflazione' nel quarto secolo d.c.: Atti dell' Incontro di Studio Roma 1988*, Rome: Istituto Italiano di Numismatica, 208–16.

Balmuth, M.S. (1971) 'Remarks on the appearance of the earliest coins', in D.G. Mitten, J.G. Pedley and J.A. Scott (eds) *Studies Presented to George M.A. Hanfmann*, Mainz: Philipp von Zabern, 1–7.

Bammer, A. (1990) 'A peripteros of the geometric period in the Artemision of Ephesus', *AS* 40: 137–60.

—— (1991) 'Les sanctuaires des VIIIe et VIIe siècles a l'Artémision d' Éphèse', *RA* 1991, 1: 63–84.

Banaji, J. (1994) 'State and aristocracy in the economic evolution of the late Empire', in *Eleventh International Economic History Congress* 1994, Milan: Università Bocconi, 107–17.

Baratte, F. (1976) 'Quelques remarques à propos des lingots d'or et d'argent du Bas Empire', in V. Kondić (ed.) *Frappe et ateliers monétaires dans l'antiquité et moyen âge*, Belgrade: Musée national, 63–71.

—— (1978) 'Lingots d'or et d'argent en rapport avec l'atelier de Sirmium', in Dj. Bošković, N. Duval, V. Popović, and G. Vallet (eds) *Sirmium VIII*, Rome and Belgrade: École française de Rome/Institut archéologique de Belgrade, 99–111.

Barron, J.P. (1966) *The Silver Coins of Samos*, London: Royal Numismatic Society.

Bernard, P. (1985) *Fouilles d'Aï Khanoum IV: Les monnaies hors trésors: Questions d'histoire Gréco-Bactrienne*, Paris: De Boccard.

Bivar, A.D.H. (1971) 'A hoard of ingot-currency of the Median period from Nūsh-i Jān, near Malayir', *Iran* 9: 97–111.

Bland, R. (forthcoming) 'Denominational relationships in the early third century AD', in C.E. King and D. Wigg (eds) *Coin Finds and Coin Use in the Roman World*.

Boardman, J. (1980) *The Greeks Overseas: Their Early Colonies and Trade*, 2nd edn, London: Thames and Hudson.

Bogaert, R. (1966) *Les origines antiques de la banque de dépôt*, Leiden: A.W. Sijthoff.

—— (1968) *Banques et banquiers dans les cités grecques*, Leiden: Sijthoff.

Boon, G. (1988) 'Counterfeit coins in Roman Britain', in J. Casey and R. Reece (eds) *Coins and the Archaeologist*, 2nd edn, London: Seaby, 102–88.

Bowman, A.K. (1980) 'The economy of Egypt in the earlier fourth century', in C.E. King (ed.) *Imperial Revenue, Expenditure and Monetary Policy in the Fourth Century AD*, Oxford: BAR, 23–40.

Boyd, T.D. and Rudolf, W.W. (1978) 'Excavations at Porto Cheli and Vicinity: Preliminary Report IV: The Lower Town of Halieis, 1970–1977', *Hesperia* 67: 333–55.

Briant, P. (1989) 'Remarques finales', in R. Descat (ed.) *L'or perse et l'histoire grecque*, *REA* 91 (1–2), 321–35.

Brooke, C.N.L., Stewart, B.H.I.H., Pollard, J.G., and Volk, T.R. (eds) (1983) *Studies in Numismatic Method Presented to Philip Grierson*, Cambridge: Cambridge University Press.

Brunt, P. (1978) 'Laus imperii', in P.D.A. Garnsey and C.R. Whittaker (eds) *Imperialism in the Ancient World*, Cambridge: Cambridge University Press, 159–91.

Burnett, A. (1977) 'The coinages of Rome and Magna Graecia in the late fourth and third centuries BC', *SNR* 56: 92–121.

—— (1983) 'Review of R. Albert, *Das Bild des Augustus auf den frühen Reichsprägungen*', *Gnomon* 55: 563–5.

—— (1987) *Coinage in the Roman World*, London: Seaby.

—— (1989) 'The beginnings of Roman coinage', *AIIN* 36: 33–64.

—— (1991) *Coins*, London: British Museum Press.

—— (1993) 'Roman provincial coinage of the Julio-Claudians', in M. Price, A. Burnett, and R. Bland (eds) *Essays in Honour of Robert Carson and Kenneth Jenkins*, London: Spink, 145–53.

Burnett, A.M. and Crawford, M.H. (eds) (1987) *The Coinage of the Roman World in the Late Republic*, Oxford: BAR.

Burnett, A.M. and Hook, D.R. (1989) 'The fineness of silver coins in Italy and Rome during the late fourth and third centuries BC', *QT* 18: 151–67.

Bursche, A. (1989) 'Contacts between the Roman Empire and the mid-European Barbaricum in the light of coin finds', in I. Carradice (ed.) *Proceedings of the 10th International Congress of Numismatics, London, September 1986*, International Association of Professional Numismatists publ. no. 11, 279–87.

Butcher, K. (1986–7) 'Two related coinages of the third century AD: Philippopolis and Samosata', *INJ* 9: 73–84.

—— (1988a) *Roman Provincial Coins: An Introduction to the Greek Imperials*, London: Seaby.

—— (1988b) 'The colonial coinage of Antioch-on-the-Orontes, *c.* AD 218–53', *NC* 148: 63–75.

Butcher, K. and Ponting, M. (forthcoming) 'Rome and the East: production of Roman provincial silver coinage for Caesarea in Cappadocia under Vespasian, AD 69–72', *OJA* 14 (1).

Buttrey, T.V. (1961) 'Dio, Zonaras and the value of the Roman aureus', *JRS* 51: 40–5.

—— (1963) ' "Old aurei" at Palmyra and the coinage of Pescennius Niger', *Berytus* 14 (2): 117–28.

—— (1972) 'Vespasian as moneyer', *NC*[7] 12: 89–109.

—— (1992) 'The denarii of Pescennius Niger', *NC* 152: iv–xxii.

—— (1993) 'Calculating ancient coin production: facts and fantasies', *NC* 153: 335–51.

—— (1994) 'Calculating ancient coin production II: why it cannot be done', *NC* 154: 341–52.

Cahn, H.A. (1989) 'Le monnayage des satrapes: iconographie et signification', in R. Descat (ed.) *L'or perse et l'histoire grecque*, *REA* 91 (1–2), 97–106.

Cahn, H.A. and Gerin, D. (1988) 'Themistocles at Magnesia', *NC* 148: 13–20.

Callataÿ, F. de (1982) 'La date des premiers tétradrachmes de poids attique émis par Alexandre le Grand', *RBN* 128: 5–25.

—— (1987) 'La politique monétaire de Mithridate VI Eupator, roi du Pont (120–63 av. J.C.)', in G. Depeyrot, T. Hackens, and G. Moucharte (eds) *Rythmes de la production monétaire, de l'antiquité à nos jours*, Louvain-la-Neuve: Numismatica Lovaniensia 7, 55–66.

—— (1989) 'Les trésors achéménides et les monnayages d'Alexandre: espèces immobilisées et espèces circulantes', *REA* 91 (1–2): 259–76.

—— (1994) 'Réflexions sur les ateliers d'Asie mineure d'Alexandre le Grand', in M. Amandry and G. Le Rider (eds), *Trésors et circulation monétaire en Anatolie antique*, Paris: Bibliothèque nationale de France.

—— (forthcoming a) *Histoire monétaire des guerres mithridatiques*.

—— (forthcoming b) 'Calculating ancient coin production: what we may hope', *NC*.

Callu, J.P. (1969) *La politique monétaire des empereurs romains de 238 à 311*, Paris: De Boccard.

—— (1978) 'Denier et Nummus (300–354)', in *Dévaluations* I: 107–21.

—— (1980) 'Silver hoards and emissions from 324 to 392', in C.E. King (ed.) *Imperial Revenue, Expenditure and Monetary Policy in the Fourth Century AD*, Oxford: BAR, 175–254.

—— (1993) 'Quantifier l'inflation du IVe siècle: modes et causes de l'évolution du volume des frappes', in L. Camilli and S. Sorda (eds) *L'"Inflazione" nel quarto secolo d.c.: Atti dell'Incontro di Studio Roma 1988*, Rome: Istituto Italiano di Numismatica, 97–113.

Callu, J.P., Brenot, C., and Barrandon, J.N. (1979) 'Analyses de séries atypiques (Aurélien-Tacite-Carus-Licinius)', *QT* 8: 241–54.

Callu, J.P. and Loriot, X. (1990) *L'or monnayé II: la dispersion des aurei en Gaule romaine sous l'empire*, Juan-les-Pins: A.P.D.C.A.

Camilli, L. and Sorda, S. (eds) (1993) *L'"Inflazione" nel quarto secolo d.c.: Atti dell'Incontro di Studio Roma 1988*, Rome: Istituto Italiano di Numismatica.

Camp, J. Mck. (1979) 'Die Ausgrabung der antiken Münzstätte Athens', *SM* 29: 52–5.

Cantilena, R. (1989) 'Rinvenimento di un'officina monetale a Laos: problemi di circolazione e di produzione monetaria', in E. Greco, S. Luppino and A. Schnapp (eds) *Laos I: scavi a Marcellina 1973–1985*, Taranto: Istituto per la storia e l'archeologia della Magna Grecia, 25–41.

Carradice, I. (1983) *Coinage and Finances in the Reign of Domitian AD 81–96*, Oxford: BAR.

—— (1987a) 'The "regal" coinage of the Persian empire', in I. Carradice (ed.) *Coinage and Administration in the Athenian and Persian Empires*, Oxford: BAR International Series 343, 73–107.

—— (ed.) (1987b) *Coinage and Administration in the Athenian and Persian Empires*, Oxford: BAR International Series 343.

—— (ed.) (1989) *Proceedings of the 10th International Congress of Numismatics, London, September 1986*, International Association of Professional Numismatists publ. no. 11.

Carradice , I.A. and La Niece, S. (1988) 'The Libyan War and coinage: a new hoard and the evidence of metal analysis', *NC* 148: 33–52.

Carradice, I. and Price, M. (1988) *Coinage in the Greek World*, London: Seaby.

Carrié, J.M. (1993) 'Observations sur la fiscalité du IVe siècle pour servir à l'histoire monétaire', in L. Camilli and S. Sorda (eds) *L'"Inflazione" nel quarto secolo d.c.: Atti dell' Incontro di Studio Roma 1988*, Rome: Istituto Italiano di Numismatica, 115–54.

Carruba, O. (1991) 'Valvel e Rkalil: monetazione arcaica della Lidia: problemi e considerazioni linguistiche', in R. Martini and N. Vismara (eds) *Ermanno A. Arslan Studia Dicata* vol. 1, Milan: Ennere, Glaux 7: 13–23.

Carson, R.A.G. (1956) 'System and product in the Roman mint', in R.A.G. Carson and C.H.V. Sutherland (eds) *Essays in Roman Coinage Presented to Harold Mattingly*, Oxford: Oxford University Press, 227–39.

Carson, R.A.G. and Kraay, C.M. (eds) (1978) *Scripta Nummaria Romana: Essays Presented to Humphrey Sutherland*, London: Spink.

Carson, R.A.G. and Sutherland, C.H.V. (eds) (1956) *Essays in Roman Coinage Presented to Harold Mattingly*, Oxford: Oxford University Press.

Carter, G.F. and Nord, R.S. (1992) 'Calculation of the average die lifetimes and the number of anvils for coinage in antiquity', *AJN* 3–4: 147–64.

Casey, J. and Reece, R. (eds) (1988) *Coins and the Archaeologist*, 2nd edn, London: Seaby.

Casson, L. (1989) *The Periplus Maris Erythraei*, Princeton: Princeton University Press.

—— (1990) 'New light on maritime loans: P. Vindob. G40822', *ZPE* 84: 195–206.

Cecco, M. de (1985) 'Monetary theory and Roman history', *Journal of Economic History* 45 (4): 809–22.

Challis, C.E. (ed.) (1992) *A New History of the Royal Mint*, Cambridge: Cambridge University Press.

Chassinat, E. (1921) 'Un type d'étalon monétaire sous l'ancien empire', *Recueil de travaux relatifs à la philologie et à l'archéologie égyptiennes et assyriennes* 39: 79–88.

Cipolla, C.M. (1989) *Money in Sixteenth-century Florence*, Berkeley: University of California Press.

Coarelli, F. (1985) *Roma*, 3rd edn, Rome: Laterza.

Consolaki, H. and Hackens, T. (1980) 'Un atelier monétaire dans un temple argien?', in *Études argiennes*, *BCH* suppl. 6, Athens and Paris: École française d'Athènes and de Boccard, 279–94.

Cook, R.M. (1958) 'Speculations on the origins of coinage', *Historia* 7: 257–62.

Corbier, M. (1976–7) 'Fiscalité et monnaie: problèmes de méthode', *Dialoghi di Archeologia* 9–10: 504–41.

Courakis, A.S. (ed.) (forthcoming) *Economic Thought and Economic Reality in Ancient Greece*.

Cowell, M.R. (1992) 'An analytical survey of British Celtic gold coinage', in M. Mays (ed.) *Celtic Coinage: Britain and Beyond*, Oxford: BAR/Tempus Reparatum, 207–33.

Cowell, M., Meekr, N., Craddock, P., and Hyne, K. (forthcoming) 'Scientific studies of the early Lydian gold, electrum and silver coinages'.

Crawford, M. (1969) 'Coin hoards and the pattern of violence in the late Republic', *PBSR* 37: 76–81.

—— (1975) 'Finance, coinage and money from the Severans to Constantine', *ANRW* II.2: 560–93.

—— (1978) 'Trade and movement of coinage across the Adriatic in the Hellenistic period', in R.A.G. Carson and C.M. Kraay (eds) *Scripta Nummaria Romana: Essays Presented to Humphrey Sutherland*, London: Spink, 1–11.

—— (1983a) 'Numismatics', in M. Crawford (ed.) *Sources for Ancient History*, Cambridge: Cambridge University Press, 185–233.

—— (1983b) 'Roman imperial coin types and the formation of public opinion', in C.N.L. Brooke *et al.* (eds) *Studies in Numismatic Method Presented to Philip Grierson*, Cambridge: Cambridge University Press, 47–64.

—— (1985) *Coinage and Money under the Roman Republic: Italy and the Mediterranean Economy*, London: Methuen.

Cribb, J. (1983) 'Investigating the introduction of coinage in India: a review of recent research', *JNSI* 45: 80–101.

Crump, T. (1981) *The Phenomenon of Money*, London: Routledge and Kegan Paul.

Davies, J.K (1984) *Wealth and the Power of Wealth in Classical Athens*, Salem: Ayer.

Dentzer, J.-M., Gauthier, P., and Hackens, T. (eds) (1975) *Numismatique antique: problèmes et méthodes*, Nancy-Louvain: Peeters.

Depeyrot, G. (1991) *Crises et inflation entre antiquité et moyen âge*, Paris: Armand Colin.

Depeyrot, G., Hackens, T., and Moucharte, G. (eds) (1987) *Rythmes de la production monétaire, de l'antiquité à nos jours*, Louvain-la-Neuve: Numismatica Lovaniensia 7.

Descat, R. (ed.) (1989) *L'or perse et l'histoire grecque, REA* 91 (1–2).

Domergue, C. (1990) *Les mines de la péninsule ibérique dans l'antiquité romaine*, Rome: Collection de l'École française de Rome 127.

Drexhage, H.-J. (1991) *Preise, Mieten/Pachten, Kosten und Löhne im römischen Ägypten bis zum Regierungsantritt Diokletians*, St Katharinen: Scripta Mercaturae Verlag.

Duncan-Jones, R. (1982) *The Economy of the Roman Empire: Quantitative Studies*, 2nd edn, Cambridge: Cambridge University Press.

—— (1990) *Structure and Scale in the Roman Economy*, Cambridge: Cambridge University Press.

—— (1994) *Money and Government in the Roman Empire*, Cambridge: Cambridge University Press.

Ehrenberg, V. (1951) *The People of Aristophanes: A Sociology of Old Attic Comedy*, Oxford: Blackwell.

Ehrhardt, C.T.H.R. (1984) 'Roman coin types and the Roman public', *JNG* 34: 41–54.

Erim, K.T., Reynolds, J., and Crawford, M. (1971) 'Diocletian's currency reform; a new inscription', *JRS* 61: 171–7.

Esty, W. (1986) 'Estimation of the size of a coinage: a survey and comparison of methods', *NC* 146: 185–215.

Finley, M.I. (1978) 'The fifth-century Athenian empire: a balance sheet', in P.D.A. Garnsey and C.R. Whittaker (eds) *Imperialism in the Ancient World*, Cambridge: Cambridge University Press, 103–26.

—— (1981) *Economy and Society in Ancient Greece*, London: Chatto and Windus.

Fittschen, K. (ed.) (1988) *Griechische Porträts*, Darmstadt: Wissenschaftliche Buchgesellschaft.

Foraboschi, D. (1984) 'Il rapporto oro/argento nel 113 d.C.', *ZPE* 57: 79–80.

Fornara, C.W. (1983) *Translated Documents of Greece and Rome 1: Archaic Times to the End of the Peloponnesian War*, 2nd edn, Cambridge: Cambridge University Press.

Foster, B.R. (1977) 'Commercial activity in Sargonic Mesopotamia', *Iraq* 39: 31–43.

Fulford, M. (1985) 'Roman material in barbarian society c. 200 BC – c. AD 400', in T.C. Champion and J.V.S. Megaw (eds) *Settlement and Society: Aspects of West European Prehistory in the First Millenium BC*, Leicester: Leicester University Press, 91–108.

Furtwängler, A. (1982) 'Griechische Vieltypenprägung und Münzbeamte', *SNR* 61: 5–29.

—— (1986) 'Neue beobachtungen zur frühesten Münzprägung', *SNR* 65: 153–65.

Gale, N.H., Gentner, W., and Wagner, G.A. (1980) 'Mineralogical and geographical silver sources of archaic Greek coinage', in D.M. Metcalf and W.A. Oddy (eds) *Metallurgy in Numismatics* vol. 1, London: Royal Numismatic Society, 3–49.

Garnsey, P. (1974) 'Aspects of the decline of the urban aristocracy in the empire', *ANRW* II.1: 229–52.

—— (1988) *Famine and Food Supply in the Graeco-Roman World*, Cambridge: Cambridge University Press.

Garnsey, P.D.A. and Whittaker, C.R. (eds) (1978) *Imperialism in the Ancient World*, Cambridge: Cambridge University Press.

Giard, J.-B. (1970) 'Pouvoir central et libertés locales, le monnayage en bronze de Claude avant 50 après J.C.', *RN*[6] 12: 33–61.

Gilliard, F.D. (1964) 'Notes on the coinage of Julian the Apostate', *JRS* 54: 135–41.

Greene, K. (1986) *The Archaeology of the Roman Economy*, London: Batsford.

Grierson, P. (1968) 'Variations in die-output', *N. Circ.* 76: 298–9.

Grunauer-von Hoerschelmann, S. (1982-3) 'The Severan emissions of the Peloponnesus', *INJ* 6–7: 39–46.

Hackens, T. and Weiller, R. (eds) (1982) *Actes du 9ème Congrès International de Numismatique: Berne, Septembre 1979*, Louvain-la-Neuve: Association Internationale des Numismates Professionnels.

Hallock, R.T. (1960) 'A new look at the Persepolis treasury tablets', *JNES* 19: 90–100.

Hanfmann, G.M.A. (1983) *Sardis from Prehistoric to Roman Times: Results of the Archaeological Exploration of Sardis 1958–1975*, Cambridge, Mass.: Harvard University Press.

Hannestad, N. (1986) *Roman Art and Imperial Policy*, Århus: Aarhus University Press.

Hansen, E.V. (1971) *The Attalids of Pergamon*, 2nd edn, Ithaca and London: Cornell University Press.

Hansen, M.H. (1991) *The Athenian Democracy in the Age of Demosthenes. Structure, Principles, and Ideology*, Oxford: Blackwell.

Hardwick, N. (1991) *The Coinage of Chios from the Sixth to the Fourth Century BC*, unpublished D.Phil. thesis, University of Oxford.

Harl, K. (1987) *Civic Coins and Civic Politics in the Roman East AD 180–275*, Berkeley and Los Angeles: University of California Press.

Harris, W.V. (1979) *War and Imperialism in Republican Rome, 327–70 BC*, Oxford: Clarendon Press.

Haselgrove, C. (1993) 'The development of British Iron-Age coinage', *NC* 153: 31–63.

Heckel, W. and Sullivan, R. (eds) (1984) *Ancient Coins of the Graeco-Roman World: The Nickle Numismatic Papers*, Waterloo, Ontario: Wilfrid Laurier University Press.

Hendy, M.F. (1985) *Studies in the Byzantine Monetary Economy c. 300–1450*, Cambridge: Cambridge University Press.

—— (1988) 'From public to private: the western barbarian coinages as a mirror of the disintegration of late Roman state structures', *Viator: Medieval and Renaissance Studies* 19: 29–78.

—— (1991) 'East and west: divergent models of coinage and its use', *Settimane di studio del Centro italiano di studi sull'alto medioevo* 38: 637–79.

—— (1993) 'From antiquity to the Middle Ages: economic and monetary aspects of the transition', in *De la antigüedad al medievo: siglos IV–VIII, III Congreso de Estudios Medievales*, Fundacion Sanchez-Albornoz: 325–60.

Hölscher, T. (1973) *Griechische Historienbilder des 5. und 4. Jahrhunderts v. Chr.*, Würzburg: Konrad Triltsch Verlag.

—— (1980) 'Die Geschichtsauffassung in der römischen Repräsentationskunst', *JdAI* 95: 265–321.

—— (1982) 'Die Bedeutung der Münzen für das Verstandnis der politischen Repräsentationskunst der späten römischen Republik', in T. Hackens and R. Weiller (eds) *Actes du 9ème Congrès International de Numismatique: Berne, Septembre 1979*, Louvain-la-Neuve: Association Internationale des Numismates Professionnels, 269–82.

—— (1984) *Staatsdenkmal und Publikum: vom Untergang der Republik bis zur Festigung des Kaisertums in Rom*, Konstanz: Konstanzer althistorische Vorträge und Forschungen 9.

Hopkins, K. (1980) 'Trade and taxes in the Roman Empire (200 BC – AD 400)', *JRS* 70: 101–25.

Houghton, A., Hurter, S., Erhart Mottahedeh, P., and Ayer Scott, P. (eds) (1984) *Festschrift für Leo Mildenberg*, Wetteren: N.R.

Howgego, C.J. (1985) *Greek Imperial Countermarks: Studies in the Provincial Coinage of the Roman Empire*, London: Royal Numismatic Society.

—— (1989) 'After the colt has bolted: a review of Amandry on Roman Corinth', *NC* 149: 199–208.

—— (1990) 'Why did ancient states strike coins?', *NC* 150: 1–25.

—— (1992) 'The supply and use of money in the Roman world 200 BC to AD 300', *JRS* 82: 1–31.

—— (1994) 'Coin circulation and the integration of the Roman economy', *JRA* 7: 5–21.

—— (forthcoming) 'The circulation of silver coins, models of the Roman economy, and crisis in the third century AD: some numismatic evidence', in C.E. King and D. Wigg (eds) *Coin Finds and Coin Use in the Roman World*.

Humphrey, C. (1985) 'Barter and economic disintegration', *Man* (n.s.) 20: 48–72.

Humphrey, C. and Hugh-Jones, S. (eds) (1992) *Barter, Exchange and Value: An Anthropological Approach*, Cambridge: Cambridge University Press.

Huvelin, H., Christol, M., and Gautier, G. (eds) (1987) *Mélanges de numismatique offerts à Pierre Bastien*, Wetteren: N.R.

Isager, S. and Hansen, M.H. (1975) *Aspects of Athenian Society in the Fourth Century BC*, Odense: Odense University Press.

Janssen, J.J. (1975) *Commodity Prices from the Ramessid Period*, Leiden: Brill.

Jenkins, G.K. (1967) 'The monetary systems in the early hellenistic time with special regard to the economic policy of the Ptolemaic kings', in A. Kindler (ed.) *The Patterns of Monetary Development in Phoenicia and Palestine in Antiquity: International Numismatic Convention, Jerusalem 27–31 December 1963*, Jerusalem: Schocken, 53–72.

—— (1984) 'Varia Punica', in A. Houghton *et al.* (eds) *Festschrift für Leo Mildenberg*, Wetteren: N.R., 127–36.

Jenkins, G.K. and Lewis, R.B. (1963) *Carthaginian Gold and Electrum Coins*, London: Royal Numismatic Society.

Johnston, A. (1982–3) 'Die sharing in Asia Minor: the view from Sardis', *LNJ* 6–7: 59–78.

—— (forthcoming a) 'Aphrodisias reconsidered', *NC*.

—— (forthcoming b) 'Greek imperial denominations in the province of Asia'.

Johnston, A.W. (1979) *Trademarks on Greek Vases*, Warminster: Aris and Phillips.

Jones, A.H.M. (1971) *The Cities of the Eastern Roman Provinces*, 2nd edn, Oxford: Clarendon Press.

—— (1974) *The Roman Economy: Studies in Ancient Economic and Administrative History*, P.A. Brunt (ed.), Oxford: Blackwell.

Jones, J.R. (1970) 'Mint magistrates in the early Roman Empire', *BICS* 17: 70–8.

Kagan, J.H. (1987) 'The Decadrachm hoard: chronology and consequences', in I. Carradice (ed.) *Coinage and Administration in the Athenian and Persian Empires*, Oxford: BAR International Series 343, 21–8.

—— (1994) 'An archaic Greek coin hoard from the eastern Mediterranean and early Cypriot coinage', *NC* 154: 17–52.

Karwiese, S. (1980) 'Lysander as Herakliskos Drakonopnigon ("Heracles the snake-strangler")', *NC* 140: 1–27.

—— (1991) 'The Artemisium coin hoard and the first coins of Ephesus', *RBN* 137: 1–28.

Kastner, W. (1986) ' "Phanes" oder "Phano"?', *SNR* 65: 5–11.

Kent, J. (1954) 'Notes on some fourth-century coin types', *NC* [6] 14: 216–17.

Kim, H.S. (1994) 'Greek fractional silver coinage: a reassessment of the inception, development, prevalence, and functions of small change during the late archaic and early classical periods', unpublished M.Phil. thesis, University of Oxford.

King, C.E. (ed.) (1980) *Imperial Revenue, Expenditure and Monetary Policy in the Fourth Century AD*, Oxford: BAR.

—— (1981) 'The circulation of coin in the western provinces AD 260–95', in A. King and M. Henig (eds) *The Roman West in the Third Century: Contributions from Archaeology and History*, Oxford: BAR, 89–126.

—— (1993a) 'The fourth century coinage', in L. Camilli and S. Sorda (eds) *L' 'Inflazione' nel quarto secolo d.c.: Atti dell'Incontro di Studio Roma 1988*, Rome: Istituto Italiano di Numismatica, 1–87.

—— (1993b) 'The role of gold in the later third century AD', *RIN* 95: 439–51.

—— (forthcoming) 'Roman copies', in C.E. King and D. Wigg (eds) *Coin Finds and Coin Use in the Roman World*.

King, C.E. and Wigg, D. (eds) (forthcoming) *Coin Finds and Coin Use in the Roman World*.

Kinns, P. (1983) 'The Amphictionic coinage reconsidered', *NC* 143: 1–22.

—— (1987) 'Asia Minor', in A.M. Burnett and M.H. Crawford (eds) *The Coinage of the Roman World in the Late Republic*, Oxford: BAR, 105–19.

—— (1989) 'Ionia: the pattern of coinage during the last century of the Persian empire', in R. Descat (ed.) *L'or perse et l'histoire grecque*, *REA* 91 (1–2), 183–93.

Klose, D.O.A. (1987) *Die Münzprägung von Smyrna in der römischen Kaiserzeit*, Berlin: Walter de Gruyter.

Kolendo, J. (1980) 'L'arrêt de l'afflux des monnaies romaines dans le "Barbaricum" sous Septime-Sévère', in *Dévaluations* II: 169–72.

Kraay, C.M. (1949) 'The coinage of Vindex and Galba, AD 68, and the continuity of the Augustan principate', *NC* [6] 9: 129–49.

—— (1964) 'Hoards, small change and the origin of coinage', *JHS* 84: 76–91.

—— (1976) *Archaic and Classical Greek Coins*, London: Methuen.

—— (1984) 'Greek Coinage and War', in W. Heckel and R. Sullivan (eds) *Ancient Coins of the Graeco-Roman World: The Nickle Numismatic Papers*, Waterloo, Ontario: Wilfrid Laurier University Press, 3–18.

Kraay, C.M. and Jenkins, G.K. (1968) *Essays in Greek Coinage Presented to Stanley Robinson*, Oxford: Clarendon Press.

Kraft, K. (1972) *Das System der kaiserzeitlichen Münzprägung in Kleinasien*, Berlin: Gebr. Mann Verlag.

Kroll, J.H. (1979) 'A chronology of early Athenian bronze coinage, ca. 350–250 BC' in O. Mørkholm and N.M. Waggoner (eds) *Greek Numismatics and Archaeology: Essays in Honor of Margaret Thompson*, Wetteren: N.R., 139–54.

Laet, S.J. de (1949) *Portorium*, Bruges: Rijksuniversiteit te Gent.

Lauffer, S. (1971) *Diokletians Preisedikt*, Berlin: de Gruyter.

Le Rider, G. (1966) *Monnaies crétoises du Ve au Ier siècle av. J.C.*, Paris: École française d'Athènes, Études crétoises 15.

—— (1975) 'Contremarques et surfrappes dans l'antiquité grecque', in Dentzer *et al.* (eds) *Numismatique antique: problèmes et méthodes*, Nancy-Louvain: Peeters, 27–56.

—— (1977) *Le monnayage d'argent et d'or de Philippe II frappé en Macédoine de 359 à 294*, Paris: Bourgey.

—— (1986) 'Les Alexandres d'argent en Asie Mineure et dans l'orient séleucide au IIIe siècle av. J.C. (*c.* 275– *c.* 225): Remarques sur le système monétaire des séleucides et des ptolémées', *JS*: 3–57.

—— (1989) 'La politique monétaire du royaume de Pergame après 188', *JS*: 163–90.

—— (1991) 'Éphèse et Arados au IIe siècle avant notre ère', *QT* 20: 193–212.

—— (1993a) 'Les deux monnaies macédoniennes des années 323–294/290', *BCH* 117: 491–500.

—— (1993b) 'Les ressources financières de Séleucos IV (187–175) et le paiement de l'indemnité aux Romains', in M. Price *et al.* (eds) *Essays in Honour of Robert Carson and Kenneth Jenkins*, London: Spink, 49–67.

Le Rider, G., Jenkins, K., Waggoner, N., and Westermark, U. (eds) (1989) *Kraay-Mørkholm Essays: Numismatic Studies in Memory of C.M. Kraay and O. Mørkholm*, Louvain-la-Neuve: Numismatica Lovaniensia 10.

Levick, B. (1982) 'Propaganda and the imperial coinage', *Antichthon* 16: 104–16.

Levy, B.E. (1987) '*Indulgentiae Augusti Moneta Inpetrata*: A Flavian episode', in H. Huvelin *et al.* (eds) *Mélanges de numismatique offerts à Pierre Bastien*, Wetteren: N.R., 39–49.

Lewis, D.M. (1987) 'The Athenian coinage decree', in I. Carradice (ed.) *Coinage and Administration in the Athenian and Persian Empires*, Oxford: BAR International Series 343, 53–63.

—— (1990) 'Public property in the city', in O. Murray and S. Price (eds) *The Greek City from Homer to Alexander*, Oxford, Clarendon Press, 245–63.

Liebeschuetz, J.H.W.G. (1972) *Antioch: City and Imperial Administration in the Later Roman Empire*, Oxford: Clarendon Press.

Lind, L. (1981) *Roman Denarii found in Sweden 2: Catalogue, Text*, Stockholm: Stockholm Studies in Classical Archaeology 11: 2.

Lo Cascio, E. (1981) 'State and coinage in the late Republic and early Empire', *JRS* 71: 76–86.

—— (forthcoming) 'How did the Romans view their coinage and its function?', in C.E. King and D. Wigg (eds) *Coin Finds and Coin Use in the Roman World*.

Luckenbill, D.D. (1924) *The Annals of Sennacherib*, Chicago: University of Chicago Press.

MacDowall, D.W. (1990a) 'Finds of Roman coins in south Asia: problems of interpretation', *Ancient Ceylon* 9: 49–74.

—— (1990b) 'The export of Roman Republican denarii to south Asia', *Ancient Ceylon* 8 (7 on cover): 62–74.

—— (1991) 'Indian imports of Roman silver coins', in Amal Kumar Jha (ed.) *Coinage, Trade and Economy, 3rd International Colloquium, January 8th–11th 1991*, Indian Institute of Research in Numismatic Studies, 145–63.

Macrakis, A.L. (1984) 'Comparative economic values in the Iliad: the oxen-worth', in A.L. Boegehold *et al.* (eds) *Studies Presented to Sterling Dow on his Eightieth Birthday*, Durham, North Carolina: Duke University, 211–15.

Malkmus, W. (1989–93) 'Addenda to Vermeule's catalog of ancient coin dies', *SAN* 17 (4): 80–5; 18 (1): 16–22; 18 (2): 40–9; 18 (3): 72–7; 18 (4): 96–105.

Martin, T.R. (1985) *Sovereignty and Coinage in Classical Greece*, Princeton: Princeton University Press.

Mate, M. (1969) 'Coin dies under Edward I and II', *NC*[7] 9: 207–18.

Mattingly, H.B. (1969) 'Athens and the Western Greeks: *c.* 500–413 BC', in *La circolazione della moneta Ateniese in Sicilia e in Magna Grecia. Atti del I Convegno del Centro Internazionale di Studi Numismatici: Napoli 5–8 Aprile 1967*, Rome: Istituto Italiano di Numismatica, 201–22.

—— (1987) 'The Athenian coinage decree and the assertion of empire', in I. Carradice (ed.) *Coinage and Administration in the Athenian and Persian Empires*, Oxford: BAR International Series 343, 65–71.

—— (1988) 'Review of T.R. Martin, *Sovereignty and Coinage in Classical Greece*', *NC* 148: 231–3.

—— (1989) 'Review of I. Carradice and M. Price, *Coinage in the Greek World*', *NC* 149: 228–32.

Mayhew, N.J. (1974) 'Numismatic evidence and falling prices in the fourteenth century', *Econ. Hist. Rev.*[2] 27: 1–15.

—— (1987) 'Money and prices in England from Henry II to Edward III', *Agricultural History Review* 35: 121–32.

Mays, M. (ed.) (1992) *Celtic Coinage: Britain and Beyond*, Oxford: BAR/Tempus Reparatum.

Meiggs, R. (1972) *The Athenian Empire*, Oxford: Oxford University Press.

Metcalf, D.M. and Oddy, W.A. (eds) (1980) *Metallurgy in Numismatics*, vol. 1, London: Royal Numismatic Society.

Metcalf, W.E. (1982) 'The Flavians in the East', in T. Hackens and R. Weiller (eds) *Actes du 9ème Congrès International de Numismatique: Berne,*

Septembre 1979, Louvain-la-Neuve: Association Internationale des Numismates Professionnels, 321–39.

—— (1987) 'From Greek to Latin currency in third-century Egypt', in H. Huvelin *et al.* (eds) *Mélanges de numismatique offerts à Pierre Bastien*, Wetteren: N.R., 157–68.

—— (ed.) (1991) *Mnemata: Papers in Memory of Nancy M. Waggoner*, New York: The American Numismatic Society.

Millar, F.G.B. (1983) 'Empire and city, Augustus to Julian: obligations, excuses and status', *JRS* 73: 76–96.

—— (1984) 'State and subject: the impact of monarchy', in F.G.B. Millar and E. Segal (eds) *Caesar Augustus: Seven Aspects*, Oxford: Clarendon Press, 37–60.

—— (1991) 'Les congiaires à Rome et la monnaie', in A. Giovannini (ed.) *Nourrir la plèbe: actes du colloque tenu à Genève les 28/29. ix. 1989 en hommage à Denis van Berchem*, Basel: Schweizerische Beiträge zur Altertumswissenschaft 22: 143–57.

—— (1993) *The Roman Near East 31 BC–AD 337*, Cambridge, Mass.: Harvard University Press.

Millett, P. (1983) 'Maritime loans and the structure of credit in fourth-century Athens', in P. Garnsey, K. Hopkins and C.R. Whittaker (eds) *Trade in the Ancient Economy*, London: Chatto and Windus, 36–52.

—— (1991) *Lending and Borrowing in Ancient Athens*, Cambridge: Cambridge University Press.

Milne, J.G. (1971) *Catalogue of Alexandrian Coins*, with a supplement by C.M. Kraay, Oxford: Visitors of the Ashmolean Museum.

Mitchell, S. (1993) *Anatolia: Land, Men, and Gods in Asia Minor*, 2 vols, Oxford: Clarendon Press.

Mørkholm, O. (1982a) 'The Attic coin standard in the Levant during the hellenistic period', in S. Scheers (ed.) *Studia Paulo Naster Oblata I: Numismatica Antiqua*, Louvain: Orientalia Lovaniensia Analecta 12, 139–49.

—— (1982b) 'The "behaviour" of dies in the hellenistic period', in T. Hackens and R. Weiller (eds) *Actes du 9ème Congrès International de Numismatique: Berne, Septembre 1979*, Louvain-la-Neuve: Association Internationale des Numismates Professionnels, 209–14.

—— (1983a) 'The autonomous tetradrachms of Laodicea ad Mare', *MN* 28: 89–107.

—— (1983b) 'The life of obverse dies in the hellenistic period', in C.N.L. Brooke *et al.* (eds) *Studies in Numismatic Method Presented to Philip Grierson*, Cambridge: Cambridge University Press, 11–21.

—— (1984) 'The monetary system in the Seleucid empire after 187 BC', in W. Heckel and R. Sullivan (eds) *Ancient Coins of the Graeco-Roman World: The Nickle Numismatic Papers*, Waterloo, Ontario: Wilfred Laurier University Press, 93–113.

—— (1991) *Early Hellenistic Coinage: From the Accession of Alexander to the Peace of Apamea (336–188 BC)*, Cambridge: Cambridge University Press.

Mørkholm, O. and Waggoner, N.M. (1979) *Greek Numismatics and Archaeology: Essays in Honor of Margaret Thompson*, Wetteren: N.R.

Morris, I. (1986) 'Gift and commodity in Archaic Greece', *Man* 21: 1–17.

—— (1991) 'The early polis as city and state', in J. Rich and A. Wallace-Hadrill (eds) *City and Country in the Ancient World*, London: Routledge, 25–59.

Morrisson, C., Brenot, C., Callu, J.-P., Barrandon, J.-N., Poirier, J., and Halleux, R. (1985) *L'or monnayé I: purification et altérations de Rome à Byzance*, Paris: Centre National de la Recherche Scientifique.

Moysey, R.A. (1989) 'Observations on the numismatic evidence relating to the great satrapal revolt of 362/1 BC', in R. Descat (ed.) *L'or perse et l'histoire grecque*, *RÉA* 91 (1–2), 107–39.

Mrozek, S. (1978) 'Les espèces monétaires dans les inscriptions latines du Haut-empire romain', in *Dévaluations* I: 79–86.

Murray, O. (1990) 'Cities of reason', in O. Murray and S. Price (eds) *The Greek City from Homer to Alexander*, Oxford: Clarendon Press, 1–25.

Murray, O. and Price, S. (eds) (1990) *The Greek City from Homer to Alexander*, Oxford: Clarendon Press.

Nash, D. (1987) *Coinage in the Celtic World*, London: Seaby.

Naster, P. (1970) '*Karsha* et *sheqel* dans les documents araméens d'Éléphantine (Ve siècle avant J.-C.)', *RBN* 116: 31–5.

Nicolaou, I. (1990) *Paphos II: The Coins from the House of Dionysos*, Nicosia: Department of Antiquities, Cyprus.

Nicolet, C. (1963) 'A Rome pendant la seconde guerre punique: techniques financières et manipulations monétaires', *Annales ESC* 18 (1): 417–36.

—— (1971) 'Les variations des prix et la "théorie quantitative de la monnaie" à Rome, de Cicéron à Pline l'Ancien', *Annales ESC* 26: 1203–27.

—— (1984) 'Pline, Paul et la théorie de la monnaie', *Athenaeum* n.s. 62: 105–35.

Nicolet-Pierre, H. (1986) 'L'oiseau d'Athéna, d'Égypte en Bactriane: quelques remarques sur l'usage d'un type monétaire à l'époque classique', in L. Kahil, C. Augé and P. Linant de Bellefonds (eds) *Iconographie classique et identités régionales*, *BCH* suppl. 14, Paris: École française d'Athènes, 365–76.

Nixon, L. and Price, S. (1990) 'The size and resources of Greek cities', in O. Murray and S. Price (eds) *The Greek City from Homer to Alexander*, Oxford: Clarendon Press, 137–70.

North, J.A. (1981) 'The development of Roman imperialism', *JRS* 71: 1–9.

Northover, J.P. (1992) 'Material issues in the Celtic coinage', in M. Mays (ed.) *Celtic Coinage: Britain and Beyond*, Oxford: BAR/Tempus Reparatum, 235–99.

Oeconomides, M. (1993) 'Ena nomismatokopeio stin archaia Pella', in *Archaia Makedonia: Pempto Diethnes Symposio*, Thessalonica: Institute for Balkan Studies, 1143–54.

Osborne, R. (1987) *Classical Landscape with Figures: The Ancient Greek City and its Countryside*, London: Philip.

—— (1988) 'Social and economic implications of the leasing of land and property in classical and hellenistic Greece', *Chiron* 18: 279–323.

—— (1991) 'Pride and prejudice, sense and subsistence: exchange and society in the Greek city', in J. Rich and A. Wallace-Hadrill (eds) *City and Country in the Ancient World*, London: Routledge, 119–46.

Pászthory, E. (1979) 'Zwei Kleinmünzen aus Athen', *SM* 29: 1–7.

Peter, M. (forthcoming) 'Some aspects of coin circulation on the Rhine in the 2nd century AD', in C.E. King and D. Wigg (eds) *Coin Finds and Coin Use in the Roman World*.

Pflaum, H.G. (1948) *Le marbre de Thorigny*, Paris: Bibl. de L'École des Hautes Études.

Picard, O. (1989) 'Innovations monétaires dans la Grèce du IVe siècle', *CRAI*: 673–87.

—— (1990) 'Philippe II et le monnayage des cités grecques', *REG* 103: 1–15.

Polański, T. (1992a) 'The imperial propaganda and historical tradition according to a selection of coins from the collection of Augustine Czartoryski. Part I: The Fides-Concordia group', *Zeszyty Naukowe Uniwersytetu Jagiellońskiego* 1067, Prace Archeologiczne 53: 47–57.

—— (1992b) 'Part II: The image of success in the foreign and interior policy of the emperor', *ZNUJ* 1072, Prace Archeologiczne 54: 45–58.

Polanyi, K. (1968) 'The semantics of money-uses', in G. Dalton (ed.) *Primitive, Archaic and Modern Economies: Essays of Karl Polanyi*, Garden City: Doubleday Anchor, 175–203.

Powell, M.A. (1978) 'A contribution to the history of money in Mesopotamia prior to the invention of coinage', in B. Hruška and G. Komoróczy (eds) *Festschrift Lubor Matouš* II, Budapest: Assyriologia 5: 211–43.

—— (1990) 'Identification and interpretation of long term price fluctuations in Babylonia: more on the history of money in Mesopotamia', *Altorientalische Forschungen* 17: 76–99.

Price, M.J. (1968) 'Early Greek bronze coinage', in C.M. Kraay and G.K. Jenkins (eds) *Essays in Greek Coinage Presented to Stanley Robinson*, Oxford: Clarendon Press, 90–104.

—— (1979a) 'The coinage of Philip II', *NC* 139: 230–41.

—— (1979b) 'The function of early Greek bronze coinage', *Atti del VI Convegno del Centro Internazionale di Studi Numismatici: Napoli 17–22 aprile 1977*, Rome: supplement to *AIIN* 25: 351–65.

—— (1980) 'The uses of metal analysis in the study of archaic Greek coinage: some comments', in D.M. Metcalf and W.A. Oddy (eds) *Metallurgy in Numismatics*, vol. 1, London: Royal Numismatic Society, 50–4.

—— (1981) 'A portrait of Alexander the Great from Egypt', *NNF-NYTT, Meddelelser fra Norsk Numismatisk Forening*, 1981 (1): 24–37.

—— (1982) 'The "Porus" coinage of Alexander the Great: a symbol of concord and community', in S. Scheers (ed.) *Studia Paulo Naster Oblata I: Numismatica Antiqua*, Louvain: Orientalia Lovaniensia Analecta 12, 75–88.

—— (1983) 'Thoughts on the beginnings of coinage', in C.N.L. Brooke *et al.* (eds) *Studies in Numismatic Method Presented to Philip Grierson*, Cambridge: Cambridge University Press, 1–10.

—— (1987a) 'Southern Greece', in A.M. Burnett and M.H. Crawford (eds) *The Coinage of the Roman World in the Late Republic*, Oxford: BAR, 95–103.

—— (1987b) 'The coinages of the northern Aegean', in I. Carradice (ed.) *Coinage and Administration in the Athenian and Persian Empires*, Oxford: BAR International Series 343, 43–52.

—— (1989) 'The Larissa, 1968 hoard (*IGCH* 237)', in G. Le Rider *et al.* (eds) *Kraay-Mørkholm Essays: Numismatic Studies in Memory of C.M. Kraay and O. Mørkholm*, Louvain-la-Neuve: Numismatica Lovaniensia 10, 233–43.

—— (1991a) *The Coinage in the Name of Alexander the Great and Philip Arrhidaeus*, Zurich and London: Swiss Numismatic Society and British Museum Press.

—— (1991b) 'Circulation at Babylon in 323 BC', in W.E. Metcalf (ed.) *Mnemata: Papers in Memory of Nancy M. Waggoner*, New York: The American Numismatic Society, 63–72.

—— (1993) 'More from Memphis, and the Syria 1989 hoard', in M. Price *et al.* (eds) *Essays in Honour of Robert Carson and Kenneth Jenkins*, London: Spink, 31–5.

Price, M., Burnett, A. and Bland, R. (eds) (1993) *Essays in Honour of Robert Carson and Kenneth Jenkins*, London: Spink.

Price, M.J. and Waggoner, N.M. (1975) *Archaic Greek Coinage: The Asyut Hoard*, London: Vecchi.

Price, S.R.F. (1979) 'The divine right of emperors', *CR* n.s. 29: 277–9.

Pritchett, W.K. (1956) 'The Attic stelai, part II', *Hesperia* 25: 178–317.

—— (1961) 'Five new fragments of the Attic stelai', *Hesperia* 30: 23–9.

Purcell, N. (1990) 'Mobility and the polis', in O. Murray and S. Price (eds) *The Greek City from Homer to Alexander*, Oxford: Clarendon Press, 29–58.

Rathbone, D.W. (1989) 'The ancient economy and Graeco-Roman Egypt', in L. Criscuolo and G. Geraci (eds) *Egitto e storia antica dell'ellenismo all'età araba*, Bologna: CLUEB, 159–76.

—— (forthcoming) 'Monetization, not price-inflation, in third-century AD Egypt?', in C.E. King and D. Wigg (eds) *Coin Finds and Coin Use in the Roman World*.

Redfield, J.M. (1986) 'The development of the market in archaic Greece', in B.L. Anderson and A.J.H. Latham (eds) *The Market in History*, London: Croom Helm, 29–58.

Reece, R. (1987) *Coinage in Roman Britain*, London: Seaby.

—— (forthcoming) 'The interpretation of site finds: a review', in C.E. King and D. Wigg (eds) *Coin Finds and Coin Use in the Roman World*.

Reekmans, T. (1948) 'Monetary history and the dating of Ptolemaic papyri', *Studia Hellenistica* 5: 15–43.

—— (1951) 'The Ptolemaic copper inflation', in E. van 'T Dack and T. Reekmans (eds) *Studia Hellenistica 7: Ptolemaica*, Louvain: Universitaires de Louvain, 61–118.

Renfrew, C. (1986) 'Introduction: peer polity interaction and socio-political change', in C. Renfrew and J.F. Cherry (eds) *Peer Polity Interaction and Socio-political Change*, Cambridge: Cambridge University Press, 1–18.

Renfrew, C. and Cherry, J.F. (eds) (1986) *Peer Polity Interaction and Socio-political Change*, Cambridge: Cambridge University Press.

Renger, J. (1984) 'Patterns of non-institutional trade and non-commercial exchange in ancient Mesopotamia at the beginning of the second millenium BC', in A. Archi (ed.) *Circulation of Goods in Non-palatial Context in the Ancient Near East*, Rome: Dell'Ateneo, 31–124.

Rich, J. and Wallace-Hadrill, A. (eds) (1991) *City and Country in the Ancient World*, London: Routledge.

Richter, G.M.A. (1984) *The Portraits of the Greeks*, abridged and revised by R.R.R. Smith, Oxford: Phaidon.

Robert, L. (1962) 'Monnaies dans les inscriptions grecques', RN^6 4: 7–24.

—— (1977) 'La titulature de Nicée et de Nicomédie: La gloire et la haine', *HSCP* 81: 1–39.

Robinson, E.S.G. (1946) 'Rhegion, Zankle-Messana and the Samians', *JHS* 60: 13–20.

—— (1960) 'Some problems in the later fifth century coinage at Athens', *MN* 9: 1–15.

Robinson, E.S.G. and Price, M.J. (1967) 'An emergency coinage of Timotheos', *NC*[7] 7: 1–6.

Rodriguez-Almeida, E. (1980) *Forma Urbis Marmorea: aggiornamento generale 1980*, Rome: Quasar.

Rutter, N.K. (1979) *Campanian Coinages, 475–380 BC*, Edinburgh: Edinburgh University Press.

—— (1981) 'Early Greek Coinage and the influence of the Athenian state', in B. Cunliffe (ed.) *Coinage and Society in Britain and Gaul: Some Current Problems*, London: Council for British Archaeology, 1–9.

Sachs, A.J. and Hunger, H. (1988) *Astronomical Diaries and Related Texts from Babylonia*, Vienna: Österreichischen Akademie der Wissenschaften.

Salmon, J. (1993) 'Trade and Corinthian coins in the west', in *La monetazione Corinzia in occidente: atti del IX Convegno del Centro Internazionale di Studi Numismatici: Napoli 27–28 ottobre 1986*, Rome: Istituto Italiano di Numismatica, 3–17.

—— (forthcoming) 'The economic role of the state in Ancient Greece', in A.S. Courakis (ed.) *Economic Thought and Economic Reality in Ancient Greece*.

Scheers, S. (ed.) (1982) *Studia Paulo Naster Oblata I: Numismatica Antiqua*, Louvain: Orientalia Lovaniensia Analecta 12.

Seaford, R. (1994) *Reciprocity and Ritual: Homer and Tragedy in the Developing City-state*, Oxford: Clarendon Press.

Sherratt, E.S. (1990) ' "Reading the texts": archaeology and the Homeric question', *Antiquity* 64: 807–24.

Sherratt, E.S. and Sherratt, A. (1993) 'The growth of the Mediterranean economy in the early first millenium BC', *WA* 24 (3): 361–78.

Sherwin-White, S. and Kuhrt, A. (1993) *From Samarkhand to Sardis: A New Approach to the Seleucid Empire*, London: Duckworth.

Shotter, D.C.A. (1983) 'The principate of Nerva: some observations on the coin evidence', *Historia* 32: 215–26.

Simon, B. (1993) *Die Selbstdarstellung des Augustus in der Münzprägung und in den Res Gestae*, diss., Universität Heidelberg 1990/91 (unseen by author).

Smith, R.R.R. (1987) 'The Imperial reliefs from the Sebasteion at Aphrodisias', *JRS* 77: 88–138.

—— (1988a) *Hellenistic Royal Portraits*, Oxford: Clarendon Press.

—— (1988b) '*Simulacra gentium*: the *ethne* from the Sebasteion at Aphrodisias', *JRS* 78: 50–77.

Snodgrass, A.M. (1986) 'Interaction by design: the Greek city state', in C. Renfrew and J.F. Cherry (eds) *Peer Polity Interaction and Socio-political Change*, Cambridge: Cambridge University Press, 47–58.

—— (1991) 'Archaeology and the study of the Greek city', in J. Rich and A. Wallace-Hadrill (eds) *City and Country in the Ancient World*, London: Routledge, 1–23.

Spaer, A. (1984) 'Ascalon: from royal mint to autonomy', in A. Houghton *et al.* (eds) *Festschrift für Leo Mildenberg*, Wetteren: N.R., 229–39.

Speidel, M.A. (1992) 'Roman army pay scales', *JRS* 82: 87–106.

Speidel, M.P. (1993) 'Commodus the God-emperor and the army', *JRS* 83: 109–14.

Spier, J. (1990) 'Emblems in Archaic Greece', *BICS* 37: 107–29.

Spufford, P. (1988) *Money and its Use in Medieval Europe*, Cambridge: Cambridge University Press.

Stancomb, W. (1993) 'Arrowheads, dolphins and cast coins in the Black Sea region', *Classical Numismatic Review* 18 (3): 5.

Stewart, A. (1993) *Faces of Power: Alexander's Image and Hellenistic Politics*, Berkeley: University of California Press.

Strack, P.L. (1931–7) *Untersuchungen zur römischen Reichsprägung des zweiten Jahrhunderts*, parts 1–3, Stuttgart: W. Kohlhammer.

Stronach, D. (1985) 'The Apadana: a signature of the line of Darius I', in J.L. Huot, M. Yon and Y. Calvet (eds) *De l'Indus aux Balkans: Recueil à la mémoire de Jean Deshayes*, Paris: Recherche sur les Civilisations, 433–45.

Sutherland, C.H.V. (1951) *Coinage in Roman Imperial Policy 31 BC–AD 68*, London: Methuen.

Szidat, J. (1981) 'Zur Wirkung und Aufnahme der Münzpropaganda (Iul. Misop. 355 d)', *Museum Helveticum* 38: 22–33.

Thompson, M. (1961) *The New Style Silver Coinage of Athens*, New York: American Numismatic Society *NS* 10.

—— (1968) *The Agrinion Hoard*, New York: American Numismatic Society *NNM* 159.

—— (1984) 'Paying the mercenaries', in A. Houghton *et al.* (eds) *Festschrift für Leo Mildenberg*, Wetteren: N.R., 241–7.

Thompson, W.E. (1970) 'The golden Nikai and the coinage of Athens', *NC*[7] 10: 1–6.

Torbagyi, M. (forthcoming) 'Umlauf der Münzen von Apollonia und Dyrrhachium im Karpatenbecken', in *Actes du XIe Congrès International de Numismatique: Bruxelles, 8–13 septembre 1991*.

Troxell, H.A. (1991) 'Alexander's earliest Macedonian silver', in W.E. Metcalf (ed.) *Mnemata: Papers in Memory of Nancy M. Waggoner*, New York: The American Numismatic Society, 49–62.

Tuplin, C. (1987) 'The administration of the Persian Empire', in I. Carradice (ed.) *Coinage and Administration in the Athenian and Persian Empires*, Oxford: BAR International Series 343, 109–66.

Turner, P. (1989) *Roman Coins from India*, London: Royal Numismatic Society.

Uchitel, A. (1988) 'The archives of Mycenaean Greece and the Ancient Near East', in M. Heltzer and E. Lipiński (eds) *Society and Economy in the Eastern Mediterranean (c. 1500–1000 BC)*, Louvain: Uitgeverig Peeters, 19–30.

van der Mieroop, M. (1992) *Society and Enterprise in Old Babylonian Ur*, Berlin: Berliner Beiträge zum Vorderen Orient Bd. 12.

Vermeule, C.C. (1954) *Some Notes on Ancient Dies and Coining Methods*, London: Spink.

Veyne, P. (1979) 'Rome devant la prétendue fuite de l'or: mercantilisme ou politique disciplinaire', *Annales ESC* 34: 211–44.

Volk, T.R. (1987) 'Mint output and coin hoards', in G. Depeyrot *et al.* (eds) *Rythmes de la production monétaire, de l'antiquité à nos jours*, Louvain-la-Neuve: Numismatica Lovaniensia 7, 141–221.

von Reden, S. (forthcoming a) *Exchange in Ancient Greece.*

—— (forthcoming b) 'Ancient money: institution as symbol. The Greek polis as a case study', in A.S. Courakis (ed.) *Economic Thought and Economic Reality in Ancient Greece.*

Waldbaum, J.C. (1983) *Metalwork from Sardis: The Finds through 1974*, Cambridge, Mass.: Harvard University Press.

Walker, D.R. (1976–8) *The Metrology of the Roman Silver Coinage*, vols 1–3, Oxford: BAR.

—— (1980) 'The silver contents of the Roman Republican coinage', in D.M. Metcalf and W.A. Oddy (eds) *Metallurgy in Numismatics*, vol. 1, London: Royal Numismatic Society, 55–72.

—— (1988) *Roman Coins from the Sacred Spring at Bath*, Oxford: Oxford University Committee for Archaeology.

Wallace-Hadrill, A. (1981a) 'The emperor and his virtues', *Historia* 30: 298–323.

—— (1981b) 'Galba's aequitas', *NC* 141: 20–39.

—— (1986) 'Image and authority in the coinage of Augustus', *JRS* 76: 66–87.

Weidauer, L. (1975) *Probleme der frühen Elektronprägung*, Fribourg: Office du livre, Typos: Monographien zur antiken Numismatik, 1.

Weigel, R.D. (1990) 'Gallienus' "animal series" coins and Roman religion', *NC* 150: 135–43.

Weinstock, S. (1971) *Divus Julius*, Oxford: Clarendon Press.

Weiss, P. (1991) 'Auxe Perge: Beobachtungen zu einem bemerkenswerten städtischen Dokument des späten 3. Jahrhunderts n. Chr.', *Chiron* 21: 353–92.

Whittaker (1978) 'Carthaginian imperialism in the fifth and fourth centuries', in P.D.A. Garnsey and C.R. Whittaker (eds) *Imperialism in the Ancient World*, Cambridge: Cambridge University Press, 59–90.

—— (1980) 'Inflation and the economy in the fourth century AD', in C.E. King (ed.) *Imperial Revenue, Expenditure and Monetary Policy in the Fourth Century AD*, Oxford: BAR, 1–22.

Wielowiejski, J. (1980) 'Der Einfluss der Devaluation des Denars auf die Annahme römischer Münzen durch die hinter der Donau ansässigen Völker', in *Dévaluations* II: 155–66.

Wigg, D. (1991) *Münzumlauf in Nordgallien um die Mitte des 4. Jahrhunderts n. Chr.*, Berlin: Studien zu Fundmünzen der Antike 8.

Will, E. (1955) 'Réflexions et hypothèses sur les origines du monnayage', *RN*[5] 17: 5–23.

—— (1988) 'Review of Thomas R. Martin, *Sovereignty and Coinage in Classical Greece*', in *Échos du monde classique/Classical Views* 32, n.s. 7 (3): 417–20.

Williams, D.J.R. (1991–3) 'The "Pot-hoard" pot from the Archaic Artemision at Ephesus', *BICS* 38: 98–104.

Woolf, G. (1990) 'World-systems analysis and the Roman empire', *JRA* 3: 44–58.

—— (1992) 'Imperialism, empire and the integration of the Roman economy', *World Archaeology* 23 (3): 283–93.

Yoffe, N. (1981) *Explaining Trade in Ancient Western Asia*, Malibu: Undena, Monographs on the Ancient Near East 2, 2.

Zanker, P. (1988) *The Power of Images in the Age of Augustus*, Ann Arbor: University of Michigan Press.

Zervos, O. (1980) 'The Demanhur hoard: addenda', *NC*[7] 20: 185–8.

Key to plates

In this key numbers in square brackets refer to pages in the text. All coins are of silver unless otherwise described. The coins illustrated are in the Heberden Coin Room of the Ashmolean Museum, Oxford, with the exception of the following, which are in the Department of Coins and Medals, British Museum: 1, 2, 38, 45–6, 48, 52, 54–5, 67, 78–9, 88, 105, 122, 130, 138, 153–4, 156, 163–4, 166–8, 171. Ingot no. 183 is in a private collection, and ingot no. 184 is in the Römermuseum Augst.

ARCHAIC AND CLASSICAL

Western Asia Minor

1 Electrum stater, before *c.* 560 BC: Stag, 'I am the badge of Phanes'/Punches [4]
2 Phocaea, electrum stater, before *c.* 560 BC: Seal/Punches [3]
3 Electrum, sixth stater, before *c.* 560 BC: Striations/Punch [2]
4 Lydia, electrum, third stater, before *c.* 560 BC: Lion's head/Punches [3]
5 Lydia, electrum, sixth stater, before *c.* 560 BC: Lion's head VALVEL/Punches [3]
6 Lydia, electrum, sixth stater, before *c.* 560 BC: Lion's head RKALIL/Punches [3]
7 Electrum, ninety-sixth stater, before *c.* 560 BC: Stag's head/Punch [7]
8 0.43g, before *c.* 500 BC: Head/Punch [7]
9 Teos, stater, *c.* 500–480 BC: Griffin/Punch [6]
10 Rhodes, tridrachm, *c.* 405–404 BC: Heracles strangling snakes/Rose [63]

Italy and Sicily

11 Velia, drachm, *c.* 535–500 BC: Forepart of lion tearing prey/Punch [4, 6]
12 Sybaris, stater, before 510 BC: Bull/Incuse bull [4, 15]
13 Zancle/Messana, tetradrachm, *c.* 490 BC: Lion's scalp/Prow of galley [6, 63]
14 Messana (Anaxilas), tetradrachm, *c.* 480 BC: Mule-car/Hare [63]
15 Acragas, gold diobol (?), *c.* 406 BC: Eagle and snake/Crab [113]

Mainland Greece

16 Aegina, didrachm, before *c.* 510 BC: Turtle/Punch [25, 97]
17 Corinth, tridrachm, before *c.* 500 BC: Pegasus/Punch [25, 97]
18 Corinth, tridrachm, *c.* 345 BC: Pegasus/Head of Athena [25, 98]
19 Athens, didrachm, before *c.* 505 BC: Gorgoneion/Punch [3]
20 Athens, tetradrachm, *c.* 490–480 BC: Head of Athena/Owl [25, 36, 97]
21 Athens, tetradrachm, *c.* 450 BC: Head of Athena/Owl [44, 97]
22 Athens, hemidrachm, *c.* 450–400 BC: Head of Athena/Owl [20]
23 Athens, gold diobol, *c.* 406 BC: Head of Athena/Two owls [111, 141]
24 Athens, base metal, *c.* 350–320 BC: Head of Athena/Two owls, heads joined [8]
25 Abdera, tetradrachm, *c.* 530–500 BC: Griffin/Punch [4, 6]
26 Derrones, dodecadrachm, *c.* 480–460 BC: Car drawn by oxen/Trisceles [96]

The Persian Empire

27 Lydia/Persia, heavy gold stater, before *c.* 520 BC: Foreparts of lion and bull/Punches [4, 46]
28 Persia, silver half stater (siglos), *c.* 520–500 BC: Foreparts of lion and bull/Punches [4, 46]
29 Persia, siglos, *c.* 510–490 BC: Half-length figure of king/Punch [4, 46]
30 Persia, gold daric, *c.* 400–330 BC: King/Punch [4, 8, 46]
31 Magnesia, obol (?), *c.* 465–450 BC (?): Head of Themistocles (?) /Monogram [64]
32 Cyzicus, electrum stater, fifth century BC: Soldier with bow/Punch [4, 8, 47]
33 Ephesos, tetradrachm, *c.* 400–330 BC: Bee/Forepart of stag [47]
34 Lycia, Mithrapata, stater, *c.* 375 BC: Forepart of lion/Head of Mithrapata [47, 64]
35 Lycia, Perikla, stater, *c.* 375 BC: Head of Perikla/Soldier [47, 64]
36 Mallos, stater (double siglos), *c.* 385–333 BC: Head of Aphrodite/Head of Satrap [47, 64]
37 Tarsos, Pharnabazos, stater (double siglos), 379–374 BC: Baal of Tarsos/Head of Ares (?) [47, 49, 66]
38 Egypt, Artaxerxes, tetradrachm, *c.* 343 BC: Head of Athena/Owl 'Artaxerxes Pharaoh' [9, 38, 53, 97]

39 Egypt, Sabaces, tetradrachm, *c.* 333 BC: Head of Athena/Owl [9, 53, 97]

Philip II and Alexander

40 Macedonia, Philip II, tetradrachm, *c.* 356–336 BC: Head of Zeus/Philip on horse [64]
41 Macedonia, Philip II, tetradrachm, *c.* 336 BC (?): Head of Zeus/Jockey on horse [49, 66]
42 Macedonia, Alexander III, tetradrachm, *c.* 336 BC (?): Head of Heracles/Zeus [49, 66]
43 Macedonia, Philip II, gold stater, *c.* 345–336 BC: Head of Apollo/Chariot [8, 48, 66]
44 'Babylon', Alexander, gold stater, *c.* 331–325 BC: Head of Athena/Nike [8, 9, 66]
45 Mesopotamia (?), Alexander, 5 shekel, *c.* 325 BC: Alexander on horse attacking Indian potentate on elephant/Alexander holding thunderbolt, crowned by Nike [39, 51, 64, 66, 79]
46 Mesopotamia (?), Alexander, 2 shekel, *c.* 325 BC: Indian with bow/Elephant [51, 66]
47 Mesopotamia, gold double-daric, *c.* 325 BC: King/Punch [51]
48 Hierapolis-Bambyce, stater, *c.* 333–325 BC: Lion/Alexander on horse [51, 48]

HELLENISTIC

Balkans

49 Eastern Celts (Danube basin), tetradrachm, early 3rd century BC: Head of Zeus/Jockey on horse [10, 103]
50 Demetrius Poliorcetes, mint of Salamis, tetradrachm, 330–295 BC: Nike on prow/Poseidon [66]
51 Demetrius Poliorcetes, tetradrachm, *c.* 290 BC: Head of Demetrius/Poseidon [65]
52 Greece, gold stater, *c.* 196 BC: Head of Flamininus/Nike [68]
53 Athens, tetradrachm, *c.* 124/3 BC: Head of Athena/Owl (the A on the amphora refers to the first month of the Athenian civil year) [31, 57]
54 Gortyn, didrachm, *c.* 322–300 BC: Goddess in tree/Bull. Overstruck on a coin of Cyrenaica (head of Zeus Ammon still visible on reverse) [89, 98]
55 Gortyn, tetradrachm, 67 BC: Head of Roma/Artemis Ephesia (*RPC* I no. 902/1) [84]

Asia Minor: regal and imperial issues

56 Lysimachus, mint of Lampsacus, tetradrachm, 297/6–282/1 BC: Head of Alexander/Athena [65]
57 Mithridates, tetradrachm, 89/88 BC: Head of Mithridates/Pegasus in ivy wreath [37]

58 Pergamum, under Eumenes I, tetradrachm, 262–241 BC: Head of Philetaerus/Athena [54, 65]
59 Ephesos, Attalus III, cistophoric tetradrachm, 138/137 BC: Mystic cista in ivy wreath/Bow-case entwined by serpents [54, 55]
60 Pergamum, cistophoric tetradrachm, 55–53 BC (C. Pulcher proconsul): Mystic cista in wreath/Bow-case entwined by serpents [57]
61 Ephesos (?), cistophoric tetradrachm, c. 39 BC: Head of Antony wearing ivy wreath, all in wreath/Bust of Octavia above mystic cista, flanked by snakes (*RPC* 2201) [57, 78]
62 Ephesos, cistophoric tetradrachm, 28 BC: Head of Octavian/Pax in wreath (*RPC* 2203) [57, 76]

Asia Minor: civic issues

63 Nicaea, bronze, 61–59 BC: Head of Dionysos/Roma [42, 84]
64 Myrina, tetradrachm, c. 155–145 BC: Head of Apollo/Apollo [55, 99]
65 Ephesos, drachm, second century BC: Bee/Stag and palm tree [55]
66 Rhodes, tetradrachm, c. 201–190 BC: Head of Alexander/Zeus [50, 51]
67 Aspendos, tetradrachm, c. 212/211 BC (year 1): Head of Alexander/Zeus [41, 50]
68 Side, tetradrachm, c. 210–170 BC: Head of Athena, countermarked at Tralles with a bow-case/Nike [41, 55]

East

69 Seleucus I, mint of Bactra, tetradrachm, c. 305–285 BC: Head of Zeus/Athena in quadriga of elephants [66]
70 Antiochus I, mint of Seleuceia on the Tigris, tetradrachm, c. 274–270 BC: Head of Antiochus/Apollo [51, 66]
71 Antiochus IV, mint of Antioch, tetradrachm, c. 169–167 BC: Head of Antiochus IV/Zeus [65]
72 Antiochus IV, Antioch ad Callirhoen, bronze, 169/8–164 BC: Head of Antiochus/Zeus [52]
73 Antiochus VI, mint of Antioch, tetradrachm, 143/142 BC: Head of Antiochus/Dioscuri on horses [65]
74 Tripolis, tetradrachm, c. 102–93 BC: Heads of Dioscuri/Tyche [41]
75 Bactria, Demetrius I, tetradrachm, c. 200–190 BC: Bust of Demetrius/Heracles [10]

Egypt and North Africa

76 Ptolemy I, tetradrachm, c. 310–305 BC: Head of Alexander/Athena [65]
77 Ptolemy I, tetradrachm, c. 300–282 BC: Head of Ptolemy/Eagle on thunderbolt [53, 65]
78 Ptolemy II, gold octodrachm (mnaeion), c. 261/260–240 BC: Busts of Ptolemy II and Arsinoe II/Busts of Ptolemy I and Berenice I [8, 65]
79 Ptolemy IV, gold octodrachm, 222–205 BC: Head of Ptolemy III/Cornucopiae [8, 65]

80   Cleopatra VII, bronze 80 drachma (?), *c.* 40–30 BC: Bust of Cleopatra/ Eagle on thunderbolt [132]
81   Carthage, gold stater, *c.* 350–320 BC: Head of Tanit/Horse [8, 113]
82   'Libya', base silver shekel, 241–238 BC: Head of Heracles/Lion [114]
83   Carthage, base silver, *c.* 209–208 BC: Head of Tanit/Horse [114]

ROMAN REPUBLICAN

Bronze

84   Bronze As, *c.* 225–217 BC: Head of Janus/Prow (*RRC* 36/1) [10, 26, 112]
85   Bronze As, after 211 BC: Head of Janus/Prow (*RRC* 56/2) [112]

The west

86   Locri, didrachm, *c.* 275 BC: Head of Zeus/Pistis crowning Roma [57, 67]
87   Cese-Tarraco, denarius, second century BC: Male head/Horseman with second horse [58]

Gold and silver

88   Gold stater, 225–212 BC: Head of Janus/Oath-taking scene (*RRC* 28/1) [10, 112]
89   60-As gold piece, from 211 BC: Head of Mars/Eagle on thunderbolt (*RRC* 44/2) [10, 112]
90   Denarius, from 211 BC: Head of Roma/Dioscuri (*RRC* 44/5) [11, 112]
91   Victoriatus, from 211 BC: Head of Jupiter/Victory crowning trophy (*RRC* 44/1) [112]
92   Denarius, *c.* 119 BC: Head of Janus/Roma crowning trophy (*RRC* 281/1) [68]
93   Denarius, *c.* 101 BC: Head of Roma/Marius (?) as *triumphator* in quadriga (*RRC* 326/1) [68]
94   Denarius, *c.* 100 BC: Head of Saturn/Two quaestors on bench (*RRC* 330/1a) [36]
95   Denarius, *c.* 90 BC: Head of Apollo/Horseman (*RRC* 340/1) [36]
96   Denarius, 84–83 BC: Head of Venus/Two trophies, jug, and lituus (*RRC* 359/2) [68, 78]
97   Denarius, 82 BC: Head of Roma/Sulla as *triumphator* in quadriga (*RRC* 367/3) [68]
98   Denarius, 76–75 BC: Bust of Genius of the Roman people/Sceptre with wreath, globe, and rudder (*RRC* 393/1b) [83]
99   Denarius, 70 BC: Heads of Honos and Virtus/Italia and Roma (*RRC* 403/1) [83]
100   Denarius, 56 BC: Head of Hercules/Globe, three small wreaths, one large wreath, aplustre, and corn-ear (*RRC* 449/4b) [68, 83]
101   Denarius, 53 BC: Bust of Roma/Curule chair; below, sceptre with wreath (*RRC* 435/1) [72]

102   Denarius, 48 BC: Head of Libertas/Roma (*RRC* 449/4) [73, 83]
103   Denarius, 47–46 BC: Head of Venus/Aeneas and Anchises (*RRC* 458/1) [73, 78]
104   Aureus, 46 BC: Female head/Lituus, jug, and axe (*RRC* 466/1) [10]
105   Denarius, 44 BC: Head of Julius Caesar/Fasces and caduceus, axe, globe, and clasped hands (*RRC* 480/6) [69, 75]
106   Denarius, 44–43 BC: Head of Cn. Pompeius Magnus with trident/Ship (*RRC* 483/2) [78]
107   Denarius, 43–42 BC: Head of Brutus/Pileus and two daggers (*RRC* 508/3) [69, 71, 73]
108   Denarius, 42–40 BC: Head of Cn. Pompeius Magnus/Neptune between two Catanacan brothers carrying parents (*RRC* 511/3a) [73]
109   Denarius, 32–31 BC: Ship/Legionary eagle and standards (*RRC* 544/24) [118]

ROMAN IMPERIAL TO AD 300

110   Octavian, denarius, *c.* 32–29 BC: Bust of Nike/Statue (*RIC* I^2 256) [77, 78]
111   Octavian, denarius, *c.* 29–27 BC: Herm with features of Octavian, thunderbolt behind/Octavian on curule chair, holding Victoria (*RIC* I^2 270) [78]
112   Octavian, denarius, *c.* 29–27 BC: Head of 'Apollo'/Statue on rostral column (*RIC* I^2 271) [77]
113   Octavian, denarius, 28 BC: Head of Octavian/Crocodile (*RIC* I^2 275a) [76]
114   Aureus, Spanish mint, *c.* 20–19 BC: Augustus/Clipeus virtutis between laurel branches (*RIC* I^2 52a) [68, 76]
115   Augustus, denarius, mint of Rome, *c.* 19 BC: Bust of Feronia, moneyer Turpilianus/Parthian kneeling, returning standard (*RIC* I^2 288) [69, 72, 76]
116   Augustus, denarius, mint of Rome, 13 BC: Head of Augustus/Head of Agrippa, moneyer Cossus Lentulus (*RIC* I^2 414) [69, 81]
117   Augustus, mint of Lugdunum, copper As, AD 12–14: Head of Tiberius/Altar (*RIC* I^2 245) [81]
118   Copper As, *c.* AD 62: Nero/Apollo (*RIC* I^2 75) [79]
119   Brass dupondius, *c.* AD 63: Nero/Victoria (*RIC* I^2 119) [79]
120   Denarius, AD 68–9: Head of Libertas/Pileus and daggers (*RIC* I^2 25) [73]
121   Denarius, AD 68–9: Victoria/SPQR in wreath (*RIC* I^2 72) [76]
122   Brass sestertius, AD 71: Vespasian/Inscription in wreath (*RIC* 456) [76]
123   Brass sestertius, AD 80–1: Titus/Vespasian handing globe to Titus (*RIC* 98) [81]
124   Domitian, denarius, AD 82–83 and later: Bust of Domitian/Baby boy on globe, surrounded by stars (*RIC* 213) [78]
125   Domitian, copper quadrans, AD 81–96: S.C./Rhinoceros (*RIC* 435) [122]
126   Brass sestertius, AD 92–4: Domitian/Victoria crowning Domitian, who holds thunderbolt (*RIC* 403) [79]

127 Brass sestertius, AD 95–6: Domitian/Triumphal arch (*RIC* 416) [72]
128 Brass sestertius, AD 97: Nerva/Two mules grazing (*RIC* 93) [72]
129 Trajan, aureus, *c.* AD 107: Head of Tiberius/Female seated, inscription states that Trajan has restored the type (*RIC* 821) [72]
130 Aureus, AD 114–17: Trajan/Jupiter and Trajan (*RIC* 250) [79]
131 Brass sestertius, AD 114–17: Trajan/Trajan presenting king to Parthia (*RIC* 667) [83]
132 Denarius, AD 117: Hadrian/Trajan and Hadrian clasping hands, ADOPTIO (*RIC* 3a) [82]
133 Aureus, AD 134–8: Hadrian/Egypt (RIC 296) [72, 83]
134 Copper As, AD 119: Hadrian/Britannia (*RIC* 577 b) [71, 72, 83, 107]
135 Copper As, AD 154–5: Antoninus Pius/Britannia (*RIC* 934) [107]
136 Brass sestertius, AD 192: Commodus as Hercules/Club and inscription in wreath (*RIC* 638) [80]
137 Denarius, Syrian mint, AD 194–5: Septimius Severus/Victoria inscribing shield on column (*RIC* 430) [109]
138 Aureus, AD 201: Caracalla/Septimius Severus and Julia Domna as the Sun and Moon (*RIC* 52) [79, 81]
139 Aureus, AD 202: Septimius Severus/Julia Domna between Caracalla and Geta (*RIC* 181 c) [81]
140 'Antoninianus', AD 215: Caracalla/Serapis (*RIC* 263 d) [11, 79, 115, 131]
141 'Antoninianus', mint of Antioch, AD 244–5: Philip I/Pax (*RIC* 69) [72, 79]
142 'Antoninianus', AD 248: Otacilia/Hippopotamus, IIII = fourth officina (*RIC* 116 b) [26, 79]
143 'Antoninianus', mint of Antioch, *c.* AD 264–5: Salonina/Ceres (*RIC* 90) [79]
144 Bronze sestertius, mint of 'Cologne', AD 260: Postumus/Trophy and captives (*RIC* 120) [82, 137]
145 Reformed radiate, mint of Siscia, AD 274–5: Aurelian/Sol (*RIC* 255) [127, 131]
146 'Antoninianus', mint of Antioch, *c.* AD 270: Aurelian/Vabalathus (*RIC* 381) [82, 137]
147 Denarius, AD 287–93: Carausius/Wolf and twins (*RIC* 571 D) [82, 137]
148 'Antoninianus', AD 287–93: Carausius with Diocletian and Maximian/Pax (*RIC* 1) [82, 137]

WESTERN CELTIC

149 Belgic Gaul, debased gold, *c.* 60–50 BC: Blank/Horse [58, 114]
150 Britain, Tincommius (southern kingdom), debased gold, late first century BC: Inscription/Horseman [10, 58, 114]
151 Britain, Cunobelin, mint of Camulodunum, debased gold, early first century AD: Corn-ear/Horse [10, 58, 114]
152 Britain, Caratacus (southern kingdom), debased silver, *c.* AD 40: Bust/Eagle [10, 58, 114]

ROMAN PROVINCIAL COINAGE

153 Magnesia ad Sipylum, bronze, early 20s BC (?): Head of Marcus Tullius Cicero/Hand holding wreath, ears of corn, and vine branch (*RPC* 2448) [84]

154 Pergamum, bronze, *c.* 10–2 BC: Bust of Livia 'Hera'/Bust of Julia 'Aphrodite' (RPC 2359) [85]

155 Syrian Antioch, tetradrachm, AD 62/3: Nero/Eagle (*RPC* 4184) [38]

156 Sicyon, bronze, AD 66–8: Nero 'Zeus Eleutherios'/Horseman (*RPC* 1238) [73, 85]

157 Alexandria, base silver tetradrachm, AD 67/8: Nero/Actian Apollo (*RPC* 5317) [85]

158 First Jewish Revolt, shekel, AD 68: Temple vessel/Stem with three pomegranates [41]

159 Second Jewish Revolt, tetradrachm, AD 134–5: Temple 'Simeon'/Bundle of lulav and ethrog 'For the freedom of Jerusalem' [41, 82]

160 Lycia, drachm, AD 98–9: Trajan/Lyres [102]

161 Chios, bronze assarion, first/second century AD: Sphinx/Amphora [57]

162 Smyrna, bronze, *c.* AD 147: Antoninus Pius/Pelops and Hippodameia in biga [86]

163 Nicaea, bronze, AD 198–212: Julia Domna/Caracalla and Geta, commemorating the Severan Philadelphian games [86]

164 Mytilene, bronze, AD 209–12: Caracalla and Geta (name and bust of Geta erased)/Caesar on horse spearing enemy [71, 86]

165 Pergamum, bronze, AD 214–17: Caracalla/Three neocorate temples [86]

166 Laodicea, bronze, AD 214–17: Caracalla/Earth and Sea raise a radiate figure of Caracalla, eagle with wreath below [86]

167 Edessa, bronze, AD 238–44: Gordian III/Emperor seated and King Abgar [85]

168 Philippopolis (minted at Antioch), bronze, AD 244–9: Otacilia/Roma [30, 42]

169 Syria (minted at Rome), tetradrachm, AD 244–6: Philip I/Eagle (MON. VRB.) [30]

170 Mopsus, bronze, AD 255/6: Valerian/Bridge [85]

171 Smyrna, bronze, AD 260–8: Gallienus (countermarked H = 8)/Inscription in wreath [122, 139]

172 Alexandria, 'copper' drachm, AD 269/70: Claudius II/Nilus [122]

173 Alexandria, base silver tetradrachm, AD 295/6: Diocletian/Serapis and Isis [59, 128, 140]

ROMAN IMPERIAL: FOURTH CENTURY AD

174 Mint of Alexandria, billon nummus, *c.* AD 300: Diocletian/Genius of the Roman people (*RIC* 30a) [119, 127, 129, 131]

175 Mint of Ticinum, argenteus, *c.* AD 300: Maximian/XCVI (= 96) in wreath (*RIC* 20 b) [116, 119, 129, 131]

176 Mint of Ticinum, gold solidus, AD 316: Constantine I/Four Seasons (*RIC* 41) [12, 116]

177 Mint of Ticinum, billon nummus, AD 316: Constantine I/Sol (*RIC* 45) [79]
178 Mint of Nicomedia, billon, AD 348–51: Constans/Emperor on galley (*RIC* 64) [131, 133]
179 Mint of Amiens, billon, AD 353: Magnentius/Chi-Rho (*RIC* 34) [70]
180 Mint of Lugdunum, billon, AD 360–3: Julian/Bull (*RIC* 236) [70, 74]
181 Mint of Rome, 'siliqua', AD 364–7: Valens/Inscription in wreath (*RIC* 10 c) [116]
182 Comitatensian mint at Milan, gold solidus, AD 394–5: Honorius/ Emperor trampling on captive (*RIC* 35 c) [30]

INGOTS

183 Silver ingot, 597.43g, from the Selinus hoard, before *c.* 500 BC, stamped with a bearded male head [35, 89]
184 Silver ingot, 952.9g, originally three Roman pounds, from the Kaiseraugst treasure, AD 350–3, stamped with facing bust of Magnentius and inscribed (80 per cent actual size) [35, 89]

1

2

3

4

5

6

7

8

9

10

11

12

13

14

15

16   17   18   19

20   21   22   23   24

25

26

27 28 29 30 31

32 33

34 35 36 37

38 39

40

41

42

43

44

45

46

47

48

49

50

51

52

53

54

55

56 57 58

59 60 61

62

63

64

65

66

67

68

69

70

71

72

73

74

75

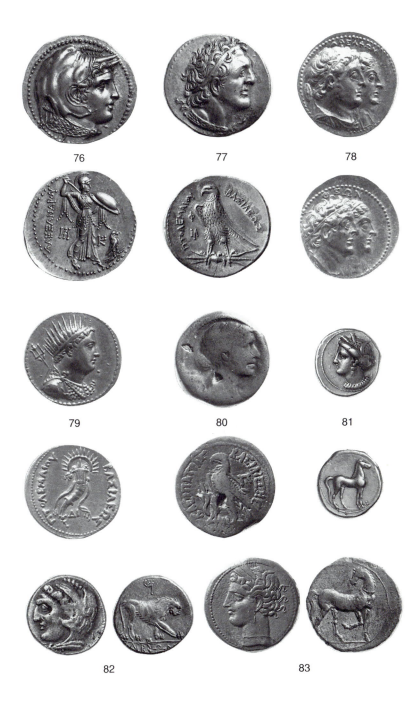

76

77

78

79

80

81

82

83

84

85

86

87

88

89

90

91

92

93

94

95

96

97

98

99

100

101

102

103

104

105

106

107

108

109

110

111

112

113

114

115

116

117

118

119

120

121

122

123

124

125

126

127

128

129   130

131

132   133

134

135

136

137   138   139   140

141   142   143

144

145   146   147   148

149

150

151

152

153

154

155

156

157

158

159

160

161

162

163

164

165

166

167

168

169

170

171

172

173

174

175

176

177

178

179

180

181

182

183

184

Index